MERLEAU-PONTY

MERLEAU-PONTY

Language and the Act of Speech

WAYNE JEFFREY FROMAN

Lewisburg
Bucknell University Press
London and Toronto: Associated University Presses

Associated University Presses, Inc.
4 Cornwall Drive
East Brunswick, N.J. 08816

Associated University Presses Ltd
27 Chancery Lane
London WC2A 1NS, England

Associated University Presses
Toronto M5E 1A7, Canada

Library of Congress Cataloging in Publication Data

Froman, Wayne Jeffrey, 1945–
  Merleau-Ponty : language and the act of
speech.

  Bibliography: p.
  Includes index.
  1. Merleau-Ponty, Maurice, 1908–1961—
Linguistics. 2. Languages—Philosophy.
I. Title.
P85.M48F76   194   81-65292
ISBN 0-8387-5015-X   AACR2

Printed in the United States of America

This book, my first, is, as is all my work,
dedicated to my parents,
Adeline and Gerard Froman,
whose loving care for one another
and for their children affords the courage to try to think.

The Word

The word
was born in the blood,
grew in the dark body, beating
and flew through the lips and the mouth.

Farther away and nearer
still, still it came
from dead fathers and from wandering races,
from lands that had returned to stone
weary of their poor tribes,
because when pain took to the roads
the settlements set out and arrived
and new lands and water reunited
to sow their word anew.

And so, this is the inheritance—
this is the wavelength which connects us
with the dead man and the dawn
of new beings not yet come to light.

Still the atmosphere quivers
with the initial word
dressed up
in terror and sighing.
It emerged
from the darkness
and until now there is no thunder
that rumbles yet with all the iron
of that word,

Pablo Neruda: Selected Poems, ed. Nathaniel Tarn, trans. Anthony Kerrigan, W. S. Merwin, Alastair Reid, and Nathaniel Tarn (New York: Dell Publishing Co., 1972).

the first
word uttered—
perhaps it was only a ripple, a drop,
and yet its great cataract falls and falls.

Later on, the word fills with meaning.
It remained gravid and it filled up with lives.
Everything had to do with births and sounds—
affirmation, clarity, strength,
negation, destruction, death—
the verb took over all the power
and blended existence with essence
in the electricity of its beauty.

Human word, syllable, combination
of spread light and the fine art of the silversmith
hereditary goblet which gathers
the communications of the blood—
here is where silence was gathered up
in the completeness of the human word
and, for human beings, not to speak is to die—
language extends even to the hair,
the mouth speaks without the lips moving—
all of a sudden the eyes are words.

I take the word and go over it
as though it were nothing more than a human shape,
its arrangements awe me and I find my way
through each variation in the spoken word—
I utter and I am and without speaking I approach
the limit of words and the silence.

I drink to the word, raising
a word or a shining cup,
in it I drink
the pure wine of language
or inexhaustible water,
maternal source of words,
and cup and water and wine
give rise to my song
because the verb is the source
and vivid life—it is blood,

blood which expresses its substance
and so implies its own unwinding—
words give glass-quality to glass, blood to blood
and life to life itself.

Pablo Neruda

Contents

Preface

IN the works of the founder of the phenomenological movement in contemporary European thought, Edmund Husserl, languge does not figure as a primary philosophical concern.[1] In much thought that has been nourished by Husserl's work, language has emerged as a major concern. In Merleau-Ponty's work in particular, language is situated centrally in the overall philosophic endeavor. In the prospectus of his work written at the time of his successful candidacy to the Collège de France,[2] Merleau-Ponty explicitly cites language as the problematic that holds the clue to interrogations, in the light of discoveries presented in *Phenomenology of Perception,*[3] of interpersonal relations, history, and ultimately, of the "Logos of the perceived world," interrogations that were to be presented in his projected future work. Presently, the problematic of language promises to be of critical importance in the determination of the philosophical destiny of phenomenology.

Originally, in addition to proceeding by way of a detailed examination of Merleau-Ponty's first major explicit treatment of the problematic of language, the chapter entitled "The Body as Expression, and Speech" in *Phenomenology of Perception,* in the context of an investigation of Merleau-Ponty's interrogation of language that assumes what work must be done in order to disengage this problematic from the body of his work, this study proceeded to Merleau-Ponty's work after *Phenomenology of Perception,* work in which language is explicitly a guiding concern, by way of detailed examinations of the preceding development in his thought in *The Structure of Behavior* and throughout the

13

entire text of *Phenomenology of Perception*.[4] Following
Merleau-Ponty step by step through the transformation in
perception that is called for by the study, in *The Structure
of Behavior,* of man in relation to his world, and that is in
fact proposed by Merleau-Ponty in *Phenomenology of Perception,* deters one from lapsing back into traditional misconceptions of perception, which deny one access to the
philosophical problematic of language. It was found that the
inclusion of detailed examinations of *The Structure of Behavior* and the entire text of *Phenomenology of Perception*
would entail a digression for the purpose of developing ar-
guments that discredit theoretical objections to Merleau-
Ponty's study of perception in general that could arise from
the scientistic frame of mind, a digression that ultimately is
not necessary inasmuch as any such objections are undermined decisively by Merleau-Ponty's findings in the course
of his investigation of perception itself. It would also entail
repetitious statements of those philosophical tasks which
arise again and again with each step taken by Merleau-
Ponty in his exposure of the original content of perception
before it is overlaid with a structure that issues from traditional misconceptions of perception. Although to include
detailed examinations of *The Structure of Behavior* and
each of the three parts of *Phenomenology of Perception,*
"The Body," "The World as Perceived," and "Being-for-
Itself and Being-in-the-World," would be to retrace the way
in which I arrived at my understanding of how Merleau-
Ponty's work after *Phenomenology of Perception* responds
to questions posed in these earlier works, and how each of
these earlier works is ultimately to be seen in the context of
the body of Merleau-Ponty's work as a whole, these exeget-
ical studies would not alter the presentation here of the
relationships among Merleau-Ponty's works. Nor would
these studies alter the presentation here of Merleau-Ponty's
overall comprehension of perception in general. Consequently, unprofitable digression and repetition could be,
and have been, avoided. In addition to the chapter entitled
"The Body as Expression, and Speech," only the three

chapters of *Phenomenology of Perception* that comprise the third part of that work, "The Cogito," "Temporality," and "Freedom," are followed here step by step in detail. Within the context of Merleau-Ponty's work considered as a whole, this concluding part of *Phenomenology of Perception*, "Being-for-Itself and Being-in-the-World," is a pivotal element that makes clear how it is that the problematic of language becomes a crucial concern for Merleau-Ponty in his work after *Phenomenology of Perception*, and how as a result of Merleau-Ponty's study of perception in general, which uproots traditional misconceptions of perception, the way is cleared for proceeding in depth with the interrogation of langauge opened in *Phenomenology of Perception*. A thorough understanding of Merleau-Ponty's philosophical interrogation of language affords the proper orientation to the investigations of specific features of the perceptual field as it is disclosed in *Phenomenology of Perception*, which, together with the investigation of language in the chapter entitled "The Body as Expression, and Speech," is found in the first two parts of that work, thus facilitating access to the details of those investigations.

In work that is concerned with language, it definitely does seem in order that it be clear that no liberties are being taken arbitrarily with respect to the language in which the work is written. Hence the following explanatory comments are provided. The use of the word *problematic* as a noun (as in "the philosophical problematic of language"), which appears frequently in work that pursues certain ways of thought that are found in contemporary European philosophy, is generally a means of designating a concern characteristic of human existence that calls for philosophical clarification, in contrast to a question or *problem* that arises by virtue of a particular theoretical framework and that one is to resolve in a manner that accords with the same theoretical framework. The word *subjectism* refers here to that mode of thinking which maintains that the human being is fundamentally a subject that, in one manner or another, is at the source of whatever the human being deals with, and

that whatever the human being deals with is what it is only
in relation to the subject. According to subjectism, therefore, all philosophical concerns are necessarily regarded
from the point of view of this subject.

I have relied on the standard English translations in citing
passages directly from Merleau-Ponty's works. However,
in certain cases, where the vocabulary becomes of particular import in the context of the body of Merleau-Ponty's
work considered as a whole, I have found it necessary to
supply my own translations in order to present the development of Merleau-Ponty's interrogation of language. In
these cases, the original French has been supplied as well.

I wish to express my thanks to Charles Kelbley, to Ken-
neth Gallagher, and to William Richardson for reading an
earlier and considerably longer version of the manuscript,
for their invaluable suggestions, and for encouragement
given me at various critical stages in the preparation of this
book, to think through the matter at hand for myself and
articulate my findings in the best way possible. Needless to
say, any shortcomings of this work are my responsibility
and mine alone.

Notes

1. In *Ideen zu einer reinen Phänomenologie und phänomenologischen Philosophie: Allgemeine Einführung in die Phänomenologie* (ed. Walter Biemel, Husserl-
iana III [The Hague: Martinus Nijhoff, 1950]; *Ideas: General Introduction to Pure
Phenomenology*, trans. W. R. Boyce Gibson [London: George Allen and Unwin,
1931]), Husserl suggests in regard to the phenomenologist's language that although it may at first be ambiguous and vague, adherence to phenomenological
rigor will assure that the phenomenologist's language will be precised in the
course of the development of phenomenology. (See the introduction to that work,
§66, and the note at the end of §84.) At the outset of the *Formale und transzendentale Logik* of 1929 (Halle a.S.: Max Niemeyer, 1929; *Formal and Transcendental
Logic*, trans. Dorion Cairns [The Hague: Martinus Nijhoff, 1969]), Husserl laid
aside the question concerning the nature of language itself and advised the reader
that the content and coherence of the investigations that comprise that work
sufficiently justify this omission. (See §2.) At the close of the article of 1933 by
Eugen Fink entitled "Die phänomenologische Philosophie Edmund Husserls in
der gegenwärtigen Kritik" bearing Husserl's foreword expressing total approval

(*Kantstudien* 38 [1933]), Fink includes the question concerning the phenomenologist's language as among those difficulties encountered when the phenomenologist seeks to communicate his findings to others. Fink describes these difficulties as paradoxes constantly obscuring the phenomenological problematic, paradoxes that bring into question the communicability of the findings of transcendental phenomenology. Merleau-Ponty, in opening his essay "On the Phenomenology of Language" (in *Signs,* trans. Richard C. McCleary [Evanston, Ill.: Northwestern University Press, 1964]), notes that, because in the philosophical tradition the problem of language does not pertain to "first philosophy," when Husserl does mention this problem he speaks of it more freely than of the problems of perception and knowledge, and Merleau-Ponty describes the little Husserl says on the subject as both original and enigmatic, making that subject a privileged opportunity to question phenomenology and recommence Husserl's efforts instead of merely repeating what Husserl did.

2. "An Unpublished Text by Maurice Merleau-Ponty: A Prospectus of His Work," trans. Arleen B. Dallery in Merleau-Ponty, *The Primacy of Perception and Other Essays,* ed. James M. Edie, Northwestern University Studies in Phenomenology and Existential Philosophy (Evanston, Ill.: Northwestern University Press, 1964).

3. *Phenomenology of Perception,* trans. Colin Smith, International Library of Philosophy and Scientific Method (London: Routledge & Kegan Paul, 1962.

4. *The Structure of Behavior,* trans. Alden L. Fisher (Boston: Beacon Press, 1963).

Acknowledgments

PERMISSION has been granted by the publishers to quote from the following copyrighted works:

Maurice Merleau-Ponty, *In Praise of Philosophy*, trans. John Wild and James M. Edie, Northwestern University Studies in Phenomenology and Existential Philosophy (Evanston, Ill.: Northwestern University Press, 1964); originally published in French under the title *Éloge de la philosophie* (Paris: Éditions Gallimard, 1953);

Maurice Merleau-Ponty, *Phenomenology of Perception*, trans. Colin Smith, International Library of Philosophy and Scientific Method (London: Routledge and Kegan Paul; New Jersey: Humanities Press, Inc., 1962);

Maurice Merleau-Ponty, *Phénoménologie de la perception* (Paris: Éditions Gallimard, 1945);

Maurice Merleau-Ponty, *The Primacy of Perception and Other Essays*, ed. James M. Edie, Northwestern University Studies in Phenomenology and Existential Philosophy (Evanston, Ill.: Northwestern University Press); essays originally published in French excerpted from *Les aventures de la dialectique* (Paris: Éditions Gallimard, 1955), *Humanisme et terreur* (Paris: Éditions Gallimard, 1947) and under the title *L'oeil et l'esprit* (Paris: Éditions Gallimard, 1964);

Maurice Merleau-Ponty, *Sense and Non-Sense*, trans. Hubert L. Dreyfus and Patricia A. Dreyfus, Northwestern University Studies in Phenomenology and Existential Phi-

Introduction

LANGUAGE is in itself a many-faceted philosophical concern that bears directly on other critical philosophical concerns, and it is also, in a sense, the all-inclusive philosophic concern because the act of philosophizing is an act of speaking. Merleau-Ponty states that "more clearly than any other [language] takes the form of both a special problem and a problem which contains all the others, including the problem of philosophy."[1] Merleau-Ponty's work allows us to focus on language itself without falling prey to two dangers. On the one hand, we avoid prejudging this problematic by framing it within the context of a hypostatized structure of one sort or another, be it a metaphysical structure in the traditional mode or an already complete human community of speakers of language. On the other hand, we avoid collapsing all philosophical concerns into language in a manner that both obscures the awareness of why language itself is philosophically problematic and does not permit the clarification of other philosophic concerns for which language has direct implications, by a sorting out of what pertains to the problematic of language proper in order to bring to bear lessons learned from the study of language while coming to grips with these other areas. This approach to language recalls Husserl's concern with the "things themselves," and it is in this spirit that we shall follow the development of Merleau-Ponty's thought concerning language even beyond the point at which phenomenological methodology appeared to Merleau-Ponty to be inadequate to interrogate what his work had disclosed. Inasmuch as his work focuses on language itself and in so doing discloses the structure of language, it meets contemporary analysis of language along scientific lines, but because of his concern with the being of language, with language's ontological import, Merleau-Ponty does not sever language from other dimensions of man's life and treat it as though it were a given system open to exhaustive analysis and manipulation.

A. "There is *the* world."

The study of perception is a vehicle whereby Merleau-Ponty presents a foundational tenet of his work: there is a world, or rather, as he corrects himself at one point in order to emphasize the point being made, there is *the* world. This affirmation lies deep in Merleau-Ponty's works. At present, we can first locate where he explicitly resorts to it in the course of the studies that contribute to the study of perception in his major completed work, *Phenomenology of Perception*. Thus we turn to the philosopher's own words. In concluding part one of that work, "The Body," Merleau-Ponty writes:

> The problem of the world, and to begin with that of one's own body consists in the fact that *it is all already there*.[2]

In part two of *Phenomenology of Perception,* "The World as Perceived," Merleau-Ponty, in speaking of "the thing," writes:

> How can any thing ever really and truly *present itself* to us, since its synthesis is never a completed process, and since I can always expect to see it break down and fall to the status of a mere illusion? Yet there *is* something and not nothing. There is a determinate reality, at least at a certain degree of relativity. Even if in the last resort I have no absolute knowledge of this stone, and even if my knowledge regarding it takes me step by step along an infinite road and cannot ever be complete, the fact re-

mains that the perceived stone is there, that I recognize it, that I have named it and that we agree on a certain number of statements about it.[3]

And speaking of the "natural world," Merleau-Ponty says:

Just as in the hearing subject, the absence of sounds does not cut off all communication with the world of sounds, so in the case of a subject deaf and blind from birth, the absence of the visual and auditory worlds does not sever all communication with the world in general. There is always something confronting him, a being to be deciphered, an *omnitudo realitatus,* and the foundation of this possibility is permanently laid by the first sensory experience, however narrow or imperfect it may be. We have no other way of knowing what the world is than by actively accepting this affirmation which is made every instant within us; for any definition of the world would be merely a summary and schematic outline, conveying nothing to us, if we did not already have access to the determinate, if we did not in fact know it by virtue of the mere fact that we are.[4]

Finally, speaking of other people and the human world, Merleau-Ponty writes:

Against the social world I can always avail myself of my sensible nature, close my eyes, stop up my ears, live as a stranger in society, treat others, ceremonies and institutions as mere arrangements of color and light, and strip them of their human significance. Against the natural world I can always have recourse to the thinking nature and entertain doubts about each perception taken on its own. The truth of solipsism is there. Every experience will always appear to me as a particular instance which does not exhaust the generality of my being, and I have always, as Malebranche said, movement left wherewith to go further. But I can fly from being only into being; for example, I escape from society into nature, or from the real world into an imaginary one made of the broken fragments of reality. The physical and social world al-

ways functions as a stimulus to my reactions, whether
these be positive or negative. I call such and such a perception into question only in the name of a truer one
capable of correcting it; in so far as I can deny each thing,
it is always by asserting that there is something in general, and this is why we say that thought is a thinking
nature, an assertion of being over and above the negation
of beings. I can evolve a solipsist philosophy but, in doing so, I assume the existence of a community of men
endowed with speech and I address myself to it.[5]

If one begins with the objectivistic position that perception
involves an automatic process of sensation by which objects affect a certain object that is also a subject, and that
the world as known comes about only with a subsequent
intervention of the subject, one may always doubt that the
world as known exists and, to go one step farther: one may
doubt whether any world exists and whether the process of
sensation and the subject exist. But by uncovering the original content of perception, which is concealed by unwarranted objectivistic prejudices, Merleau-Ponty discloses
man's original situatedness in the world prior to any theoretical representations of the world. Once this original situation is affirmed, one recognizes that the fact that there is
the world is the basis for any attempt to arrive at knowledge. The affirmation that there is the world is not identical
to the common-sense notion that what is perceived is what
is, or is at least all we have to work with. The common-
sense notion ignores man's original situation in the world,
which is never given as a totality in explicit perception. The
affirmation of man's original situatedness in the world allows the philosopher to affirm the transcendence of the
world as well as man's direct access to it, and it is only
these two aspects together that constitute the "worldness"
of the world. Common sense does not fully affirm that there
is the world.

At the outset of his final, unfinished work entitled *The
Visible and the Invisible,*[6] Merleau-Ponty returns to the affirmation *there is the world,* and discusses it as "perceptual

faith," the mute character of man's being situated in the world, of man's "being-in-the-world" prior to any reflection. *There is the world* appears to be an extremely simple statement. But this is deceptive. The depth of content of this affirmation can be appreciated by recognizing that in the light of Merleau-Ponty's analyses it may come as somewhat of a surprise. According to *Phenomenology of Perception,* existence is dynamic; perceiver and perceived cannot be accounted for in terms of an objectivistic theory that portrays them as complete objects found within a world that is an objective totality.

> The union of soul and body is not an amalgamation between two mutually external terms, subject and object, brought about by arbitrary decree. It is enacted at every instant in the movement of existence. . . .[7]

> This dialectic of form and content is what we have to restore, or rather, since "reciprocal action" is as yet only a compromise with causal thought, and a contradictory principle, we have to describe the circumstances under which this contradiction is conceivable which means existence, the perpetual reordering of fact and hazard by a reason nonexistent before and without those circumstances.[8]

This thesis is radicalized in *The Visible and the Invisible.* Not even the structure perceiver-perceived is treated as given. Here the genesis of this structure is elucidated. We are not dealing with the origin of a particular perceiver or thing perceived or with the origin of perceivers and perceived in general. That is to say, we are not dealing ex post facto with the structure perceiver-perceived. Rather, we are dealing with the coming into being of such a structure.[9] The source, Being, is radically dynamic.[10] The upshot of this ontological thesis could be nihilism. But Merleau-Ponty maintains the opposite,[11] and here is where this affirmation *there is the world* comes as somewhat of a surprise and reveals its depth.

In the prospectus of his work submitted in support of his candidacy to the Collège de France, Merleau-Ponty states concerning work that was to follow *Phenomenology of Perception:*

> Finally, [our inquiries] should lead us to a study of the Logos of the perceived world which we encountered in our earliest studies in the evidence of things. Here we rejoin the classical questions of metaphysics, but by following a route which removes from them their character as *problems*—that is to say, as difficulties which could be solved cheaply through the use of a few metaphysical entities constructed for this purpose. The notions of Nature and Reason, for instance, far from explaining the metamorphoses which we have observed from perception up to the more complex modes of human exchange, make them incomprehensible. For by relating them to separated principles, these notions mask a constantly experienced moment, the moment when an existence becomes aware of itself, grasps itself, and expresses its own meaning.[12]

This should serve as a warning to those who wish to understand Merleau-Ponty's endeavor, that when he speaks of Being in *The Visible and the Invisible* he is not speaking of a level of reality employed classically in order to resolve philosophic problems and thus he does not become ipso facto a metaphysician by speaking of Being. The task proposed by Merleau-Ponty calls for an act of philosophizing that does not "mask [this] constantly experienced moment . . . when an existence becomes aware of itself, grasps itself, and expresses its own meaning," but rather takes it up as it is, that is, an act that does not transmute the Logos of the perceived world into a metaphysical contrivance that allegedly explains the Logos, but rather makes manifest that Logos and in so doing is an act that itself "expresses its own meaning" and contributes to the Logos of the perceived world.[13] This act is metaphysics itself.[14] Merleau-Ponty's philosophic stance is not that of metaphysical nihilism. Nor is it that of ethical nihilism. Certain acts are appropriate. Hence the full force of the word *the* in the affirmation "there is *the* world." But such acts are appropriate not in the sense that having reconstructed the world in a theoretical fashion, man can decide what would be "correct" theoretically. Nor would such acts conform to a constructed system of values. The return to the Logos of the perceived world, which does not proceed by way of "constructed metaphysical entities" that allegedly provide an explanation of that world but rather proceeds by way of the affirmation of Being as radically dynamic, would not allow the quietism of relying on Being to determine man's acts. Man would act, and his acts would be appropriate in the sense that they would maintain man in the position in which not even those acts themselves could become a technology of acting, so to speak—another constructed system that would obscure the world that is and divert man's acts into a quietism of reliance on such a system. In the prospectus of his work Merleau-Ponty wrote that the act of metaphysics would provide us with the "principle of an ethics."[15] Although this step still lay in the future, when Merleau-Ponty's work was ended, we can say that we are dealing with a philosophical stance that is not nihilistic, in either a metaphysical or an ethical sense.

One of the simplest of everyday facts thus joins one of the deepest of philosophical affirmations in the recognition that "there is the world."[16] Merleau-Ponty opens *The Visible and the Invisible* thus:

> We see the things themselves, the world is what we see: formulae of this kind express a faith common to the natural man and the philosopher—the moment he opens his eyes; they refer to a deep-seated set of mute "opinions" implicated in our lives.[17]

And he writes a bit later:

> If the philosopher questions, and hence feigns ignorance of the world and of the vision of the world which are

operative and take form continually within him, he does
so precisely in order to make them speak, because he
believes in them and expects from them all his future
science.[18]

The problematic of perception provides Merleau-Ponty
with a vehicle that he uses to communicate his thesis, there
is the world. The study of perception provides us with the
key, in the sense of the key to a code, that allows us to
decipher Merleau-Ponty's studies ranging through art, politics, the physical sciences, the human sciences, and other
areas, and receive the communication *there is the world*.
Because the "natural man" accepts what is perceived as
what is, or at least as all that man has to work with, or in
short, because the "natural man" takes perception for
granted, the problematic of perception is the appropriate
vehicle.[19] Hence the full meaning of Merleau-Ponty's statement before the Société française de philosophie:

> The perceived world is the always presupposed foun-
> dation of all rationality, all value and all existence. This
> thesis does not destroy either rationality or the absolute.
> It only tries to bring them down to earth.[20]

Perception naively accepted is perception falsified, hence
the need for rationality, but not a rationality that loses itself
in an absolute constructed in order to overcome the paradoxes inherent in perception. There is the world. Thus this
absolute must be brought down to earth.

B. Language

Merleau-Ponty's thesis *there is the world,* once affirmed,
abruptly poses the problematic of language. If this thesis is
the starting point of philosophy, does not the philosopher,
in attempting to examine the world and give an account of
it, thereby falsify it in transmuting it into philosophy?
Should not the philosopher remain silent in this world that

is? But silence as a refusal to speak is tantamount to an admission that the philosopher cannot assert that there is the world or at least is tantamount to an admission that the philosopher cannot know or say how the world is; this latter really means that one cannot assert that there is *the* world, this particular world. What is called for is a silence that would not be the opposite of speaking but that would be coincident with speaking. Such a silence would not be a refusal to speak and such a speaking would not be a falsification of the world.

Thus Merleau-Ponty writes in a working note for *The Visible and the Invisible:*

> Therefore very important, from the introduction on, to introduce the problem of the tacit cogito and the language cogito   Naïveté of Descartes who does not see a tacit cogito under the cogito of *Wesen,* of significations—But naïveté also of a silent cogito that would deem itself to be an adequation with the silent consciousness, whereas its very description of silence rests entirely on the virtues of language. The taking possession of the world of silence, such as the description of the human body effects it, is no longer this world of silence, it is the world articulated, elevated to the *Wesen,* spoken—the description of the perceptual λόγος is a usage of λόγος προφορικός. Can this rending characteristic of reflection (which, wishing to return to itself, *leaves itself*) come to an end? There would be needed a silence that envelops the speech anew, after one has come to recognize that speech enveloped the alleged silence of the psychological coincidence. What will this silence be? As the reduction finally is not for Husserl a transcendental immanence, but the disclosing of the *Weltthesis,* this silence will *not be the contrary* of language.[21]

But what will this silence that is not the absence of speaking be, and how is it to be spoken? These questions are asked explicitly by Merleau-Ponty only after *Phenomenology of Perception.* The present task is to trace how these

questions come to be posed by Merleau-Ponty's work and
then to trace the steps taken by Merleau-Ponty toward answering them.

C. Itinerary

Chapter 1 of this study, "Language as Original Content of
Perception," is devoted to Merleau-Ponty's explicit discussion of language in *Phenomenology of Perception.* The
chapter is divided into two sections. The first, "Languagely
Meaning," disengages Merleau-Ponty's concept of meaning
developed in the studies in *Phenomenology of Perception*
that lead to the chapter devoted to language, "The Body as
Expression, and Speech." There is no extended discussion
in Merleau-Ponty's work devoted explicitly to this concept
of meaning, and yet one may find here the point of departure for understanding Merleau-Ponty's account of language. It is necessary to root out the assumption that all
meaning is the result of arbitrary construction of linguistic
systems. The second section, "The Body as Expression,
and Speech," is devoted to the chapter that bears that title
in *Phenomenology of Perception.* Here it is revealed that
language is not a fixed system, available as a tool for use
and reinvention by man, but rather is a radically dynamic
dimension of man's life which, through processes of mutual
determination with other dimensions of man's life, brings
about man's situation-in-the-world, which man can transform only via an act that does not avoid that situation by
resorting to contrived theoretical systems interposed between man and his situation, but rather takes up that situation as it is.

Chapter 2 of this study, "The Linguistic Act," consists of
two sections, "The Overcoming of Subjectism" and "The
Philosophic Act of Speaking." The first is devoted to part
three of *Phenomenology of Perception,* "Being-for-Itself
and Being-in-the-World." Here Merleau-Ponty's studies of
the *Cogito,* temporality, and freedom reveal that man must

be understood simultaneously as fully "in-the-world," situated prior to any act by man, and as acting so as to bring about the existence of the world such as it is. Even those acts whereby man brings about the existence of the world such as it is must be understood as originating not in a subject conceived somehow as apart from the world, but rather as originating in the world. The second section of this chapter discusses the implications for the linguistic act, in particular for the philosophical act of speaking called for in order to say fully what language is. At this point it becomes evident that Merleau-Ponty's claim for the "primacy of perception" does not confine the philosopher to a single dimension of existence and blind him to those aspects of language which do not fall within the province of the problematic of perception as traditionally conceived but, on the contrary, opens the way toward understanding all dimensions of existence. In particular it poses the problematic of language in its singular importance and full relief, making apparent the hazards that threaten an attempt to give a full account of language and thus suggesting a way toward arriving at one.

Chapter 3 of this study, "Living Language," focuses on Merleau-Ponty's essay "On the Phenomenology of Language." Here Merleau-Ponty turns from the disclosure of language as original content of perception to an explicitly ontological effort at determining what language is. Disclosures made here concerning what language is help to precise further the nature of the philosophical act of speaking called for in order to say fully what language is. Thus they suggest a way of proceeding that Merleau-Ponty does adopt in his last works and in particular they suggest why it is that the domain of art, if properly understood, should shed further light on the nature of the requisite philosophical act of speaking.

The fourth and final chapter of this study, "Toward an Originary Act of Speaking," is divided into three sections. The first, entitled "Art," presents Merleau-Ponty's effort to determine what art is, and proceeds by way of an exploration of the artistic gesture. The second and third sections, entitled respectively "The Flesh" and "The Visible and the Invisible," are devoted to discoveries that bring the philosopher closer to saying fully what language is, discoveries made in the course of Merleau-Ponty's study of art and then presented in his last work, *The Visible and the Invisible*.

Notes

1. *Signs*, p. 93.
2. "Le problème du monde, et pour commencer celui du corps propre, consiste en ceci que *tout y demeure*." *Phénoménologie de la perception* (Paris: Gallimard, 1945), p. 230; my translation. This anticipates the discussion in section B of this introduction of how the thesis "there is *the* world" poses the problematic of language. If "[the world] is all already there" how then is the philosopher to utter the truth of the world without hypostatizing an ideality of one sort or another that allegedly is to provide the explanation of the world, that is, without transmuting the world into philosophy and thereby falsifying it?
3. *Phenomenology of Perception*, p. 330.
4. Ibid., p. 328.
5. Ibid., p. 360.
6. *The Visible and the Invisible*, ed. Claude Lefort, trans. Alphonso Lingis, Northwestern Studies in Phenomenology and Existential Philosophy (Evanston, Ill.: Northwestern University Press, 1968). The title for this posthumously published unfinished work was suggested by working notes found with the unfinished manuscript and published with it.
7. *Phenomenology of Perception*, pp. 88–89.
8. Ibid., p. 127.
9. See *The Visible and the Invisible*, pp. 31–35. Here Merleau-Ponty offers a critique of philosophies of reflection. Kant, for example, laid out his transcendental philosophy as an account of what must be the case if a world is to be possible. Hence he begins with the assumption of the structure that is the world and does not go to the originating dynamism that is the source of the world.
10. See *The Visible and the Invisible*, p. 174. Here Merleau-Ponty speaks of that which is (e.g., "the being-rose of the rose, the being-society of society, the being-history of history," in Heidegger's terminology, beings considered in their Being dimension) as dynamic. The German *Wesen* is employed to speak of that which is. Following Heidegger's recognition of the original meaning of the term, Merleau-Ponty takes it in its verbal sense—i.e., not as static essence but as the process of "essencing." Thus that which is is not stable structure in motion, but is radically dynamic.
11. In a working note to *The Visible and the Invisible*, Merleau-Ponty writes: ". . . the *Ablaufsphänomen* that Husserl describes and thematizes contains . . . the 'simultaneity,' the *passage*, the *nunc stans*, the Proustian corporeity as guardian of the past, the immersion in a Being in transcendence not reduced to the 'perspectives' of the 'consciousness'—it contains an intentional reference which is

not only from the past to the factual, empirical present, but also and inversely from the factual present to a dimensional present or *Welt* or Being, where the past is 'simultaneous' with the present in the narrow sense. This *reciprocal* intentional reference marks the limit of the intentional analytic: the point where it becomes a philosophy of transcendence. We encounter this *Ineinander* each time the intentional reference is no longer that from a *Sinngebung* to a *Sinngebung* that motivates it but from a 'noema' to a 'noema' " (*The Visible and the Invisible*, pp. 243–44; working note). Thus not only may we say there is the world *now*, we may say there is the world in the sense that all "noemata" are simultaneous. Being is fully determinate. This is the "vertical Being" of which Merleau-Ponty speaks in *The Visible and the Invisible*. This is the complete opposite of metaphysical nihilism.

In another working note Merleau-Ponty writes: "I call the evolutionist perspective in question[—]I replace it with a cosmology of the visible in the sense that, considering endotime and endospace, for me it is no longer a question of origins, nor limits, nor of a series of events going to a first cause, but one sole explosion of Being which is forever. Describe the world of the 'rays of the world' beyond every serial-eternitarian or ideal alternative—Posit the existential eternity—the eternal body" (*The Visible and the Invisible*, p. 265; working note). Once again, Being is fully determinate—the complete opposite of metaphysical nihilism.

12. *The Primacy of Perception and Other Essays*, pp. 10–11.

13. Once again this anticipates the discussion in section B of this introduction of how the thesis "there is *the* world" poses the problematic of language. This act of philosophizing that would lay bare the Logos of the perceived world is an act of speaking. How is it to be performed?

14. See *The Primacy of Perception*, p. 11. R. Kwant writes in *From Phenomenology to Metaphysics: An Inquiry into the Last Period of Merleau-Ponty's Philosophical Life*, Duquesne Studies: Philosophical Series, vol. 20 (Pittsburgh, Pa.: Duquesne University Press, 1966), p. 240: "Merleau-Ponty's philosophy is truly metaphysical because its last word is Being." I would rather say that the first word is Being in the sense that "there is the world" is a foundational affirmation of Merleau-Ponty's thought. He becomes a metaphysician by engaging in the task of performing the above-described act.

15. *The Primacy of Perception*, p. 11.

16. "No *absolute* difference, therefore, between philosophy or the transcendental and the empirical (it is better to say: the ontological and the ontic)—No absolutely pure philosophical word. No purely philosophical politics, for example, no philosophical rigorism, when it is a question of a Manifesto.

"Yet philosophy is not immediately non-philosophy—It rejects from non-philosophy what is positivism in it, militant non-philosophy—which would reduce history to the visible, would deprive it precisely of its depth under the pretext of adhering to it better: irrationalism, *Lebensphilosophie*, fascism and communism, which do indeed have philosophical meaning, but hidden from themselves" (*The Visible and the Invisible*, p. 266; working note). It is interesting to note that Merleau-Ponty points out that there is no absolute difference between the ontological and the ontic, employing Heidegger's terminology to refer respectively to beings in their Being dimension and beings as beings. Here we are closer to the later Heidegger who, despite the extreme forgetfulness of Being that characterizes our age, does not remain silent but speaks haltingly of such concerns as language, painting, poetry, and technology, and indeed speaks less and less of the difference between Being and beings.

17. *The Visible and the Invisible,* p. 3.

18. Ibid., p. 4.

19. Acceptance and affirmation of the attitude that the world as it is perceived is the world as it is, or at least that what is perceived is all man has to work with, is a conspicuous ingredient in the manner in which man seeks to come to terms with the world today. Merleau-Ponty's study of perception involves a clarification of the modern frame of mind. It also involves a clarification of a foundational orientation of modern philosophy. Beginning with Descartes, we can trace the development of this feature of modern philosophy. The reason for the possibility of Descartes's doubting the world as our senses disclose it rests on a prejudged acceptance of sensation as our only possible access to the real world. Descartes's very problem arises from this acceptance. Hume's skepticism, the culmination of the empiricist school of thought, is this acceptance of perception as our only access to the world, shorn of any speculative metaphysical means of ascertaining that it is the "real world" that we perceive. On this point, Kant follows Hume and declares that we have knowledge only of what we experience through our senses and that this is knowledge only of the world of representation, not of the world as it is in itself. Seeking to refute this limitation which he regards as imposed by Kant, Hegel begins with our immediate sense contact with the object of knowledge and proceeds to trace a process by which he claims this contact is transformed into absolute knowledge. Each state of the process is *aufgehoben,* taken up, transformed, and overcome in the succeeding stage. Inasmuch as the original sense contact is the origin of the process, the entire process is, in a sense, contained within that original moment and we may say that Hegel's entire effort is a clarification of that moment. However, perception itself is left behind as a relatively preliminary stage of the process of arriving at knowledge. If however, as does Merleau-Ponty, one remains suspicious of the dialectic inasmuch as it tends toward an intellectual maneuver, introduced in order to resolve the paradoxes inherent in each stage of the process (see *The Visible and the Invisible,* pp. 89–95, 183), one must begin anew by determining precisely what perception is. After Hegel, the turn away from "idealism" and the return to Hume characteristic of the Anglo-Saxon tradition maintain the taking-for-granted of perception as the only possible means of access to the real world and eventually issue in claims that this access is severely limited if not a misconception from the start, in which case philosophy can deal only with the body of scientific knowledge that finds its source in the empirical, or can deal only with the systems employed to talk about the world, no access to the world being possible.

20. "The Primacy of Perception and Its Philosophical Consequences," trans. James M. Edie, in *The Primacy of Perception and Other Essays,* p. 13.

21. *The Visible and the Invisible,* p. 179. Another working note: "Silence of perception = the object made of wires of which I could not say what it is, nor how many sides it has, etc. and which nonetheless is there. . . .

"There is an analogous silence of language i.e. a language that no more involves acts of reactivated signification than does this perception—and which nonetheless functions, and inventively   it is it that is involved in the fabrication of a book—" (*The Visible and the Invisible,* p. 268). Peculiarities in punctuation and spacing in the working notes for *The Visible and the Invisible* are due to the rough nature of these notes in Merleau-Ponty's manuscript.

MERLEAU-PONTY

1 Language as Original Content of Perception

Absolute Knowledge contains within itself this necessity of relinquishing itself from the form of the pure notion, and necessarily involves the transition of this notion into consciousness. For Spirit that knows itself is, just for the reason that it grasps its own notion, immediate identity with itself; and this in the distinction that it implies, is the certainty of what is immediate or is sense-consciousness—the beginning from which we started. This process of releasing itself from the form of its self is the highest freedom and security of its knowledge of itself.[1]

—Hegel

The Idea which is independent or for itself, when viewed on the point of this its unity with itself, is Perception or Intuition, and the percipient Idea is Nature.[2]

—Hegel

MERLEAU-PONTY turns to perception in response to what is learned from his first book, *The Structure of Behavior*. At the outset of that work, Merleau-Ponty states its goal:

Our goal is to understand the relations of consciousness and nature: organic, psychological, or even social. By nature we understand here a multiplicity of events external to each other and bound together by relations of causality.[3]

In the course of the work Merleau-Ponty makes it evident that he is not dealing with a "relationship" between consciousness and nature if relationship is conceived as a link between two terms external to one another. The intent of the work is posed, not in terms of Descartes's *res cogitans* and *res extensa,* but rather in terms of consciousness and nature, which suggests the intermingling of the two, inasmuch as consciousness, following the Husserlian interpretation of Descartes and development of the concept of intentionality, is always consciousness of something, and nature is a term applied not only to material bodies but to psychological and social realities as well. Behavior is chosen as the ground on which to study the human being because "behavior" does not connote a reduction of mind to body or vice versa but rather does connote a dynamic interplay of man and environment. In the concluding part of *The Structure of Behavior,* the "Problem of Perceptual Consciousness," Merleau-Ponty makes it evident that his study in that work of the analysis of behavior offered by the school of psychology called behaviorism allows him to affirm what Descartes disclosed, inasmuch as Descartes opened the field of consciousness, so to speak; but it does not allow him to follow Descartes insofar as Descartes posited the "thinking thing" as a subject set apart from a world of objects and in so doing opened the way for the hypostatization of a pure consciousness that posits the world. At the same time, Merleau-Ponty's study of the behavioristic analysis of behavior, from the simplest to the higher forms, demonstrates the impossibility of adopting a materialistic, causal ontology in accounting for human beings and their relationship to the world. The classical notion of the body as the sum of the materialistic parts operating on one another via mechanistic causality is a misconception. The body is a whole unequal to the sum of parts. Furthermore, the so-called stimulus of traditional behavioristic theory is not isolable as an objective, elementary cause. It is elaborated by the organism. Similarly, the so-called reaction is elaborated by the orientation of the organism in its environment. Hence it is ultimately impossible to objectively divide behavior into organism and environment involved in a cause-effect mechanism. As an alternative to materialistic, mechanistic ontology, Merleau-Ponty offers an account of this whole in which organism and environment are subsumed, according to which this unity is to be conceived as "form," a notion that Merleau-Ponty borrows from Gestalt psychology. *Form* refers to a totality that is not the sum of parts but rather within which the various elements subsumed dynamically determine each of the others and each is in turn dynamically determined by the others. *Form* implies that this unity is not a homogeneous One but is indeed determinate, structured. Ordering occurs within the form, and is not the result of an external influence such as mind, conceived of as separated from the rest of the organism.

Traditional interpretations of the concept of form developed in Gestalt psychology tend to relapse into categories derived from materialism when ontology is the issue. Merleau-Ponty points out that this is a betrayal of the radically new nature of the concept of form and demonstrates that a philosophy of form can account for the physical order, the vital order, and the human order without succumbing to materialism, or to mentalism, that is, the positing of a pure consciousness that arranges behavior, or to vitalism, that is, an attempt to complete an objectivistic theory by hypostatization of some sort of element—call it life, consciousness, or a vital élan—that would fuse together the apparently distinct levels of the physical, biological, and mental. In each case, the particular order, the physical, the vital, or the human,[4] is actually constituted by the type of form peculiar to it. The forms are not the pure constructs of an activity of pure consciousness. Nor are they the framework of a universe that is in-itself. In each case the forms in question are perceived forms and cannot be theoretically built up from an opaque physical layer in itself. The full ontological import of the notion of form is that it integrates idea or essence and existence and requires no attempts to find an exterior source for the ordering process, which takes place inherently. Since the body of knowledge of man and his world derives from the integration of the contents of our perception at the time of experimental observation with structures borrowed as well from perceptual consciousness, it is the existent dynamic process of structuralization within perceptual consciousness that must be interrogated in order to pursue the philosophical investigation of man and his world begun in *The Structure of Behavior*. Merleau-Ponty's intent in *Phenomenology of Perception* is to disclose the original content of perception before it is overlaid with an objectivistic structure in accord with realism and not to replace traditional theories of perception with another theory. He makes this point in comparing empiricism with the view he offers:

> there is no phenomenon which can be adduced as a crucial proof against [empiricism]. Generally speaking, the description of phenomena does not enable one to refute thought which is not alive to its own existence, and which resides in things. The physicist's atoms will always appear more real than the historical and qualitative face of the world, the physico-chemical processes more real than the organic forms, the psychological atoms of empiricism more real than perceived phenomena, the intellectual atoms represented by the "significations" of the Vienna Circle more real than consciousness, as long as the attempt is made to build up the shape of the world (life, perception, mind) instead of recognizing, as the source which stares us in the face and as the ultimate court of appeal in our knowledge of these things, our *experience* of them. The adoption of this new way of looking at things . . . must be undertaken by everyone, whereupon it will be seen to be justified by the abundance of phenomena which it elucidates. Before its discovery, these phenomena were inaccessible.[5]

A. Languagely Meaning

In order to effect the transformation of perception that discloses the original content of perception, Merleau-Ponty must displace from an unwarranted dominating role, objectivistic characteristics as reflected in traditional empiricist and intellectualist theories of perception.[6] Traditional accounts of perception employ the notion of a unit of sensation, supposedly the elementary building block of the world as perceived. Merleau-Ponty points out one fatal fault of any account that relies on this notion: we never do have an experience of such a simple unit. As far as theory is concerned, either one or both of two mistakes are made in hypostatizing these units of sensation. In one case the actual content of perception is stripped of its structure in order to claim that this structure is the result of the combination, through a process, of which an account is never really given, of elementary units of sensation. In the other case the detailed, fixed structure that is the end product of a gradual process of perceiving is imposed upon the original content of perception in order to claim that this content consists of an established framework of isolable elementary units of sensation. Turning to perception itself we find that both are indeed mistaken accounts. For example:

> Instead of providing a simple means of delimiting sensations, if we consider [quality] in the experience itself which evinces it, it is as rich and mysterious as the object, or indeed the whole spectacle, perceived. This red patch which I see on the carpet is red only in virtue of a shadow which lies across it, and hence as an element in a spatial configuration. Moreover the color can be said to be there only if it occupies an area of a certain size, too small an area not being describable in these terms. Finally this red would literally not be the same if it were not the "woolly red" of a carpet.[7] Analysis, then discovers in each quality meanings which reside in it.[8]

Divesting perception of structure by reducing it in theory to isolated units of sensation is falsifying it. Imposing on it the fixed, detailed framework of the world as known after the process of clarification is equally to falsify perception. For example:

> Suppose we construct, by the use of optics and geometry, that bit of the world which can at any moment throw its image on our retina. Everything outside its perimeter,

since it does not reflect upon any sensitive area, no more affects our vision than does light falling on our closed eyes. We ought, then, to perceive a segment of the world precisely delimited, surrounded by a zone of blackness packed full of qualities with no interval between them, held together by definite relationships of size similar to those lying on the retina. The fact is that experience offers nothing like this, and we shall never, using the world as our starting-point, understand what a *field of vision* is. Even if it is possible to trace out a perimeter of vision by gradually approaching the center of the lateral stimuli, the results of such measurement vary from one moment to another, and one never manages to determine the instant when a stimulus once seen is seen no longer. The region surrounding the visual field is not easy to describe, but what is certain is that it is neither black nor grey. There occurs here an *indeterminate vision, a vision of something or other,* and to take the extreme case, what is behind my back is not without some element of visual presence.[9]

Both of the above-described mistakes stem from a single source, namely, the attributing of characteristics proper to a fixed objective world, such as that conceived by classical physics, to the content of original perception. When this content is portrayed as consisting of no more than isolated elementary units of sensation, the concept of these units that are not to be found in our experience derives from the concept of the completed physical object. When the original content of perception is portrayed as a fixed, detailed framework of completed objects, the entire world as it would be focused in a scientific objective account is transferred to original perception. In both cases, the transfer is unwarranted. Classical theories make the mistake of working in reverse, that is, of beginning with an end product, a detailed, completed, objective world, and hypostatizing a content of original perception that could easily be thought of as eventually yielding such a world, rather than turning immediately to the content of perception itself.

If we do put aside the prejudices deriving from classical theories of perception and come face-to-face with the original content of perception, exactly what do we find?[10] Merleau-Ponty does describe particular instances of original content of perception. For example:

> If I walk along a shore towards a ship which has run aground, and the funnel or masts merge into the forest bordering on the sand dune, there will be a moment when these details suddenly become part of the ship, and indissolubly fused with it. As I approached, I did not perceive resemblances or proximities which finally came together to form a continuous picture of the upper part of the ship. I merely felt that the look of the object was on the point of altering, that something was imminent in this tension, as a storm is imminent in storm clouds. Suddenly the sight before me was recast in a manner satisfying to my vague expectation. Only afterwards did I recognize, as justification for the change the resemblance and contiguity of what I call "stimuli"—namely the most determinate phenomena, seen at close quarters and with which I compose the "true" world. "How could I have failed to see that these pieces of wood were an integral part of the ship? For they were of the same color as the ship, and fitted well enough into its superstructure." But these reasons for correct perception were not given as reasons beforehand. The unity of the object is based on the foreshadowing of an immanent order which is about to spring upon us a reply to questions merely latent in the landscape. It solves a problem set only in the form of a vague feeling of uneasiness, it organizes elements which up to that moment did not belong to the same universe and which, for that reason, as Kant said with profound insight, could not be associated.[11]

The order that at first is only latent but becomes manifest as the unified object perceived, serves as guide, so to speak, for effecting the transformation of perception proposed by Merleau-Ponty. This order is meaning. Merleau-Ponty approaches this concept in *The Structure of Behavior* in speaking of structure in which signification and existence coincide. Structure has now become meaning, and the shift of emphasis is from "existence," understood primarily as offsetting the traditionally idealistic notion of "significance," to "existence" understood primarily as "facticity," hence underlining the quality of contingency. Meaningfulness does not only connote a structure of signification but also connotes the particularity of the various contents of perception. These various contents of perception cannot be substituted one for another in theory without losing sight of this quality of facticity. To attempt so to substitute these contents would be tantamount to assuming that the structure discerned in perception preexists the process of perception, thus predetermining that any contingent content of perception fits into this structure. This is an example of the unwarranted transfer, made in classical theories of perception, of a completed, determinate structure to the original content of perception.

Meaningfulness thus refers to the contingent unity of perception.

> Let us imagine a white patch on a homogeneous background. All the points in the patch have a certain "function" in common, that of forming themselves into a "shape." The color of the shape is more intense, and as it were more resistant than that of the background: the edges of the white patch "belong" to it, and are not part of the background although they adjoin it: the patch appears to be placed on the background and does not break it up. Each part arouses the expectation of more than it contains; and this elementary perception is therefore already charged with *meaning*.[12]

Once the unwarranted transference characteristic of traditional intellectualist and empiricist theories of perception, of a completed determinate structure to the original content of perception, is abandoned, the perception of the "human world" can no longer be conceived of as a second-order problem. Civilization is one determining feature of the contingent unity of perception. In overturning traditional empiricist theories of perception, Merleau-Ponty makes this point in terms of specific description, included here in its entirety because it is important to realize that failure to recognize this aspect of original content of perception is due to persistence of objectification of original content of perception in terms of bare atomic sense data.

By way of guarding against myths it is . . . desirable to point out everything that is made incomprehensible by empiricist constructions and all the basic phenomena which they conceal. They hide from us in the first place "the cultural world" or "human world" in which nevertheless almost our whole life is led. For most of us, Nature is no more than a vague and remote entity, overlaid by cities, roads, houses and above all by the presence of other people. Now, for empiricism, "cultural" objects and faces owe their distinctive form, their magic power, to transference and projection of memory, so that only by accident has the human world any meaning. There is nothing in the appearance of a landscape, an object or a body whereby it is predestined to look "gay" or "sad," "lively" or "dreary," "elegant" or "coarse." Once more seeking a definition of what we perceive through the physical and chemical properties of the stimuli which may act upon our sensory apparatus, empiricism excludes from perception the anger or the pain which I nevertheless read in a face, the religion whose essence I seize in some hesitation or reticence, the city whose temper I recognize in the attitude of a policeman or the style of a public building. There can no longer be any *objective spirit:* mental life withdraws into isolated consciousness devoted solely to introspection, instead of extending, as it apparently does in fact, over human space which is made up by those with whom I argue or live, filling my place of work or the abode of my happiness. Joy and sadness, vivacity and obtuseness are data of introspection, and when we invest landscapes or other people with these states, it is because we have observed in ourselves the coincidence between these internal perceptions and the external signs associated with them by the accidents of our constitution. . . . If on the other hand we admit that all these "transferences" are based on some intrinsic character of the object, the "human world" ceases to be a metaphor and becomes once more what it really is, the seat and as it were the *homeland* of our thoughts.

But not only does empiricism distort experience by making the cultural world an illusion, when in fact it is in it that our existence finds its sustenance. The natural world is also falsified and for the same reasons . . . the nature about which empiricism talks is a collection of stimuli and qualities, and it is ridiculous to pretend that nature thus conceived is, even in intention merely, the primary object of our perception: it does in fact follow the experience of cultural objects, or rather is one of them.[13]

One additional feature of the meaningful content of perception noted by Merleau-Ponty that dispels any possible remnants of prejudice deriving from realism, any possible conception of the original meaningful content of perception as affecting the perceiver or changing within itself in a manner in accord with realism, is the fact that the genesis of the meaningful content of perception involves a creative act on the part of the perceiver.

[P]erception is just that act which creates at a stroke, along with the cluster of data, the meaning which unites them— indeed which not only discovers the meaning *which they have,* but moreover *causes them to have a meaning.*[14]

Merleau-Ponty's conception of meaning is further precised by his investigation of the spatiality of one's own body and motility. Objectivistic theories of space are derived from the precognitive orientation of the body in the world. Before any such account of geometrical space is constructed, the body is already spatially situated in a determinate fashion. Before such words as *on, under, beside,* or *against* assume meaning in an intellectualist geometrical framework, these words refer to the features of the body's primary orientation in space. Indeed it is precisely because these words refer to the features of the body's primary orientation in space that they can assume meaning in an intellectualist framework. For example:

> When I say that an object is *on* a table, I always mentally put myself either in the table or in the object, and I apply to them a category which theoretically fits the relationship of my body to external objects. Stripped of this anthropological association, the word *on* is indistinguishable from the word "under" or the word "beside."[15]

Prior to any type of intellectual act of organization, the body is oriented toward certain directions and away from others. Before being objectified intellectually, the entities toward which and away from which the body is oriented are terms of the "intentional threads"[16] that form the structure of man's situation in the world prior to any objective cognition, prior to any response to the world. Merleau-Ponty calls this preobjective situation man's being-in-the-world.[17] Being-in-the-world is structured in the sense given to the word *structure* in *The Structure of Behavior*. That is, it involves determinate signification but it is not ideal. In the language of *Phenomenology of Perception*, being-in-the-world is laden with meaning, the contingent unity of the content of perception, in which each element is dynamically determined by every other. This primordial orientation of the body escapes all acounts that portray space as a separate element interposed between isolated objects located at particular spots at particular moments. The phenomenal body, that is, the body as involved in the original content of perception and not the body as objectified in classical theory, the "intentional threads" that bind it to the ends toward which man is directed, and the phenomena that are terms within this intentional structure, cannot be isolated in theory without distorting them. The contiguity of these elements found within man's being-in-the-world renders inadequate all accounts of meaning as a mere deriva-

tive of the arrangement of isolated entities. Meaning is coincident with being-in-the-world.

The original content of perception is radically dynamic.
This is why Merleau-Ponty does reject preconceived notions of the nature of the process of perception that amount
to objectifications of the preobjective, original content of
perception. This is to say that here it is not a question of
existing elements that are in motion. Rather, the process
involved in man's being-in-the-world is the process of ontogenesis. While describing the "phenomenal field" that is
opened for investigation once the objectivistic prejudices of
classical theories have been rejected, Merleau-Ponty
writes:

> Our task will be . . . to rediscover phenomena, the layer
> of living experience through which other people and
> things are first given to us, the system "Self-others-
> things" *as it comes into being.*[18]

The process involved in being-in-the-world is the ontogenesis of the perceiver-perceived structure. Merleau-Ponty's
study of motility reveals that motility is neither a mechanistic process whereby the body would be physicalistically
caused to move nor is it a process whereby a subject, conceived of as apart from the world that it would order, somehow causes the motion of the body. Rather, the source of
motility lies within man's being-in-the-world. Hence the
concept of being-in-the-world begins to take on the significance of a move beyond the subject, so to speak, not to a
world as portrayed by realism, and not to a middle ground
between subject and object, since the dualism is erroneous,
but rather to that medium in which both perceiver and perceived find their source, that medium which Merleau-
Ponty, in his study of the spatiality of one's own body and
motility, calls existence. Merleau-Ponty's study reveals
that any intellectual analysis of motion is derived from
strains or tensions that already exist within the structure of
man's original, preobjective situation in the world:

These elucidations enable us clearly to understand motility as basic intentionality. Consciousness is in the first place not a matter of "I think that" but of "I can."[19] Schneider's [a patient described in psychological studies from which Merleau-Ponty draws in his study of the spatiality of one's own body and motility] motor trouble cannot, any more than his visual deficiency, be reduced to any failure of the general function of representation. Sight and movement are specific ways of entering into relationship with objects and if, through all these experiences, some unique function finds its expression, it is the momentum of existence, which does not cancel out the radical diversity of contents, because it links them to each other, not by placing them all under the control of an "I think," but by guiding them towards the intersensory unity of a "world." Movement is not thought about movement, and bodily space is not space thought of or represented. "Each voluntary movement takes place in a setting, against a background which is determined by the movement itself. . . . We perform our movements in a space which is not 'empty' or unrelated to them, but which on the contrary, bears a highly determinate relation to them: movement and background are, in fact, only artificially separated stages of a unique totality."[20] In the action of the hand which is raised towards an object is contained a reference to the object, not as an object represented, but as that highly specific thing towards which we project ourselves, near which we are, in anticipation, and which we haunt. Consciousness is being towards the thing through the intermediary of the body.[21]

When Merleau-Ponty says that the "momentum of existence" links together the radical diversity of contents and guides them toward the intersensory unity of a world, man himself is subsumed *in the world*. Existence, which in *The Structure of Behavior* was attributed as a characteristic of the "forms" of behavior in order to emphasize that they are not ideal, and which thus far in the development of Merleau-Ponty's conception of meaning has connoted the contingent facticity of meaning within man's being-in-the-world, now refers to the dynamic medium that subsumes perceiver and perceived.

Existence is radically dynamic. The process involved in the medium that subsumes perceiver and perceived is the process of ontogenesis. Insofar as man's actions are the resolution of strains or tensions within the structure of being-in-the-world and these actions involve determinate means, such as, for example, particular tools directed toward determinate ends, these actions are amenable to objective analysis, and it may seem that action eliminates strains within being-in-the-world—that is, that through action being-in-the-world collapses into a state that could be thoroughly accounted for by realism. However, being-in-the-world never loses its inherent structure, its inherent meaning. Being-in-the-world is never reduced to a state in which meaning would subsequently arise from haphazard associations or by impositions from without. Consequently, although motility involving actions that realize determinate ends via determinate means is not illusory, and does not have to be left behind in order for being-in-the-world to be known as it truly is but rather must be fully affirmed as contributing to being-in-the-world, it must also be affirmed that motility itself is founded upon the more fundamental process of ontogenesis. Insofar as space, even when not distorted by conceiving of it as a separate element interposed between isolated objects located at particular spots at particular moments, does, like motility, always display features amenable to objective analysis, that is, always reveals itself as relational, as fixing a structure comprised of identifiable although nonisolable elements, and inasmuch as the process involved in being-in-the-world is the radically dynamic process of ontogenesis, it must be affirmed that space itself is founded upon a more fundamental level. When we acknowledge that perceiver and perceived are subsumed within one structure, and thus rather than speaking of being-in-the-world we speak of that medium which Merleau-Ponty now calls existence, we can affirm that existence is the primordial level upon which space is founded. With the concept of existence expanded in this manner, existence no longer refers only to a characteristic of meaning; rather, existence and meaning are coincident. Ontogenesis and the genesis of meaning are the same process. This is the point at stake in the following passage, given that motility is founded upon the primordial process of ontogenesis. The passage occurs at the conclusion of Merleau-Ponty's analysis of motility and the spatiality of one's own body.

> "Already motility, understood in its pure state, possesses the basic power of giving a meaning *(Sinngebung)*."[22] Even if subsequently, thought and perception of space are liberated from motility and from being-in-space, for us to be able to form a representation of space, it is first necessary that we should have been introduced into space through our body and that our body should have provided the first model of the transpositions, the equivalences, and the objectifications that make of space an objective system and allow our experience to be an experience of objects, opening out on an "in itself." "Motility is the primary sphere in which initially the meaning of all significations in the domain of represented space is engendered."[23]

Merleau-Ponty's analysis of the body in its sexual being furthers the disclosure of meaning as inherent in the original content of perception. By turning to man's sexuality, to man's affective life, Merleau-Ponty discloses a mode of determinateness that resists all objective analysis precisely because it is the fabric, so to speak, woven of the intentional threads through which one's own bodily consciousness comprehends other incarnate subjects. This "erotic comprehension" cannot be plotted on an objectivistic grid. Unlike primordial motility, which involves relationships between the phenomenal body on the one hand and on the other, certain terms of the motor intentions that radiate

from the body, sexual attraction does not extend from one
particular point to another particular point. True, sexual
intentionality aims from a body to another body. But the
bodies, inasmuch as they are involved in this affective intentionality, are not amenable to analyses that locate objects at particular points at particular times in the way that
the terms of motor intentionality, including the body, yield
to such analysis almost immediately upon the acknowledgment of primordial motility—that is, motility originating
within man's being-in-the-world prior to any attempt at theoretical analysis.[24]

> [O]ne begins to suspects a mode of perception distinct from
> objective perception, a kind of significance distinct from
> intellectual significance, an intentionality which is not
> pure "awareness of something." Erotic perception is not
> a *cogitatio* which aims at a *cogitatum;* through one body
> it aims at another body, and takes place in the world, not
> in a consciousness. A sight has a sexual significance for
> me, not when I consider, even confusedly, its possible
> relationship to the sexual organs or to pleasurable states,
> but when it exists for my body, for that power always
> available for bringing together into an erotic situation, the
> stimuli applied, and adapting sexual content to it. There
> is an erotic "comprehension" not of the order of under-
> standing, since understanding subsumes an experience,
> once perceived, under some idea, while desire compre-
> hends blindly by linking body to body.[25]

Furthermore, the radical contingency of the original content of perception is accented by the study of sexuality. The
topology of the "erotic situation" arises from the sexual
schema of the body understood as phenomenal body, the
body as involved in the original content of perception,
never totally within the grasp of the perceiver and thus
impossible to fix objectivistically.

> [T]he visible body is subtended by a sexual schema, which
> is strictly individual, emphasizing the erogenous areas,

outlining a sexual physiognomy, and eliciting the gestures of [the body of the other sex] which is itself integrated into this emotional totality.[26]

There is no recourse to an idealism that would be instantiated in the original content of perception. This position,
although not a type of realism, is another form of ground-
less objectification inasmuch as it claims that a completed
framework of ideal meaning does subsist in some manner.
Merleau-Ponty provides a description of the meaningfulness of the content of dreams that demonstrates that if one
theoretically divorces sexual signification from the meaningful content of dreams and portrays sexuality as though it
were a ready-made completed framework of significations,
the meaning of dreams is misrepresented.

> The dreamer does not first visualize the latent content of
> his dream, the one, that is, which is to be revealed with
> the help of suitable images by the "second account"; he
> does not first perceive "in clear" the stimuli of genital
> origin as being genital, only subsequently translating the
> text into figurative language. For the dreamer, indeed,
> who is far removed from the language of the waking
> state, this or that genital excitation or sexual drive *is*
> without more ado this image of a wall being climbed or
> cliff-face being scaled, which are seen as the obvious
> content. Sexuality becomes diffused in images which de-
> rive from it only certain typical relationships, only a cer-
> tain general emotional physiognomy. The dreamer's
> penis *becomes* the serpent which appears in the obvious
> content.[27]

It is in this way, the way in which meaning comes into
being with the dream, the way in which sexuality becomes
diffused in the images, that meaning permeates original
content of perception. It is in this way that meaning permeates language that we speak and hear. This is why in his
essay entitled "On the Phenomenology of Language"
Merleau-Ponty describes language as "pregnant with

meaning" and speaks of "languagely meaning."[28] Here the
appropriate passage will simply be quoted at length. Full
comprehension of what is involved requires the study that
follows in this chapter, of Merleau-Ponty's extended discussion, in *Phenomenology of Perception,* of language.

The speaking power the child assimilates in learning
his language is not the sum of morphological, syntactical,
and lexical meanings. These attainments are neither necessary nor sufficient to acquire a language, and once the
act of speaking is acquired it presupposes no comparison
between what I want to express and the conceptual arrangement of the means of expression I make use of. The
words and turns of phrase needed to bring my significative intention to expression recommend themselves to
me, when I am speaking, only by what Humboldt called
innere Sprachform (and our contemporaries call *Wort-
begriff*) that is, only by a certain style of speaking from
which they arise and according to which they are organized without my having to represent them to myself.
There is a "languagely" meaning of language which effects the mediation between my as yet unspeaking intention and words, and in such a way that my spoken words
surprise me myself and teach me my thought. Organized
signs have their immanent meaning, which does not arise
from the "I think" but from the "I am able to."
    This action at a distance by language, which brings
significations together without touching them, and this
eloquence which designates them in a peremptory fashion without ever changing them into words or breaking
the silence of consciousness, are eminent cases of corporeal intentionality. I have a rigorous awareness of the
bearing of my gestures or of the spatiality of my body
which allows me to maintain relationships with the world
without thematically representing to myself the objects I
am going to grasp or the relationships of size between my
body and the avenues offered to me by the world. On the
condition that I do not reflect expressly upon it, my consciousness of my body immediately signifies a certain
landscape about me, that of my fingers a certain fibrous
or grainy style of the object. It is in the same fashion that

the spoken word (the one I utter or the one I hear) is pregnant with a meaning which can be read in the very texture of the linguistic gesture (to the point that a hesitation, an alteration of the voice, or the choice of a certain syntax suffices to modify it), and yet is never contained in that gesture, every expression always appearing to me as a trace, no idea being given to me except in transparency, and every attempt to close our hand on the thought which dwells in the spoken word leaving only a bit of verbal material in our fingers.[29]

The "attempt to close our hand on the thought which dwells in the spoken word" would be analogous to an attempt to theoretically divorce sexual signification from the meaningful content of the dream as described in the passage quoted earlier, and the "bit of verbal material left in our fingers" by such an attempt would be analogous to a nonsensical juxtaposition of images impoverished beyond recognition, which would be the remains of a dream if the attempt is made to theoretically divorce signification from it and claim that such signification is localizable in an already-completed framework.

It is precisely the meaningfulness of the original content of perception as revealed by Merleau-Ponty's study of man's being-in-the-world that is overlooked by traditional theories of perception. At the close of his study of the spatiality of the body and motility Merleau-Ponty writes:

In sum, what we have learned from the study of motility is a new meaning of the word *meaning*. The strength of intellectualist psychology, like that of idealist philosophy, comes from the fact that they have no difficulty in showing that perception and thought have an intrinsic meaning and cannot be explained in terms of the external association of fortuitously grouped contents. The *Cogito* was the coming to awareness of this interiority. But all signification was thereby conceived as an act of thought, as the operation of a pure I, and if intellectualism easily overcame empiricism, it was itself incapable of accounting for the variety of our experience, for that within it which is nonsense, and for the contingency of the contents. The experience of the body makes us acknowledge an imposition of meaning that is not accomplished by a universal constituting consciousness, a meaning that adheres to certain contents.[30]

As we now turn to Merleau-Ponty's description of how language itself is revealed by the proposed transformation of perception that displaces objectivistic characteristics from an unwarranted dominant role and thus discloses the original content of perception, it is meaning recognized in the above-described manner that will serve as guide, so to speak, for effecting this transformation. Ultimately, the overcoming of objectivism will require that the philosopher abandon the point of view of a subject who perceives what is already there to be perceived and begin at the point so to speak, where the perceiver-perceived structure comes into being, that point which in *Phenomenology of Perception*, as we have seen, Merleau-Ponty calls "existence." Ultimately, as we shall see, what will be required is an originary act of philosophical speaking, one that is neither an act performed on content of perception already laid out before a perceiver nor an act performed on an undifferentiated in-itself, the in-itself of Sartre's *Being and Nothingness*. Nevertheless, on the basis of what has been established concerning "languagely meaning," it will be impossible to portray the effort required of the philosopher as a futile attempt to speak a language in which meaning, which by the nature of things always remains hidden behind spoken language, is made explicit. Nor will it be possible to portray the effort required of the philosopher as an attempt to speak a language in which an ideal framework of meaning is made explicit. Nor will it be possible to portray this effort in terms of a hypostatized symbolic infrastructure which, even if said to be generated in and through language, would nevertheless be metalinguistic in nature, in the sense that it would have to be comprehended in order to comprehend the meaning of language, and thus would again pose a framework that would have to be represented to oneself in order to comprehend the meaning of language. In describing "languagely meaning" Merleau-Ponty points out that the act of speaking simply "presupposes no comparison between what I want to express and the conceptual arrangement of the means of expression I make use of." "Languagely meaning" is coincident with language. As will now be made clear with the disclosure of language itself as original content of perception, the genesis of meaning in language and the ontogenesis of language are the same process.

B. The Body as Expression, and Speech

At the outset of the chapter of *Phenomenology of Perception* entitled "The Body as Expression, and Speech," Merleau-Ponty acknowledges that the study of language should play a decisive role in the displacement of objectivistic characteristics from an unwarranted dominating role in the content of perception. He writes that here "we shall have the opportunity to leave behind us, once and for all, the traditional subject-object dichotomy."[31] Only the study itself will reveal if this is the outcome and, if so, why. However, before we engage in the study, it is possible to realize why Merleau-Ponty acknowledges at least this opportunity as such. Comparison with currents of man's being-in-the-world, already considered by Merleau-Ponty, is of help. Primordial motility has been disclosed as the phenomenal body's precognitive orientation toward certain phenomena and away from others. Sexuality has been disclosed as the phenomenal body's precognitive "erotic comprehension" of other bodies. Both motility and sexuality show up on a background of phenomena that contribute to the structuralization of the intentionality involved. For example, primordial motility is displayed by a situation in which the phenomenal body is oriented toward phenomena

that play determinate roles in the accomplishment of a particular task and away from phenomena that would be obstacles. This characteristic of primordial motility was cited as
amenable to objectification. In the case of sexuality, bodily
intentionality is directed toward another person, and although a careful exploration is called for in order to determine precisely what this entails, we can acknowledge the
fact that the other person does contribute to the structuralization of the sexual relationship. Unlike both motility and
sexuality, language, be it spoken, written, or thought, is a
feature of man's existence that does not appear to be directed toward existent phenomena that contribute to its
structuralization. That is, there is no apparent causal effect,
no apparent direct determining effect whatsoever, exerted
upon language by phenomena found in man's world. This is
why for contemporary common sense, language is self-
enclosed, a stock of always-available, always-understood
words and phrases that a person repeats habitually. One
cannot go so far as to say that for common sense language is
not determined in any way by phenomena found in the
world, because for common sense the question never
arises. As for rhetorical language, at first glance one may
say that language is here employed as a tool. But upon
consideration the analogy breaks down. Whereas a tool is
physically suited to the task at hand, there is a strong ten-
dency for rhetoric to degenerate into sophistry of the sort
that, while achieving its polemical end, all other motivation
is lost. Once again, language appears as a stock of habitual
devices.

Philosophically, one may draw the conclusion that,
bluntly, language says nothing about the world but says
something only about itself. Or one may allow that language
does say something about the world but only when it com-
plies with scientific findings. In such instances language
would say something about the world only within the strict
limitations of scientific empirical verifiability. Any translation of theoretical scientific statements and application of
scientific findings to the world of man's pragmatic affairs

would proceed according to the requisites for man's well-being, empirically determined.

But what if the philosopher "slackens the intentional threads which attach us to the world," "steps back to watch the forms of transcendence fly up like sparks from a fire," and thus performs the phenomenological reduction as described by Merleau-Ponty?[32] If the philosopher, in confronting language, suspends his complicity with the world, refuses to sustain the attitude according to which man's world consists of prescribed givens, what then could be said concerning the apparent immunity of language from causal determination, from direct determination of any sort by the phenomena found in man's world? The philosopher would have to look again in order to determine precisely what this observation indicates about language. Any ontological judgment, such as that which would distinguish language ontologically from a realm of phenomena that may or may not have a determining effect on language, is suspended. It is precisely this judgment that is tacitly assumed when the claim is made that language says nothing about the world, despite the fact that the additional claim may follow that all ontology is nonsensical because it involves statements purportedly about the world.

If it were to be demonstrated that language is fundamentally a mode of intentionality that does contribute to man's being-in-the-world and is neither a purely physical process nor a product of a pure consciousness conceived of as apart from the world, all objectification would collapse. As a current of man's being-in-the-world, language would be involved in mutually determining processes with phenomena that play a role in the structuralization of the intentionality of other currents of man's being-in-the-world. Language itself resists any objectification. Although categories of objectivity are at times imported in order to study language, it is not implied that language is an object or is a composite of objects. Specifically, although language may be treated as an already completed system of words and grammatical rules that may change by additions, substitutions, or disappearances of the same, this is not to say that language is an object as portrayed by realism. If language is involved in mutually determining processes with phenomena found in man's world, these phenomena cannot be regarded as objects to any degree. That is, these phenomena cannot be regarded as instances of an ontological type that is distinct from language, or from some ontological type of which language would be an instance, such that no interaction would be possible. In short, the original observation to the effect that language is immune to causal determination, to direct determination of any sort by phenomena found in man's world, involves the assumption of an erroneous ontological dualism derived from the objectification of such phenomena. The study of language holds open the possibility of abandoning the concept of object. Ultimately, the phenomenon of the phenomenon, and of the unified world of phenomena, would have to be clarified.

As for the other member of the subject-object dichotomy, the subject, the study of language offers an opportunity to abandon this traditional concept. Even if one were to admit that the two aspects of man's being-in-the-world already considered by Merleau-Ponty, motility and sexuality, cannot be accounted for on the basis of a pure consciousness that orders an external world in one manner or another, one may still maintain man's linguistic ability as the exclusive domain of pure consciousness. Spoken and written language may be regarded as the by-product of a process of thought that is interior to a pure consciousness employing the components of language and ordered according to the rules of language. The components of language and the rules of language may be regarded as produced by decree by a community of pure consciousnesses. If it is demonstrated that this one theoretical stronghold of pure consciousness is a fallacy, the notion of a self-enclosed subject set apart from objects would no longer be tenable. It is not a question of disproving the subject-object dichotomy; it is a question of abandoning it. Nor is it a question of demonstrating that subject and object are really continuous. There would be no reason to begin with the dichotomy in the first place.

All this may appear to be abstract speculative metaphysics, which is incongruous with Merleau-Ponty's effort at actually transforming perception. This discussion is abstract and speculative because only Merleau-Ponty's analyses of language could possibly fulfill the promise that the problematic of language holds. This discussion is not metaphysical, however, if by calling it such one understands that it has been suggested that there is a specific structure underlying all of reality, and that all phenomena are fundamentally parts, in some sense, of this metaphysical structure or that all phenomena must be regarded as ways in which this fundamental structure appears to man. By suggesting that the claim that language and the phenomena found in man's world cannot possibly be mutually determining is founded on a false assumption of an ontological dualism, one is not necessarily claiming that language and the phenomena found in man's world are fundamentally involved in the same metaphysical structure that ipso facto accounts for their interaction. No theoretical metaphysical device has been introduced in order to give an account of what cannot be explained employing objectivistic concepts. For example, it has not been said that language, be it thought, spoken, or written, is fundamentally composed of "monads" that are related through a "preestablished harmony" to "monads" that comprise the phenomena found in man's world, and that this accounts for the interaction. If it is demonstrated that language and the phenomena found in man's world are mutually determining, the question remains as to precisely what the process of mutual determination is.

Merleau-Ponty's first step in this study of language is to note the inadequacies of the traditional empiricist and intellectualist interpretations. One empiricist theory is that language consists of "traces" left in the neurological system which, when reactivated by the appropriate physical stimuli, which set off the particular neurological mechanism, then yield the appropriate word. Another empiricist theory is that language consists of "traces" left in the unconscious psychic life of a person, which, when recalled to consciousness because of associations with present states of consciousness, yield the appropriate word to be articulated. Speech is thus a third-person process. According to these theories speech does not involve any action on the part of the subject. Psychology has revealed the inadequacy of these empiricist theories by discovering that certain abnormalities pertaining to language indicate that speech does involve an act of some sort on the part of the speaker. It is the speaker's ability to perform this act that is impaired in such cases. For example, a patient who retains the use of certain words in contexts bearing on his immediate situation has lost the use of the same words when the opportunity is at hand to speak about something other than his immediate situation. This indicates a breakdown in an activity of thought on the part of the speaker that plays a role in determining the speaker's language. This breakdown is not that of an automatic third-person process. In other cases patients who cannot name colors set before them are also incapable of sorting samples according to color. What is impaired in this case is the ability to subsume particulars under a category. This disability is manifested in both the linguistic disability and the incapacity to sort samples, and once again points to an activity of thought on the part of the speaker that plays a role in determining the speaker's language.[33]

Experimental evidence thus points the way toward an intellectualist account of language. According to such a theory, significance is decided by an internal thought process and is imparted to the components of language, words and grammatical forms, through some as-yet-unclarified process. Once again, empiricist and intellectualist accounts are derived from an unexamined assumption. Both assume an already-established system of meaning and try to determine the conditions that make it possible for there to be such a system. These theoretical conditions turn out to be

either the automatic association of neurological or psychological "traces," or an activity of thinking that purportedly
imparts significance to the components of language. Neither theory questions the original assumption. Neither
theory accounts for the coming into being of meaning in
language itself, but rather each assumes the meaning in
language and gives what amounts to an abstract attempt at
explanation, after the fact, of the conditions of possibility.
Both theories fail to affirm the fact that "the word has a
meaning" and is not an empty shell deriving any significance that may accrue to it from the gratuitous association
of neurological or physiological "traces" or from a thought
process that proceeds independently of the elements of language themselves. Intellectualism suggests an activity on
the part of the speaker, but ultimately can offer no account
of precisely how it is that the thought process it portrays
ultimately produces a word that is meaningful. Since the
meaningfulness of language is the forgotten original assumption, the need to relate the suggested activity on the
part of the speaker to the actual coming-into-being of meaning in language remains unnoticed.

As far as speech itself is concerned, intellectualism is
hardly any different from empiricism, and is no better
able than the latter to dispense with an explanation in
terms of involuntary action. Once the categorial operation is performed, the appearance of the word which
completes the process still has to be explained, and this
will be done by recourse to a physiological or psychic
mechanism, since the word is a passive shell. Thus we
refute both intellectualism and empiricism by simply saying that *the word has a meaning*.[34]

What is meant by saying that "the word has a meaning"?
Merleau-Ponty points out that one must affirm that the
word has a meaning once one takes cognizance of the fact
that the appearance of a word qualitatively changes a person's situation in relation to things and in relation to other

people. Both a speaker's and a hearer's situation is modified with the appearance of a word. When I name a thing, my relation with that thing is fixed in a manner in which it had not previously been fixed. Here Merleau-Ponty draws on experimental work in child psychology, in particular Piaget's, which demonstrates that "for the child the thing is not known until it is named, the name is the essence of the thing and resides in it on the same footing as its color and its form."[35] If significance were imparted to words by a thought process intended to devise representations of what is found in the world, the child would already know the things that he or she names. Furthermore, the child would be aware of the source of the significance, namely, the internal thought process, and therefore could not regard the name of the thing as a quality of the thing. The appearance of the word does alter the meaning inherent in the child's world. It may be objected that the child simply learns to know things when the child comes into possession of the linguistic device, the word, and then subsequently discovers the "natural existence" of the things. The childish belief that this process involves a qualitative modification of the world, a change other than the mere acquisition of a new linguistic device, is one that the child would acquire from the linguistic community. Merleau-Ponty replies that this view already assumes that the child is aware of being a member of a linguistic community such that he or she receives meanings from words, meanings that alter the child's situation in the world. If this were not the case, the childish account would never be related, for the child, to the world.

The listener's situation also undergoes qualitative changes with the appearance of a word. There are instances in which words heard (or read) alter the meaning of a person's world. Here one cannot say that the words are linguistic devices designed by our consciousness to call up the same thoughts in another consciousness that would associate the words with the appropriate thoughts that are already its own. In such instances the words have thoroughly altered the thoughts of the hearer (or reader). The appearance of the word itself alters the hearer's (or reader's) situation in relation to things and other people. Merleau-Ponty offers the child uttering a first word, the lover revealing his feelings, and the writer and philosopher who "reawaken primordial experience anterior to all traditions" as clearest illustrations of such an event.[36]

The word has a meaning. How does the word with its meaning come into being? Just as motility could not be explained on the basis of a purely physical process or on the basis of a hypothetical prior organization on a geometrical grid of the body and the things surrounding it, accomplished by a pure consciousness, so the act of speech cannot be understood on the basis of a purely physical process or on the basis of a "verbal image" that would be present to a pure consciousness prior to the act of speaking. Words are in no way given in themselves apart from the meanings intervolved with them. If it were necessary to reconstruct "verbal images," words or phrases would not be easier to recall than thoughts. Just as it was necessary to conclude that the actual motion of the body follows from a prior dynamic situation or orientation of the body, so it is necessary to acknowledge that speech follows from a prior dynamic orientation of the body in the speaker's world of meanings. In the case of speech the phenomena toward which and away from which the body is already oriented are words, and these words are inhabited by meaning.

> Words cannot be "strongholds of thought," nor can thought seek expression, unless words are in themselves a comprehensible text, and unless speech possesses a power of significance entirely its own. The word and speech must somehow cease to be a way of designating things or thoughts, and become the presence of that thought in the phenomenal world, and, moreover, not its clothing but its token or its body.[37]

Experimental psychology supports this interpretation of speech in terms of a prior orientation of the body toward words that are inhabited by meaning.[38] A patient who suf-

fers from amnesic aphasia in respect to the names of colors
is also incapable of sorting color samples. Both disabilities
stem from a breakdown in the patient's orientation toward
meaning that was previously available in the patient's world
and with which the patient has now lost touch. When confronted with the samples, the patient cannot achieve the full
categorial attitude because his experience of the samples
never is such that the color quality appears the same in
various instances. Categories can never become fixed. The
experience is reduced to the immediacy of each sample and
the patient actually never gets beyond the stage of a separate category for each sample. The categorial attitude never
arises because there is a breakdown in the experience. It is
not the case that a breakdown in a purely physical system
or a breakdown in the thinking process causes the disturbance. Categorial thinking derives from a prior orientation
toward meaning in a person's world.

The speech disability is therefore not attributable to a
malfunction of a purely physical system or a disturbance in
a process of pure thought, but must ultimately be attributed
to the breakdown that occurs in the patient's orientation
toward meaning in his world. What happens to the names of
the colors, the words? Many patients retain the ability to
repeat the words. When confronted with the samples patients repeat the names of the colors as though expecting
the word to accomplish something for them and it even
happens that the name of the color will recall the name of an
object that displays this color, but the patient remains incapable of selecting a sample of this color among samples of
other colors. Thus the patient exhibits the thought process
of associating words but the words have lost meaning.
There is a qualitative change in the words. The words are
phenomena that are inhabited by meaning with which the
patient has lost touch. The fact that the original disturbance
in the orientation in a patient's world of meanings is manifested in a breakdown in speech and a breakdown in the
patient's apprehension of things such as color samples indicates that the two are not mutually independent. Each does

retain its specificity. Disturbances of either one may be brought about by physiological alterations. Each mutually determines the other, as each of the senses determines the others and is so determined, within the process that is the genesis of meaning.[39] The phenomena apprehended in speaking, words, and the phenomena apprehended in sensing, things such as color samples, are not mutually independent. Once again, each type of phenomenon does retain its specificity. Words and things are not reducible to a metaphysical logos that is ontologically homogeneous. Words and things are mutually determining elements within the process that is ontogenesis. The question still remains at this point as to precisely how this process works. But given the fact of the interaction between things and words, things found in man's world cannot be regarded as instances of an ontological type that is totally distinct from an ontological type instanced in words and that therefore cannot interact with words. Objectification collapses.

Speaking comes about from a prior orientation of the body toward and away from words.

> [Words] are behind me, like things behind my back, or like the city's horizon round my house, I reckon with them or rely on them, but without having any "verbal image." . . . I do not need to visualize the word in order to know and pronounce it. It is enough that I possess its articulatory and acoustic style as one of the modulations, one of the possible uses of my body. I reach back for the word as my hand reaches towards the part of my body which is being pricked; the word has a certain location in my linguistic world, and is part of my equipment. I have only one means of representing it, which is uttering it, just as the artist has only one means of representing the work on which he is engaged: by doing it.[40]

Just as the actual locomotion and posturing of the body are, in one sense, the resolution of strains or tensions within the precognitive orientation of the body toward and away from things, speaking is, in one sense, a resolution of strains or tensions within the body's orientation toward and away from words. On the other hand, just as it cannot be said that locomotion or posturing resolve strains and tensions within the precognitive orientation of the body in such a way that the body and the things toward which and away from which it is orientated relapse into objects in themselves as portrayed by realism, it cannot be said that speaking brings about the relapse of the body to such a state and the relapse of words into mere entries in a dictionary. Bodily intentionality directed toward words persists.

> The body's function in remembering is that same function of projection which we have already met in starting to move: the body converts a certain motor essence into vocal form, spreads out the articulatory style of a word into audible phenomena, and arrays the former attitude, which is resumed, into the panorama of the past, projecting an intention to move into actual movement, because the body is a power of natural expression.[41]

"The spoken word is a gesture. . . ."[42] At first glance it may appear that a gesture, such as pointing to a thing, is determined only by the structure of the body and the structure of the world in which the gesture is performed. Thus the gesture of pointing to a thing is determined by the structure of the hand and arm and by the upright position of the human body plus the position and size of the thing to which the person is pointing. But the gesture also acts. Pointing to something brings that thing from the periphery of the world to the center. This gesture finalizes the situation in the sense that previously the person may have been thinking about various qualities of the thing and now replaces in his attention such abstract qualities with the thing itself as present. Translated into words, this gesture could say: "There, *that* is what I have been thinking about." In bringing the thing to which the person is pointing to the center of the world, this gesture yields a new periphery, which calls for clarification. Analogously, the spoken word is not the mere transference of a thought, interior to a pure consciousness, about a thing found in the world, into an audible vehicle. The spoken word has meaning; it marks a qualitative change in the world, which includes the speaker's body and things. The spoken word itself acts.

The process involved in comprehending a gesture provides Merleau-Ponty with an opportunity to precise the sense in which a gesture may be said to act. I do not comprehend a gesture I witness by associating it with feelings I recall that I experienced when I performed the type of gesture that I see another performing at the moment. There is no intervening cognitive process that finally reveals to me the meaning of the gesture. I do not make a judgment to the effect that behind this gesture performed by the other person there is a psychic state that is the same as a psychic state that I have experienced. When I comprehend an angry gesture, for example, "[the] gesture *does not make me think* of anger, it is anger itself."[43] An adult will comprehend a sexual gesture because it effects a modification in the adult's world of which he has a precognitive bodily comprehension, which includes an "erotic comprehension" of other bodies. A sexual scene that a child happens to witness may disturb the child's world, but the child will not comprehend the gestures as an adult would, because the child's sexuality has not yet developed the specificity it exhibits in adults. There is no cognitive significance transmitted by gestures. To comprehend a gesture is to take it up in one's precognitive bodily comprehension of the world. It was noted above in the case of pointing to a thing how a gesture modifies the world experienced by a person who performs the gesture. A gesture modifies the world experienced by a person who witnesses it before that person engages in the cognitive process of making a judgment about what has occurred. An angry gesture may evoke a response from me before I have determined why the person who performs it is angry, if the anger is specifically directed at me, what the possible responses are and which would be appropriate, what the precise significance of my response is, what anger is, and whether or not all people have the same experience when it is said that they are angry. The gesture itself acts; it brings about a qualitative change in the world; it has meaning.

This analysis of the spoken word as a gesture that follows, as do locomotion and posturing, upon a prior orientation of one's body in the world is not yet complete. Does the statement that the gesture acts necessarily involve the claim that the philosopher somehow has stepped out of the commerce with gestures and can view the process as an external observer? In order to state that the gesture acts, must the philosopher ultimately claim to know the gesture as a completed entity that then comes to play a role in the meaning structure of the world—in other words, as an ideal object? Must the philosopher ultimately claim that there is an ideal system of gestures that is instantiated somehow in the world? Finally, in order to state that the gesture acts, must the philosopher ultimately claim knowledge of an actor, such as Absolute Spirit, that directs the interplay between man and gesture? This claim would contradict Merleau-Ponty's conception of meaning as contingent structure, not ideal but rather existing.

Merleau-Ponty turns to a study of the origin of language that demonstrates that an account can be given of the fact that "[the] linguistic gesture, like all the rest, delineates its own meaning,"[44] without recourse to metaphysical explanatory devices. At first glance, it may appear that words are arbitrary signs agreed upon by man in order to communicate thoughts about the world in which he finds himself. The existence of a number of languages may be offered as evidence. Merleau-Ponty points out that this view of language derives from a consideration of only "the conceptual and delimiting meanings of words," the dictionary entries that, although based on spoken language, also represent an effort to fix usage and thus play a role of arbitrary authority. But if the emotional content of words is taken into account, that content which is evident in poetry, one recognizes that words are not mere arbitrary signs agreed upon by man in order to represent things found in the world, but rather present emotional essences extracted from the world. When speaking of the "emotional content" of words, the reference is not to a stock of sociologically adopted conventional responses to the world. *Emotional* must be taken in its literal sense as motion carrying man beyond himself, beyond the world as man has organized it and has taken control of it. In other words, although there is an act on man's part involved in the origin of language, it is not a gratuitous act but one that accords with the world. This is by no means to claim that there is a naturalistic causal process at work, according to which particular stimuli produce particular responses, namely, words and gestural behavior in general. In the first place, different languages exist. But even if the issue is pushed back a step and the claim is made that the various languages are ultimately the end product of naturalistically caused emotional reactions by man, it must be acknowledged that the general emotional behavior that is classified by inclusion in one or another category of emotion differs among people from different cultures.

> The fact is that the behavior associated with anger or love is not the same in a Japanese and an Occidental. Or, to be more precise, the difference of behavior corresponds to a difference in the emotions themselves. It is not only the gesture which is contingent in relation to the body's organization, it is the manner itself in which we meet the situation and live it. The angry Japanese smiles, the westerner goes red and stamps his foot or else goes pale and hisses his words. It is not enough for two conscious subjects to have the same organs and nervous system for the same emotions to produce in both the same signs. What is important is how they use their bodies, the simultaneous patterning of body and world in emotion.[45]

The meaning a word has is neither reducible to an end product of a naturalistic causal process nor is it transported by man from thought to the word conceived of as an arbitrarily devised sign. It is impossible to find the meaning of the word anywhere but in the word itself. The word has a meaning.

> If it were possible, in any vocabulary, to disregard what is attributable to the mechanical laws of phonetics, to the influences of other languages, the rationalization of grammarians, and assimilatory processes, we should probably discover in the original form of each language a somewhat restricted system of expression, but such as would make it not entirely arbitrary, if we designate night by the word "nuit," to use "lumière" for light. The predominance of vowels in one language, or of consonants in another, and constructional and syntactical systems, do not represent so many arbitrary conventions for the expression of one and the same idea, but several ways for the human body to sing the world's praises and in the last resort to live it.[46]

Once a word comes into existence it is there to be taken up in a linguistic gesture and spoken again. Since the meaning of the word never derived from a thought transported into an arbitrarily devised sign, it is not possible to say that words become conventional signs. When a word is spoken again it has meaning; it does not represent a thought that was at one time assigned to it. Besides the historical origin and chronological development of language, an origin in the present, a genesis of meaning is at work in language.

> Strictly speaking . . . there are no conventional signs, standing as the simple notation of a thought pure and clear in itself, there are only words into which the history of a whole language is compressed, and which effect communication with no absolute guarantee, dogged as they are by incredible linguistic hazards. . . . The meaning of a sentence appears intelligible throughout, detachable from the sentence and finitely self-subsistent in an intelligible world, because we presuppose as given all those exchanges, owed to the history of the language, which contribute to determining its sense. . . . But in fact, as we have said, the clearness of language stands out

from an obscure background, and if we carry our research far enough we shall eventually find that language is equally uncommunicative of anything other than itself, that its meaning is inseparable from it.[47]

Although the linguistic gesture, the word, has its meaning and thus is not man's arbitrary creation used as a sign for a thought, it does involve an act on man's part. Speech, although it is in a sense the resolution of strains or tensions within the body's orientation toward and away from words, is not an automatic process, but one that involves an act that man himself initiates.

Language certainly has an inner content, but this is not self-subsistent and self-conscious thought. What then does language express, if it does not express thoughts? It presents or rather it *is* the subject's taking up of a position in the world of his meanings. . . . The meaning of the gesture is not contained in it like some physical or physiological phenomenon. The meaning of the word is not contained in the word as a sound. But the human body is defined in terms of its property of appropriating, in an indefinite series of discontinuous acts, significant cores which transcend and transfigure its natural powers. This act of transcendence is first encountered in the acquisition of a pattern of behavior, then in the mute communication of gesture: it is through the same power that the body opens itself to some new kind of conduct and makes it understood to external witnesses.[48]

The fact that there is a genesis of meaning at work in language at present precludes the possibility of conceiving of words as completed phenomena. Hence it must be affirmed that the radically dynamic process of ontogenesis is at work here as well. This fact is most evident in originary instances of language such as those already noted—those of the child uttering a first word, the lover revealing his feelings, the "first man who spoke," or the writer and philosopher reawakening primordial experience anterior to all traditions. Merleau-Ponty describes such an event:

The new meaningful intention only knows itself by recovering already available significations, which result from prior acts of expression. The available significations suddenly link up following an unknown law, and once and for all a new cultural entity has begun to exist. . . . We live in a world where speech is an *institution*. . . . We become unaware of what is contingent in expression and in communication, whether it be that of the child learning to speak, that of the writer saying and thinking something for the first time, or that of anyone transforming a certain type of silence into speech. It is, however, quite clear that constituted speech, such as is at play in everyday life, presupposes that the decisive step of expression has been accomplished. Our view of man will remain superficial as long as we do not return to that origin, as long as we do not rediscover, under the noise of words, the primordial silence, as long as we do not describe the gesture that breaks this silence.[49]

In view of the fact that words cannot be regarded as completed phenomena, what sense did it make to describe speech as following upon an orientation of the body toward and away from words? Here we encounter words as original content of perception. The difficulty in speaking of that original content of perception which escapes objectification was already encountered in the case of original content of perception that exhibits sexual meaning. At that point Merleau-Ponty suggested the analogy of the content of dreams.[50] Here, although Merleau-Ponty does not use the specific example, an analogy with what is at work in the creative activity of a craftsman is of help. As the craftsman works with his material, the development of the piece of work will determine his movements while his movements determine the development of the piece of work. The actual crafting of the piece is not directed by a purely abstract form or image about which the craftsman thinks, but rather is directed by the piece of work coming into being, toward which the craftsman's body orients itself.

The effort called for in order to speak of the original

content of perception without covering it over with objectifications now appears as the task of speaking. The study
of language itself has revealed that the philosophical act of
speaking, reawakening primordial experience anterior to all
traditions, is one of speaking words that have their meanings in the sense just described. How is this philosophical
act of speaking to be performed? Philosophies of language
and scientific linguistics, to the extent that they turn away
from the issue of ontogenesis at work in language, do not
meet this crisis. If the attempt is made to divorce the genesis of meaning from the process of ontogenesis, the historical modifications of a language and the fluctuations of the
language as it is spoken today, which are scientifically discovered, cannot complete our understanding of language;
they are steps toward clarifying the very origin of language,
the ontogenesis of language and of man as speaker of language.

The question concerning how the fact that language has
its meaning, and is not the receptacle of meanings transported from the speaker's thoughts, is cotenable with the
fact that man's act of speaking brings about language such
as it is, remains unanswered at this point in Merleau-
Ponty's work. There is no recourse to the perspective of an
external observer who would be capable of objectively
viewing a cooperation, so to speak, between language and
man. What is involved in speaking can only be apprehended
in accomplishing the act itself. In a passage that draws together the disclosure of language as having its meaning, and
thus marks the overturning of the empiricist and intellectualist accounts, Merleau-Ponty's own language reveals the
extreme tension at work in attempting to find a vantage
point from which the act of speaking can be described without resorting to metaphysical devices such as an ideal
framework of language that would guarantee a prior knowledge of the result of the act of speaking or an Absolute
Spirit that would direct the entire process and thus perform
the same function. At the same time, this passage makes it
evident that language cannot be taken for granted as a "natu-

ral" process, which would be tantamount to default in the face of the task of speaking, and hence in the face of the task of philosophizing. Merleau-Ponty writes:

> Everything is manufactured and everything is natural in man, as it were, in the sense that there is not a word, not an instance of behavior that does not owe something to purely biological being—and that at the same time does not elude the simplicity of animal life and divert the vital forms of behavior from their proper direction through a sort of *escapement* and through a genius for the equivocal that might serve to define man. Already the mere presence of a living being transforms the physical world, brings about the appearance here of "food," elsewhere a "hiding place," giving to "stimuli" a meaning they did not have. A fortiori is this true of the presence of man in the animal world. Instances of behavior create meanings that are transcendent in relation to the anatomical apparatus, and yet immanent in the behavior as such since it makes itself known and is understood. It is impossible to restrict this irrational power that creates meanings and communicates them. Speech is only one particular case of it.[51]

This passage indicates why the study of language may be regarded as a nodal point of Merleau-Ponty's endeavor in terms of how the various projects in which he engages are related. *The Structure of Behavior* indicated the need for a study of the original content of perception in order to disclose the source of those structures which serve science in its efforts to explain man and this world in which he finds himself. The study of language has disclosed the fact that speaking, originary speaking such as philosophy in particular, effects an alteration of speaker, hearers, and their world, a "modulation of existence."[52] Merleau-Ponty is encountering a critical difficulty in attempting to maintain the perspective of the perceiver who describes the content of perception. But if the philosopher comes to turn aside from description toward a creative philosophical act, this is not to say that philosophy becomes gratuitous. Words have their meanings, and it is only when this fact is ignored that the philosophical act becomes gratuitous and perhaps ultimately impossible. These disclosures call upon the philosopher to begin from that point, so to speak, where perceiver and perceived, man and world, originate. This is precisely what we shall see Merleau-Ponty attempt after *Phenomenology of Perception.*

This study of language was begun by Merleau-Ponty as a step in the disclosure of the phenomenal body as involved in the original content of perception. But by further clarifying the genesis of meaning and ontogenesis, this study disclosed processes that preclude any attempt to portray man in terms of an already established hierarchy of faculties, or even "currents of existence" such as the various senses, motility, sexuality, and language itself, and thus has implications that carry the philosopher beyond the context in which the study originates. The psychological study of language disturbances, from which Merleau-Ponty drew as support of the statement that words have meaning, indicated that words and things found in man's world mutually determine one another. Words and things could no longer be regarded as instances of totally distinct ontological types that cannot interact. The consideration of words as gestures led to the acknowledgment of an "irrational power"—of which speech is only one particular instance—that transforms both man and world. This imprecise terminology resulted from the fact that at this point the question as to how it is philosophically cotenable that man is already in a world of things and words that have meaning prior to any act on man's part, and that man's actions bring about the existence of the world such as it is, has not been resolved. This question now presents itself as a primary concern. The entire problematic of perception is undergoing transformation in the course of Merleau-Ponty's work. Only if one begins with the unexamined assumption that perception involves the reception of sense data that are subsequently ordered in some manner to yield that which is known does one arrive at an abstract theory of a hierarchy of faculties and at the theoretical problem of how they function together. At the outset, Merleau-Ponty overturned this view of perception, and his study of the phenomenal body as involved in the original content of perception has provided support for the affirmation that the original content of perception is meaningful. Now, as he draws together the study of language, Merleau-Ponty poses the question that his study of perception has yielded, namely, the question as to how the fact that man is already in a world that has meaning prior to any act by man is philosophically cotenable with the fact that man's actions bring about the existence of the world such as it is.

Merleau-Ponty points out the need to discover a "function" that subsumes both motility—that form of intentionality which is directed toward things—and "intelligence," which is associated with linguistic processes and thus is portrayed as directed, so to speak, toward words. Experimental psychology provides evidence of this necessity. Linguistic disturbances range from a breakdown in what previously may have been called the purely physiological process involved in speech but that we now know as motility, a form of intentionality directed in this case toward words as things, to breakdowns in the ability to categorize, which we now know rests upon a form of intentionality directed toward the meanings that both things and words have. However, even in cases in which the disturbance is primarily a motor disturbance, there is some breakdown in the patient's grasp of the meaning of words.[53] In cases of this type the patient's "[articulatory] and syntactical accuracy always stand in inverse ratio to each other, which shows that the articulation of a word is not merely a motor phenomenon, but that it draws upon the same energies which organize the syntactical order."[54]

Merleau-Ponty depicts the "function" that subsumes motility and "intelligence" as follows:

[T]he intention to speak can be found only in an open experience; it appears like the boiling of a liquid, when, in the density of being, vacuous volumes are built up and move outward. "As soon as man uses language to establish a living relation with himself or with his fellows, language is no longer an instrument, *no longer a means; it is a manifestation, a revelation of intimate being and of the psychic link which unites us to the world and to our fellow men.* The patient's language may display considerable knowledge and it may be utilizable for determined activities, but it totally lacks this productivity that is man's deepest essence and that perhaps is not revealed in any other creation of civilization with as much evidence as it is revealed in the creation of language itself."[55] One might say, taking up again a celebrated distinction, that *languages,* that is, constituted systems of vocabulary and syntax, "means of expression" that exist empirically, are the depository and the sedimentation of acts of speech, in which unformulated meaning not only finds the means of being conveyed outwardly, but moreover acquires existence for itself, and is truly created as meaning. Or again one may distinguish between a *word in the speaking* and a *spoken word.* The former is the one in which the meaningful intention is at the stage of being born. Here existence is polarized into a certain "meaning" ["sens"] that cannot be defined by any natural object. It is beyond being that it seeks to catch up with itself and that is why it creates speech as an empirical support for its own nonbeing. Speech is the excess of our existence over natural being. But the act of expression constitutes a linguistic world and a cultural world, and allows to fall back into being that which was attempting to go beyond being. Hence the spoken word that enjoys available significations as an acquired fortune. From this point, other acts of authentic expression—those of the writer, the artist, or the philosopher—become possible. This ever-recreated opening in the plenitude of being is that which conditions the child's first speech as it does the writer's speech, the construction of the word and that of concepts. Such is this function that one intuits through language, which reiterates itself, serving as its own foundation, or which, like a wave, regathers itself and takes hold of itself in order to hurtle beyond itself.[56]

Once again, Merleau-Ponty's language is not precise and the passage requires some unraveling. When Merleau-Ponty speaks of existence becoming polarized, the reference is to the strains or tensions that the study of language has disclosed as preceding the spoken word.[57] Speaking does not resolve these strains or tensions in the sense that man falls back into being an object in-itself and words fall back into being no more than entries in a dictionary. Thus Merleau-Ponty states that what was attempting to go beyond being falls back into being and new strains or tensions take shape that are a source of new acts of authentic expression. These tensions or strains do not occur only within man's orientation toward and away from words but occur throughout the "psychic link that unites us to the world and to our fellow men," throughout existence. Not only does such an event give rise to the authentic expression of the writer and philosopher, whose medium is words, but to the authentic expression of the artist as well, whose medium may be, for example, the body in space in the case of a dancer, or things in the case of a sculptor. Here there is no theoretical classification of ontological types that would be the proper domain of separate human faculties. There are no "natural objects" that would be instances of an ontological type totally distinct from that of which words would be instances such that "natural objects" and words could not possibly interact. Language is not the exclusive domain of an intellectual faculty that would be totally distinct from a faculty of perception that would have the world of objects, including other people insofar as they are objectifiable, as its proper domain. There are only this "function" from which authentic expression arises, and existence—or as Merleau-Ponty now says, being—which integrates the various currents of existence within which this "function" is at work. This "function" is precisely that "irrational power" that Merleau-Ponty mentioned previously, which creates meanings and communicates them.[58] The question is now: what is the relationship between this "function" and man's "productivity," man's act of authentic expression? How is man simultaneously in the world, on the one hand, situated prior to any act on man's part in a manner that gives rise to man's acts, including speaking, and, on the other hand, the one who acts so as to bring about the existence of the world such as it is?

Only if one begins with the assumption that perception is a bare contact with the world that is to be known is one subsequently forced to add further theoretical dimensions to man, an "intellectual" dimension and perhaps a "spiritual" dimension, in order to explain how man comes to know himself, to know his place in reality, so to speak, and to become truly free. For example, the dialectic appears in Hegel's work as a necessary process at work in reality because it becomes a theoretical necessity at each moment in the dialectic to import structures that develop the meaningfulness of the content of knowledge. Just as it was pointed out in *The Structure of Behavior* that the structures imported by science and then claimed to be objective structures are imported from the content of perception, so it may be the case that the structures imported in theory at each moment in the Hegelian dialectic originate in perception. The "Absolute Concept" may be a theoretical edifice built up from structures imported from original content of perception. The accumulation of what is theoretically left behind as each moment of the Hegelian dialectic is *aufgehoben*—simultaneously taken up, transformed, and left behind—may be original meaningful content of perception which was never affirmed. The ambiguity concerning whether man or Absolute Spirit is responsible for history may arise from not having affirmed the meaningfulness of the original content of perception because this affirmation leads, as we have seen, directly to the question of how man can be conceived as in the world, situated prior to any act by man, and at the same time as the one who acts so as to bring about the existence of the world such as it is. Ultimately, the structures that appear at each step in the Hegelian dialectic, and that serve to develop the meaningfulness of the content of knowledge, must all be unified within an

Absolute Spirit that directs the process. Ultimately, the
base postulate of the Hegelian system, the inexplicable ani-
mating force of the process involved, namely, the "fact"
that Absolute Spirit empties itself into Nature and History
in order to become conscious of itself, provides a means of
accounting for how it is that the supposed original bare
contact with that which is to be known does not pose an
insurmountable obstacle in the way of full knowledge (i.e.,
is not bare sensation of a *Ding-an-sich* about which nothing
can be known), but is only a first step toward full consciousness of self, which is knowledge. Thus bare nature is
not an ontological type that is totally distinct from Spirit but
rather lies within the homogeneous ontological medium
which is the body so to speak, of Absolute Spirit: Substance, in a Spinozistic sense. But if no bare nature is to be
found at the outset, there is no need to seek a homogeneous
ontological medium. There is no need to add further theoretical dimensions to man. Then the question encountered
in all areas of life is how it is that man is in the world,
situated prior to any act by man, and is simultaneously the
one who acts so as to bring about the existence of the world
such as it is. Here we can return to a passage in *The Structure of Behavior* in which Merleau-Ponty's entire endeavor
is prefigured:

> [T]he life of consciousness outself of self . . . on the one
> hand, and, on the other, the consciousness of self and of
> a universe . . . in Hegelian terms, consciousness in-itself
> and consciousness in-and-for-itself—cannot be purely
> and simply juxtaposed. The problem of perception lies
> completely in this duality.[59]

For Merleau-Ponty, "consciousness in-itself" is already
meaningful, it is the "life of consciousness outside of self,"
man in the world, situated prior to any act by man. "Consciousness in-and-for-itself" is man's acting in the fullest
sense, taking up being-in-the-world such as it is, and bringing about the existence of the world such as it is. Ulti-

mately, in the Hegelian system, man's responsibility is qualified by, if not lost in the march of Absolute Spirit in such a way that in the last analysis, man's recourse lies in adherence to that political state which, at long last, reconciles man's projects to that of Absolute Spirit. Ultimately, Merleau-Ponty brings man face-to-face with man's responsibility.[60] Merleau-Ponty's return to the original content of perception does not eliminate other dimensions but rather opens the way to consideration of those dimensions as they are lived by man, not as they are subsequently objectified in a theoretical hierarchy that is superimposed on life. Chapter 2 will demonstrate this aspect of Merleau-Ponty's work.

This study of language does conclude Merleau-Ponty's exploration of the body as involved in the original content of perception. The body is not an object as portrayed by empiricist theories. Nor is the body a construct of a pure consciousness that cannot gain access to a body in-itself that lies behind the body as known. A fortiori it is not the case that the claim that the body exists is an unwarranted theoretical step, in which case the body would be entirely taken up into a pure consciousness. The body as lived prior to any cognitive act is already meaningful. It is already oriented in the world. This is not to say that the body is an object in-itself located at a particular point on a geometric coordinate system. Such theoretical accounts of space, as well as locomotion and posturing of the body, sexual behavior, speech, and the other modes of human behavior, find their origin in a structured bodily intentionality that reveals the structures of its termini—the body and the world. To say that the lived body is already structured is not necessarily to say that it is static. The study of language has revealed that the coming into being of the word that has its meaning, which is not an instantiation of a signification contained in an ideal system, structures both body and world. Bodily structure is radically dynamic. It is contingent.

The analysis of speech and expression makes us acknowledge the enigmatic nature of our own body even more effectively than did our remarks on bodily spatiality and unity. It is not a collection of particles, each one remaining in itself, nor yet a network of processes defined once and for all—it is not where it is, it is not what it is—since we see it secreting in itself a "meaning" that comes to it from nowhere, projecting it upon its material surroundings and communicating it to other incarnate subjects. It has always been noted that gesture or speech transfigure the body, but it was thought sufficient to say that they develop or disclose another power, thought or soul. It was overlooked that in order to be able to express it, the body must in the final analysis become the thought or the intention that it signifies for us. It is the body that points out, and that speaks: this is what we have learned in this chapter.[61]

It is as that which speaks that the body contributes to the meaningfulness of the original content of perception. To the act whereby the body "[secretes] in itself a 'meaning' that comes to it from nowhere, projecting it upon its material surroundings and communicating it to other incarnate subjects" Merleau-Ponty gives the name *transcendence*.

Existence is indeterminate in itself, by reason of its fundamental structure, and in so far as it is the very process whereby the hitherto meaningless takes on meaning, whereby . . . chance is transformed into reason; in so far as it is the act of taking up a *de facto* situation. We shall give the name transcendence to this act in which existence takes up, for its own purposes, and transforms such a situation. Precisely because it is transcendence, existence never utterly outruns anything, for in that case the tension which is essential to it would disappear. It never abandons itself. What it is never remains external and accidental to it, since this is always taken up and integrated into it.[62]

Here it is not a question of transcendence in any sense outside the body as objectivistically portrayed, affording the philosopher a point of view from which he can discern and articulate a metaphysical structure of reality including man as traditionally conceived. Merleau-Ponty does not seek such a point of view. Nor does he understand the body as an unsurpassable obstacle that prevents such transcendence. He is not seeking such a point of view in the first place. Traditionally, because the body as involved in the original content of perception was itself covered over by objectification, it was found to present an obstacle that either had to be overcome in order to arrive at knowledge of reality, overcome by finding a point of view outside it, or could not be overcome. Merleau-Ponty's effort to displace objectivistic characteristics from an unwarranted dominating role in the content of perception, in particular in one's original perception of one's own body—culminating in the study of the body as expression, and speech that demonstrates the need to abandon the traditional concept of the object—has disclosed that the problem posed by the body is none other than the problem posed by other meaningful content of perception, namely, how to speak of incomplete, nonobjectifiable phenomena without turning away from them and distorting them by transmuting them into structures imported to explain them in accord with an unwarranted assumption that they are amenable to such "explanation," that is, that they are objects that can be reflected in a system of "knowledge" imported to "explain them." This has now appeared as the task of philosophical speaking.

Ultimately, as has already been noted, the overcoming of objectivism will require that the philosopher abandon the point of view of a subject who perceives and begin at the point, so to speak, where the perceiver-perceived structure comes into being, that point which, in *Phenomenology of Perception,* Merleau-Ponty calls existence. That is, ultimately what will be required is an originary act of philosophical speaking, one that is neither an act performed on content of perception already laid out before a perceiver, nor an act performed on an undifferentiated in-itself—the in-itself of Sartre's *Being and Nothingness.*

However, just as, on the basis of what was discussed in the
first segment of this chapter concerning "languagely meaning" it was contended that this effort could not possibly be
portrayed in terms of an attempt to speak a language in
which meaning that lay anywhere else than in language itself would be made explicit, so now we may conclude that
this effort could not possibly be portrayed as a search for
the meaning of speaking anywhere else than in the body as
what speaks. To affirm that it is the body that speaks is not
to affirm that "nature" or "spirit" or any other hypostatized
ground of being speaks through man. It is to affirm that it is
the body, understood as the locus of man's being-in-the-
world, as man's opening onto the world, which speaks.

Conclusion

Merleau-Ponty's first extended treatment of language
forms a part of his effort to disclose the role of the phenomenal body within the original content of perception.
Language is one of the currents of man's being-in-the-
world. Language finds its source in man's original bodily
intentionality. Specifically, language finds its source in
man's original bodily intentionality directed toward words.
Words are phenomena. They *have* meaning. This meaning
is not static. It is radically dynamic. As a current of man's
being-in-the-world, language is involved in processes of
mutual determination at work among the various currents
of man's being-in-the-world. The genesis of meaning at
work in language is coincident with the process of ontogenesis. Both empiricist theories, which portray language
as an automatic causal process whereby external stimuli
cause a subject to pronounce particular words, and intellectualist theories, according to which a pure consciousness
transfers, in some unexplained manner, meanings from itself to a constructed linguistic system, are inadequate accounts of language.

What Merleau-Ponty has accomplished in opening the

problematic of language within the context of the study of man's being-in-the-world is to make evident the full import of the problematic of language, which is missed by other views of language. Theories that involve the assumption that language is a self-contained total system and then suggest that this system can be altered by fiat, by simply changing definitions of words and grammatical rules, by subtracting and adding words, such that by the progressive application of scientific procedures philosophical issues would be exposed as no more than solvable semantic problems, miss the fact that language has its meaning, in the sense disclosed by Merleau-Ponty, and that this meaning is involved in man's world, in processes of mutual determination with other phenomena. Theories that portray all language as ultimately reducible to a priori permanent categories miss the radically dynamic nature of language. Such theories miss the fact that the genesis of meaning in language is coincident with the process of ontogenesis. Such theories lose sight of the inherent dynamism of man's being-in-the-world and the act on man's part that brings about the existence of the world, including language, such as it is. The question concerning the possibility of new instances of originary language, described by Merleau-Ponty, is never raised in such theories. By disclosing language as having its meaning, as acting, and as coming into being through acts by man, Merleau-Ponty has made it evident how the advent of language, not only in the historical sense but also in reference to all instances of language, all acts of speaking, marks a change in man and in his world. The full import of language is not to be found in conceiving of language as a means of transcending the world but rather in affirming language as a way in which man is in-the-world.

Having slackened the intentional threads that attach us to the world, having stepped back to watch the forms of transcendence "fly up like sparks from a fire," in short, having performed the phenomenological reduction as described by Merleau-Ponty, the prejudice according to which language does not exist in the same way in which the world exists was put out of play. Words are among the phenomena that "fly up like sparks" once the reduction is performed. We learn that man is inseparable from language, that the subject-object dualism is no more adequate in accounting for the domain of language than it is in accounting for other dimensions of man. This inseparability of man from language does not refer to an ideal structure of "linguisticality" that would be automatically instantiated in each person. Nevertheless, the inseparability of man from language is not fortuitous. "Everything in man is a necessity" but "this human manner of existence is not guaranteed to every human child through some essence acquired at birth."[63] Existence, the radically dynamic medium that is where the perceiver-perceived structure comes into being, consistently transforms contingency into necessity. When the strains and tensions involved in the context of man's being-in-the-world give rise to an act of speech as described by Merleau-Ponty, man is not set apart or released, so to speak, from the tensions and strains that give rise to acts of speech. In this sense, language is a necessary dimension of man's existence.

> Human existence will force us to revise our usual notion of necessity and contingency, because it is the changing of contingency into necessity by the act of taking up again. All that we are, we are on the basis of a *de facto* situation that we make ours and that we transform ceaselessly through a sort of *escape* that is never unconditioned liberty.[64]

Merleau-Ponty's study of the contribution made by the body to the original content of perception, culminating in the study of the body as expression, and speech, recasts the traditional context for the usual notion of necessity and contingency in opening up the fundamental question concerning how it is philosophically cotenable that there is *the* world and that existence, the medium that subsumes perceiver and perceived, is radically dynamic. It is not a question of determining what could be otherwise and how and why it could be otherwise and what could not be otherwise and why it could not be otherwise. There is no dimension of man's existence that in any sense preexists the context of man's being-in-the-world and that is automatically instantiated in each person and thus permits one to substitute, in theory, contexts of being-in-the-world one for the other. How the prior question, that concerning how it is philosophically cotenable that there is *the* world and that existence is radically dynamic, is to be pursued will be disclosed in chapter 2 in the course of examining "the act of taking up again" whereby human existence "is the transformation of contingency into necessity." Merleau-Ponty neither seeks to replace a theory of necessity and contingency with another theory of necessity and contingency, nor does he seek to demonstrate that contingency is a necessary unsurpassable limit to the philosophical effort. Merleau-Ponty undertook the task of disclosing the original content of perception in pursuing the investigation of man and world begun in *The Structure of Behavior*. By effecting the transformation of perception called for in order to displace objectivistic characteristics from an unwarranted dominating role in the content of perception, he has disclosed both that man cannot be portrayed in terms of an already-established hierarchy of faculties or in terms of "currents of existence," including language, that would surmount one another and that the structuralization of the various "currents of existence" involves an act—the "act of taking up again," whereby contingency is ceaselessly transformed into necessity, an act initiated by man, which is thus, considered in itself, neither "contingent" nor "necessary." The act of speaking that would disclose how it is that there is *the* world while existence is radically dynamic, a philosophic act reawakening primordial experience anterior to all traditions, would be such an act initiated by man and would reveal the origin and limitations of the usual notion of necessity and contingency, which maintains a distinction between what could be otherwise and what could not be otherwise.

Man neither transcends a necessity that the world imposes nor succumbs to a contingency of bodily existence in and by means of language. Language neither affords man a metaphysical independence from a realm of "natural objects and processes" nor demonstrates a "natural" dependence of man on "natural objects and processes," which would confine man to a realm in which such "natural objects and processes" could be understood as stimuli that produce language thus conceived as a "natural process" of response to stimuli comprised of "natural objects and processes." This is because there are no "natural objects and processes" that would be instances of an ontological type totally distinct from that of which words would be instances, or to which words as phenomena involved in the original meaningful content of perception—before being overlaid with objectivistic prejudices deriving from theories that turn away from the original content of perception in order to import structures intended to explain perception— can be reduced. The inseparability of man from language pointed up by Merleau-Ponty in *Phenomenology of Perception,* an inseparability antecedent to what has been called necessity and contingency, the ultimate inadequacy of the subject-object dualism in accounting for the domain of language, permits us now to say specifically of language what Merleau-Ponty said in describing the body: it is "a current of given existence, with the result that we never know whether the forces which bear us on are its or ours—or with the result rather that they are never entirely either its or ours."[65] Language can no longer be taken for granted as a tool that man can manipulate at will. Language must be respected. Man must speak with care.

Notes

1. *The Phenomenology of Mind,* trans. with an Introduction and Notes by Sir James Baillie, Muirhead Library of Philosophy, 2d ed. rev. (London: George Allen & Unwin Ltd., 1949), p. 806.

2. *The Logic of Hegel,* trans. William Wallace, 2d ed. rev. and aug. (London: Oxford University Press, 1892), p. 379.

3. *The Structure of Behavior,* p. 3.

4. Physical forms are equilibria obtained with respect to particular existing conditions, the "boundary conditions" within which physical laws are applicable. Vital forms are equilibria obtained with respect to virtual conditions, preferred orientations of organisms in their respective milieus. In such instances, the structure itself actively reorganizes in order to realize the preferred orientation. The organism plays an active role. The human order also involves projection by the organism, in this case the human being, into the milieu. Merleau-Ponty describes the human order thus:

". . . What defines man is not the capacity to create a second nature—economic, social or cultural—beyond biological nature; it is rather the capacity of going beyond created structures in order to create others.

"[The] power of choosing and varying points of view permits man to create instruments, not under the pressure of a *de facto* situation, but for a virtual use and especially in order to fabricate others. The meaning of human work therefore is the recognition, beyond the present milieu, of a world of things visible for each 'I' under a plurality of aspects, the taking possession of an indefinite time and space. . . . Thus, the human dialectic is ambiguous: it is first manifested by the social or cultural structures, the appearance of which it brings about and in which it imprisons itself. *But its use-objects and its cultural objects would not be what they are if the activity which brings about their appearance did not also have as its meaning to reject them and to surpass them.*

"Correlatively, perception, which until now has appeared to us to be the assimilation of consciousness into a cradle of institutions and a narrow circle of human 'milieus,' can become, especially by means of art, perception of a universe" (*The Structure of Behavior,* pp. 175–76).

5. *Phenomenology of Perception,* p. 23. There is much more involved in *Phenomenology of Perception* than a fulfillment of Husserl's phenomenological program in the one area of perception. With the shift to an internal interrogation of perceptual consciousness as required by *The Structure of Behavior,* phenomenology suggests itself as the proper methodology. Husserl's phenomenological reduction, taking the phenomenologist out of the role of external spectator of a world as conceived in realism, and allowing him to investigate constituting consciousness and its contents, poses itself as an extremely useful tool for Merleau-Ponty's continuing endeavor. However one decides concerning the validity of Merleau-Ponty's interpretation of Husserl, beginning in the preface to *Phenomenology of Perception* and continuing in the essay entitled "The Philosopher and His Shadow" (in *Signs*) and in the chapter of *The Visible and the Invisible* entitled "Interrogation and Intuition," we learn as early as the preface to *Phenomenology of Perception* that Merleau-Ponty is not interested in employing phenomenology solely as a means of acquiring knowledge of essences. He rather is interested in accounting for knowledge of the various "forms of transcendence"—the thing or the other person, for example. In short, Merleau-Ponty is interested in how we know these "forms of transcendence" as existing. Essences may be regarded as threads that bind man to the world and that can be scrutinized when one loosens one's inherence in the world in order to provide some distance from which to know the world. Merleau-Ponty's intent in *Phenomenology of Perception* was ontological, even if this did not become apparent to him until later: "I must show

that what one might consider to be 'psychology' *(Phenomenology of Perception)* is in fact ontology" *(The Visible and the Invisible,* p. 176). In spite of what Merleau-Ponty finds to be Husserl's own refusal to separate essence from existence *(Phenomenology of Perception,* p. xv), Husserl repeatedly maintained that ontological considerations must be put off as only a last step for phenomenological philosophy. See Edmund Husserl, *Ideas: General Introduction to Pure Phenomenology,* trans. W. R. Boyce Gibson (New York: Cromwell-Collier Publishing Co., Collier Books, 1962), pp. 161–62; idem, *Cartesian Meditations: An Introduction to Phenomenology,* trans. Dorion Cairns (The Hague: Martinus Nijhoff, 1964), pp. 136–39. When Merleau-Ponty reaches the point at which he regards it as necessary to do ontology and wishes to clarify the ontological significance of the results of *Phenomenology of Perception* (see *The Visible and the Invisible,* pp. 165, 183)—a process that begins in essays such as "On the Phenomenology of Language" (in *Signs*), and "Eye and Mind" (trans. Carleton Dallery, in *The Primacy of Perception and Other Essays*), but was to issue in a full-blown ontology in *The Visible and the Invisible*—Husserl's phenomenological methodology becomes inadequate.

6. In part two of *Phenomenology of Perception,* "The World as Perceived," Merleau-Ponty reveals the source of these objectivistic characteristics that conceal the original content of perception. In perceiving a thing, the perceiver does not interpret the perspectives in which the thing is perceived and arrive at a conclusion that these are perspectives of that thing; rather, he already knows these perspectives as perspectives of the thing itself that is perceived. But the thing is not thoroughly determinate in explicit perception. The thing resists the perceiver. It could possibly be fully determinate only if the perceiver's body and the world in which the perceiver's body is situated were fully determinate in explicit perception, and this is not the case. This is not to say that the intellectualist position is vindicated according to which the objectivity of a thing is attributed as a final characterization by a pure consciousness. It is precisely in one's experience of the thing as that to which one already has direct access, and yet at the same time as that which is not fully determinate in experience, that the thingness of the thing for us is found. Perception is distorted by turning away from this double nature of the thing and representing the thing as a complete totality in a world represented as the sum of such objects. This step, taken in objectivistic theories, is unwarranted and unjustifiable. (See *Phenomenology of Perception,* pp. 317–34.)

7. J.-P. Sartre, *L'Imaginaire,* p. 241; Merleau-Ponty's note.

8. *Phenomenology of Perception,* pp. 4–5.

9. Ibid., pp. 5–6.

10. From the negative route, what we do not find: Our efforts would be misdirected if we mistakenly conclude that having rejected the unwarranted presupposition of an already completed, fully determinate world which is there to be perceived, no phenomena displaying objectlike, scientifically analyzable qualities are to be found in the content of perception. This is not the case. There is, and Merleau-Ponty will later make this explicit, a historicity of perception, which is to say that the features that have come to dominate perception, those conceptualized in the traditional theoretical accounts, do not constitute a false layer imposed gratuitously by man on perception and removable in an equally facile manner. (See, e.g., what Merleau-Ponty says regarding the historicity of Euclidean geometry, *Phenomenology of Perception,* pp. 393–94.) If we take seriously what is

learned from *The Structure of Behavior* and is supported by the descriptions offered by Merleau-Ponty that uproot the general characteristics imposed upon perception by traditional theories (see above, this section) to the effect that signification and existence coincide in the structure of perception (characterized in *The Structure of Behavior* in terms of Merleau-Ponty's notion of form), and that this structure is dynamically ordered from within, not by any external source such as consciousness conceived as apart from that which it would order, then we must affirm that those features of perception amenable to the traditional theories involving one form or another of realism are to be found to some degree in the content of perception, where they do not constitute a superimposed false layer. Merleau-Ponty's effort is directed toward establishing within perception itself the proper balance between such characteristics and those others which have been ignored as the result of the dominance of objective analysis and which are affirmed again once perception itself—rather than the body of theory devoted to perception—becomes the focus of study. Merleau-Ponty is indeed interested in removing traditional prejudices, but he is not interested in replacing them with another or others.

To suspend the traditional prejudices and thereby presume that what will be encountered in the content of perception will have diametrically opposite characteristics would result in falsifying that content in a manner that is merely the inverse of the traditional prejudices. For example, given the fact that meaningfulness has come to be taken as synonymous with the laws that ultimately are said to govern the already-completed, objectively analyzable world, with the removal of this prejudice, there is a danger of concluding that the content of perception consists of phenomena that are neutral as regards meaning and that await organization. But this collapses into the traditional theory of units of sensation, which has already been revealed as inadequate.

Given the fact that the traditional prejudice has been suspended, according to which the already-completed, objectively analyzable world consists of bodies, located in a static geometrical coordinate system, that change position and place when acted upon by certain forces but remain identical qualitatively, there is a danger of concluding that the original content of perception is a flux that is still conceived of in a manner in keeping with realism. That is to say, the nature of the flux is preconceived, and thus one is not speaking of a radically dynamic process. Merleau-Ponty explicitly guards against this error by distinguishing what one encounters as the original content of perception and the experience of that content from Bergson's notion of the inner core, so to speak, of that which is known through intuition and his notion of intuition itself as coincidence. Merleau-Ponty also guards against the concept of a flow of consciousness as contained within a transcendental Ego, as it is suggested in much of Husserl's works. This "flow" would also tend to involve presuppositions concerning the nature of the process of perception and as such would fail to take account of the radically dynamic nature of the process. (Physico-chemical analysis also does not pertain to the original content of perception because it involves a transfer of objective categories from the macroscopic to the microscopic level. Even if one speaks of transformation of matter into energy and vice versa, one is still confined by physicalistic language and by the permanent laws said to govern this process.)

11. *Phenomenology of Perception*, p. 17.
12. Ibid., pp. 3–4.
13. Ibid., pp. 23–24.

14. Ibid., p. 36.

15. Ibid., p. 101.

16. Merleau-Ponty describes the phenomenological reduction as the process of stepping "back to watch the forms of transcendence fly up like sparks from a fire," a process that "slackens the intentional threads which attach us to the world and thus brings them to our notice," rather than a withdrawal "from the world towards the unity of consciousness as the world's basis" (*Phenomenology of Perception*, p. xiii).

17. Merleau-Ponty locates man's being-in-the-world via an analysis of that situation in which a person who has lost a limb continues to feel a "phantom limb" until the nerve pathways that originally led from the limb to the brain are rendered inactive. Both the purely physical account and the purely psychological account are inadequate (see *Phenomenology of Perception*, pp. 76–89). The former ignores symptoms that are clearly psychological and that have been known to arise under these circumstances (Merleau-Ponty relies on a study by Lhermitte, "L'Image de notre corps," *Nouvelle Revue critique* [1939]). For example, emotions or circumstances that recall the moment in battle when a soldier suffered a wound that led to the amputation of a limb have been known to produce a phantom limb in subjects who had none. On the other hand a purely psychological explanation overlooks the fact that rendering certain nerves inactive does away with the phantom limb. In order to comprehend this situation, it is necessary to affirm that man is already in-the-world in a determinate manner prior to any objectifying cognition, prior to any response to the world, and that the purely psychic and purely physical, isolable in theory only, are thoroughly integrated within this preobjective situation, this being-in-the-world. Merleau-Ponty writes:

This phenomenon [of the phantom limb], distorted equally by physiological and psychological explanations, is, however, understood in the perspective of being-in-the-world. What it is in us which refuses mutilation and disablement is an *I* committed to a certain physical and inter-human world, who continues to tend towards his world despite handicaps and amputations and who, to this extent, does not recognize them *de jure*. The refusal of the deficiency is only the obverse of our inherence in a world, the implicit negation of what runs counter to the natural momentum which throws us into our tasks, our cares, our situation, our familiar horizons. To have a phantom arm is to remain open to all the actions of which the arm alone is capable; it is to retain the practical field which one enjoyed before mutilation. The body is the vehicle of being in the world, and having a body is, for a living creature, to be intervolved in a definite environment, to identify oneself with certain projects and be continually committed to them. (*Phenomenology of Perception*, pp. 81–82)

Being-in-the-world is not materialistic. Neither is it pure ideality. The phenomenal body, the body as it contributes to the original content of perception and not an objectivistic body as portrayed by theories in accord with realism, is a constant element in man's being-in-the-world. Being-in-the-world must be affirmed as an original ontological level in which the psychic and the physical are thoroughly integrated. The phantom limb is obviously not a physiological component of the patient's body. Nor is it a representation, by a positing consciousness, of the lost limb. The phantom limb does indeed exist within the patient's being-in-the-world.

18. *Phenomenology of Perception*, p. 57; emphasis added.

19. This term is the usual one in Husserl's unpublished writings; Merleau-Ponty's note.

20. K. Goldstein, "Über die Abhängigkeit der Bewegungen von optischen Vorgängen," p. 163; Merleau-Ponty's note.

21. *Phenomenology of Perception*, pp. 137–39.

22. Grünbaum, "Aphasie und Motorik," *Zeitschrift für das gesamte Neurologie und Psychiatrie* (1930), pp. 397–98; Merleau-Ponty's note.

23. Ibid., p. 394 (Merleau-Ponty's note).

" 'Déjà la motricité, prise à l'état pur, possède le pouvoir élémentaire de donner un sens *(Sinngebung).*' Même si, dans la suite, la pensée et la perception de l'espace se libèrent de la motricité et de l'être à l'espace, pour que nous puissions nous représenter l'espace il faut d'abord que nous y ayons été introduits par notre corps et qu'il nous ait donné le premier modèle des transpositions, des équivalences, des identifications qui font de l'espace un système objectif et permettent à notre expérience d'être une expérience d'objets, de s'ouvrir sur un 'en soi.' 'La motricité est la sphère primaire où d'abord s'engendre le sens de toutes les significations *(der Sinn aller Signifikationen)* dans le domaine de l'espace représenté" *(Phénoménologie de la perception,* p. 166; my translation).

24. In a footnote to his disclosure of motility as originating within man's being-in-the-world, a note dealing with the development of the understanding of apraxis, Merleau-Ponty acknowledges how easy it is to fall into the misunderstanding that the dynamism of being-in-the-world is either a causal, mechanistic process or an indeterminate flux that would amount to no more than the inverse concept. He states: "It is not easy to reveal pure motor intentionality: it is concealed behind the objective world which it helps to build up. The history of apraxia would show how the description of Praxis is always contaminated and finally made impossible by the notion of representation" *(Phenomenology of Perception,* p. 138).

25. Ibid., pp. 156–57.

26. Ibid., p. 156.

27. Laforgue, *L'Echec de Baudelaire,* p. 126; Merleau-Ponty's note. *Phenomenology of Perception,* p. 168.

28. In addition to meaning that permeates dreams and "languagely meaning," Merleau-Ponty describes musical meaning, which permeates the original content of perception of the organist who plays a particular organ for the first time *(Phenomenology of Perception,* pp. 145–46). The process of adapting to the new instrument is not one of mechanically executing many repetitions of the same movements in order to develop mechanical reflexes. The organist simply adapts too quickly to different instruments for this to be the case. Furthermore, the organist does not memorize the location, in an abstract intellectual framework, of each key, stop, and pedal on the new instrument. Rather the musician alters bodily habits already formed. The space in which he operates is not a system as portrayed by realism in which each object, in this case the keys, stops, and pedals, are located. Nor is it an abstract, intellectual, spatial framework. Rather it is space as contiguous with the musician's body, the space that is already structured in a manner determined in part by the orientation of the musician's body prior to any intellectual formulation. This spatial structure is coincident with musical significance. The musician's being-in-the-world is permeated with musical meaning. It is precisely this musical meaning that calls for appropriate motions by the organist.

29. *Signs,* pp. 88–89.

30. "Ce que nous avons découvert par l'étude de la motricité, c'est en somme un nouveau sens du mot 'sens.' La force de la psychologie intellectualiste comme

96 　　　　　　　　　　　　　　　　　　　MERLEAU-PONTY

de la philosophie idéaliste vient de ce qu'elles n'avaient pas de peine à montrer que la perception et la pensée ont un sens intrinseque et ne peuvent être expliquées par l'association extérieure de contenus fortuitement assemblés. Le Cogito était la prise de conscience de cette intériorité. Mais toute signification était par la même conçue comme un acte de pensée, comme l'opération d'un pur Je, et, si l'intellectualisme l'emportait aisément sur l'empirisme, il était lui-même incapable de rendre compte de la variété de notre expérience, de ce qui en elle est non-sens, de la contingence des contenus. L'expérience du corps nous fait reconnaître une imposition du sens qui n'est pas celle d'une conscience con-stituante universelle, un sens qui est adhèrent à certains contenus" (*Phénoménologie de la perception*, pp. 171–72; my translation).

31. *Phenomenology of Perception*, p. 174. The studies of various aspects of the body that precede "The Body as Expression, and Speech" in *Phenomenology of Perception* already contribute to the overcoming of this dichotomy. The spatiality of one's own body is revealed not as the body's location in the objective space of Cartesian coordinates viewed somehow from outside any particular observer, nor as location in space as a system manufactured by the intellect, but rather as the way in which man is already in-the-world. Thus there is no subject set off in space from objects that constitute the world. The motility of the body is revealed not as the result of the causal processes of the world conceived as the sum of objects, nor as a process directed in some fashion by decisions of the intellect, but rather as the momentum of one's being-in-the-world. Once again, there is no subject set off from objects. The "synthesis of one's own body" is not the material totality of the body conceived as an object. It is not the abstract result of an intellectual process of constructing a totality out of the various parts of the body. Rather, it is the grouping together of the various aspects of the phenomenal body into our being-in-the-world. Again, the subject-object distinction fades. Finally, sexuality is not the result of causal processes in the physiology of the body objectively conceived. It is not the result of intellectual decisions to conceive the physiological structure and respond to it in a certain manner. Rather, sexuality is our way of being-in-the-world with other bodies through the phenomenal body.

The body on the one hand, and the world as perceived on the other hand, may be regarded as two poles of the intentional structure of man's being-in-the-world. Part two of *Phenomenology of Perception* is a study of the world as perceived, the structure of which is implicated in this intentional structure. In this sense, the study of the world as perceived is an extension of the study of the body. The studies that comprise part two of *Phenomenology of Perception*, which is entitled "The World as Perceived," do reflect the effort to overcome the subject-object dichotomy. Merleau-Ponty begins with a study of sense experience, which is revealed as neither a physical, causal process nor the process of intellection whereby a subject organizes accumulated sense data. In short, sense experience is not a middle term between subject and object. Sense experience is the dynamic, structured field of man's being-in-the-world. Man is not confined within an interiority of mind or body. Man is outside himself, in the world. Next follows a discussion of space, which is revealed as neither a physical medium between objects, including an object that is also a subject, nor the result of an intellectual construction employed to order the world of objects. Man's spatial orientation is his manner of being-in-the-world. Once again, man is not confined within an interiority of mind or body. The thing and the natural world are considered next. These "forms of transcendence" are not material objects and the sum of material objects respectively. Nor are they the conclusions of intellectual processes of synthesizing sensuous experiences. Rather, the thing and the world are correlates, within my being-in-the-world, of my body, my opening onto the world. Again this confirms that man is not confined within the interiority of mind or body. Finally, access to other people can only be explained in terms of man's being-in-the-world. People are not physical objects set apart from each other nor are they minds confined to the interiority of intellection, but rather are perceptual consciousnesses in the world through the medium of the body. The other is a different manner or style of being-in-the-world whom I meet in the world. To pose the difficult issue of the accessibility of other consciousnesses, and even to reach the conclusion, as some do, that the other is inaccessible, is to admit some knowledge of the other, some access to the other. Access to the human world, inclusive of national and ethnic groups that are other than one's own, of civilizations that are other than one's own, even of other times, is explicable only in terms of man's being-in-the-world. These different styles of being-in-the-world meet in the world.

As we shall see in chapter 2 of this study, part three of *Phenomenology of Perception*, "Being-for-Itself and Being-in-the-World," demonstrates that the *Cogito*, temporality, and freedom must be understood in terms of man's being-in-the-world and not in terms of a subject set apart somehow from an objectivistic world.

There is a striking convergence between this theme in Merleau-Ponty's *Phenomenology of Perception* and Heidegger's endeavor in *Being and Time* to overcome the subject-object dualism prevalent in epistemology by revealing *Dasein* as in-the-world. (See *Being and Time*, trans. John Macquarrie and Edward Robinson [New York: Harper & Row, 1962], pp. 86–90. *Dasein:* Heidegger's name for man, the only being whose existence is an issue for it.) This convergence may be clarified in terms of the stand taken by both philosophers vis-à-vis Immanuel Kant. For Heidegger and Merleau-Ponty, Kant remains caught in the subjectism begun by Descartes to the degree that, for Kant, we know a world of representations, the result of the workings of reason upon the intake of sensuous experience. For Heidegger, the clue to overcoming Kant's subjectism lies in Kant's recognition of time as the ground of the transcendental unity of the world of representations. The task of *Being and Time* is to reveal temporality as the meaning of the Being of *Dasein* and as the horizon for an understanding of the meaning of Being. Once this is accomplished our philosophic perspective shifts. Having begun by questioning the Being of *Dasein*, the one who asks the question concerning Being, we would be enabled to ask the question concerning Being itself. *Dasein* and Being would not be opposed as subject and object but rather their relatedness would be understood by exploring temporality as the horizon for an understanding of Being. Ontology would no longer be restricted by subjectism, one would begin not from a viewpoint as subject but with Being itself. (This was to be the task of a second half of *Being and Time*. It is taken up in a lecture by Heidegger entitled "Zeit und Sein," in *L'Endurance de la pensée: Pour saluer Jean Beaufret* [Paris: Plon, 1968], pp. 12–71.)

For Merleau-Ponty, the clue to overcoming Kant's subjectism lies in recognizing the body as our opening upon the world.

The analysis of bodily space has led us to results which may be generalized. We notice for the first time, with regard to our own body, what is true of all perceived things: that the perception of space and the perception of the thing, the spatiality of the thing and its being as a thing are not two distinct problems.

The Cartesian and Kantian tradition already teaches us this; it makes the object's spatial limits its essence; it shows in existence *partes extra partes,* and in spatial distribution, the only possible significance of existence in itself. But it elucidates the perception of the object through the perception of space, whereas the experience of our own body teaches us to realize space as rooted in existence. Intellectualism clearly sees that the "motive of the thing" and "the motive of space" [Cassirer, *Philosophie der symbolischen Formen,* III, Second Part, Chap. II; Merleau-Ponty's note] are interwoven, but reduces the former to the latter. Experience discloses beneath objective space, in which the body eventually finds its place, a primitive spatiality of which experience is merely the outer covering and which merges with the body's very being. To be a body, is to be tied to a certain world, as we have seen; our body is not primarily *in* space: it is of it. (*Phenomenology of Perception,* p. 148)

32. *Phenomenology of Perception,* p. xiii.
33. Ibid., pp. 175–76.
34. Ibid., p. 177.
35. Ibid., pp. 177–78.
36. Ibid., p. 179.
37. Ibid., p. 182.
38. Merleau-Ponty draws on A. Gelb and K. Goldstein, "Über Farbennamenamnesie," *Psychologische Forschung* (1925).
39. Any analysis that theoretically isolates the senses and then proceeds to reconstruct experience as a mechanically functioning system composed of isolable contributions from each of the senses loses sight of the presupposed source for intellectual reconstruction of the process at work in each of the senses and thus ultimately of the intellectual reconstruction of experience, namely, man's inherently radically dynamic original situation in the world, man's being-in-the-world. "The connecting link between the parts of our body and that between our visual and tactile experience are not forged gradually and cumulatively. I do not translate the 'data of touch into the language of seeing' or *vice versa*—I do not bring together one by one the parts of my body; this translation and this unification are performed once and for all within me: they are my body itself" (*Phenomenology of Perception,* pp. 149–50).
40. Ibid., p. 180.
41. Ibid., p. 181.
42. Ibid., p. 184.
43. Ibid., p. 184.
44. Ibid., p. 186.
45. Ibid., p. 189.
46. Ibid., p. 187.
47. Ibid., p. 188.
48. Ibid., p. 193.
49. ". . . L'intention significative nouvelle ne se connaît elle-même qu'en se recouvrant de significations déjà disponibles, résultat d'actes d'expression antérieurs. Les significations disponibles s'entrelacent soudain selon une loi inconnue, et une fois pour toutes un nouvel être culturel a commencé d'exister. . . . Nous vivons dans un monde où la parole est *instituée.* . . . Nous perdons conscience de ce qu'il y a de contingent dans l'expression et dans la communication, soit chez l'enfant qui apprend à parler, soit chez l'écrivain qui dit et pense pour la première

fois quelque chose, enfin chez tous ceux qui transforment en parole un certain silence. Il est pourtant bien clair que la parole constituée, telle qu'elle joue dans la vie quotidienne, suppose accompli le pas décisif de l'expression. Notre vue sur l'homme restera superficielle tant que nous ne retrouverons pas, sous le bruit des paroles, le silence primordial, tant que nous ne décrirons pas le geste qui rompt ce silence" (*Phénoménologie de la perception*, pp. 213–14; my translation).

50. See above, this chapter, section A.

51. "Tout est fabriqué et tout est naturel chez l'homme, comme on voudra dire, en ce sens qu'il n'est pas un mot, pas un conduite qui ne doive quelque chose à l'être simplement biologique—et qui en même temps ne se dérobe à la simplicité de la vie animale, ne détourne de leur sens, les conduites vitales, par une sorte *d'échappement* et par un génie de l'équivoque qui pourraient servir à définir l'homme. Déjà la simple présence d'un être vivant transforme le monde physique, fait apparaître ici des 'nourritures,' ailleurs une 'cachette,' donne aux 'stimuli' un sens qu'ils n'avaient pas. A plus forte raison la présence d'un homme dans le monde animal. Les comportements créent des significations qui sont transcendentes à l'égard du dispositif anatomique, et pourtant immanentes au comportement comme tel puisqu'il s'enseigne et se comprend. On ne peut pas faire l'économie de cette puissance irrationelle qui crée des significations et qui les communique. La parole n'en qu'un cas particulier" (*Phénoménologie de la perception*, p. 221; my translation). *Échappement* is translated by "escapement," the English word derived from it. *Escapement* is rarely used. Here it is a noun referring to the new meaning yielded by words and other instances of behavior. It also connotes the action involved.

52. *Phenomenology of Perception*, p. 193.

53. "In pure alexia, if the subject can no longer recognize the letters of a word, it is through inability to pattern the visual data, or constitute the word's structure, or apprehend its visual significance. In motor aphasia, the list of words lost and preserved does not correspond to their objective characteristics (length or complexity), but to their value from the subject's point of view: the patient is unable to pronounce, in isolation, a letter or word within a familiar motor series, through being incapable of differentiating between the 'figure' and 'background' and freely conferring upon a certain word or letter the value of a figure" (*Phenomenology of Perception*, p. 195).

54. Ibid.

55. K. Goldstein, "L'Analyse de l'aphasie et l'essence du langage," *Journal de Psychologie* (1933), p. 496, our emphasis; Merleau-Ponty's note.

56. ". . . l'intention de parler ne peut se trouver que dans une expérience ouverte, elle apparaît, comme l'ébullition dans un liquide, lorsque, dans l'épaisseur de l'être, des zones de vide se constituent et se déplacent vers le dehors. 'Dès que l'homme se sert du langage pour établir une relation vivante avec lui-même ou avec ses semblables, le langage n'est plus un instrument, *n'est plus un moyen, il est une manifestation, une révélation de l'être intime et du lien psychique qui nous unit au monde et à nos semblables.* Le langage du malade a beau révéler beaucoup de savoir, il a beau être utilisable pour des activités determinées, il manque totalement de cette productivité qui fait l'essence la plus profonde de l'homme et qui ne se révèle peut-être dans aucune création de la civilisation avec autant d'évidence que dans la création du langage lui-même.' On pourrait dire, en reprenant une célèbre distinction, que les *langages,* c'est-à-dire

les systèmes de vocabulaire et de syntaxe constitués, les 'moyens d'expression' qui existent empiriquement, sont le dépôt et la sédimentation des actes de parole dans lesquels le sens informulé non seulement trouve le moyen de se traduire au dehors, mais encore acquiert l'existence pour soi-même, et est véritablement créé comme sens. Ou encore on pourrait distinguer une *parole parlante* et une *parole parlée*. La première est celle dans laquelle l'intention significative se trouve à l'état naissant. Ici l'existence se polarise dans un certain 'sens' qui ne peut être défini par aucun objet naturel, c'est au-delà de l'être qu'elle cherche à se rejoindre et c'est pourquoi elle crée la parole comme appui empirique de son propre non-être. La parole est l'excès de notre existence sur l'être naturel. Mais l'acte d'expression constitue un monde linguistique et un monde culturel, il fait retomber à l'être ce qui tendait au-delà. De là la parole parlée qui jouit des significations disponibles comme d'une fortune acquise. A partir de ces acquisitions, d'autres actes d'expression authentique,—ceux de l'écrivain, de l'artiste ou du philosophe,—deviennent possibles. Cette ouverture toujours recréée dans la plénitude de l'être est ce qui conditionne la première parole de l'enfant comme la parole de l'écrivain, la construction du mot comme celle des concepts. Telle est cette fonction que l'on devine à travers le langage, qui se réitère, s'appuie sur elle-même, ou qui, comme une vague, se rassemble et se reprend pour se projeter au-delà d'elle-même" (*Phénoménologie de la perception*, pp. 229–30; my translation).

57. See above, this section.

58. Ibid.

59. *The Structure of Behavior*, p. 176.

60. Within the confines of the present task, the significance of Merleau-Ponty's position vis-à-vis Hegel can not be developed so extensively as the dialogue of the two philosophers merits. This dialogue is clarified in the chapter "Interrogation and Dialectic" in *The Visible and the Invisible*.

61. "Mieux encore que nos remarques sur la spatialité et l'unité corporelles, l'analyse de la parole et de l'expression nous fait reconnaître la nature énigmatique du corps propre. Il n'est pas un assemblage de particules dont chacune demeurerait en soi, ou encore un entrelacement de processus définis une fois pour toutes—il n'est pas où il est, il n'est pas ce qu'il est—puisque nous le voyons secréter en lui-même un "sens" qui ne lui vient de nulle part, le projeter sur son entourage matériel et le communiquer aux autres sujets incarnés. On a toujours remarqué que le geste ou la parole transfiguraient le corps, mais on se contentait de dire qu'ils développaient ou manifestaient une autre puissance, pensée ou âme. On ne voyait pas que, pour pouvoir l'exprimer, le corps doit en dernière analyse devenir la pensée ou l'intention qu'il nous signifie. C'est lui qui montre, lui qui parle, voilà ce que nous avons appris dans ce chapitre" (*Phénoménologie de la perception*, p. 230; my translation).

62. *Phenomenology of Perception*, p. 169.

63. Ibid., p. 170.

64. "L'existence humaine nous obligera à reviser notre notion usuelle de la nécessité et de la contingence, parce qu'elle est le changement de la contingence en nécessité par l'acte de reprise. Tout ce que nous sommes, nous le sommes sur la base d'une situation de fait que nous faisons nôtre et que nous transformons sans cesse par une sorte *d'échappement* qui n'est jamais une liberté inconditionée" (*Phénoménologie de la perception*, p. 199; my translation).

65. *Phenomenology of Perception*, p. 171.

2   The Linguistic Act

> At the proper time it becomes unavoidable to think of
> how mortal speech and its utterance take place in the
> speaking of language as the peal of the stillness of the
> dif-ference. Any uttering, whether in speech or writing,
> breaks the stillness. On what does the peal of stillness
> break? How does the broken stillness come to sound in
> words? How does the broken stillness shape the mortal
> speech that sounds in verses and sentences?[1]
>
> —Heidegger

OUR focus in this chapter will be part three of *Phenomenology of Perception,* entitled "Being-for-Itself and Being-
in-the-World." This concluding part of *Phenomenology of
Perception* is devoted to a question that surfaces repeatedly
in the course of Merleau-Ponty's study of perception and
that was explicitly posed by the study of the body as expression, and speech: How is it to be understood that man
is simultaneously in a situation prior to any acts on man's
part and yet is the one who acts so as to bring about the
existence of the world such as it is?[2] Being-in-the-world
refers to man's original situation. Being-for-itself refers to
that aspect of man by which he acts so as to bring about the
existence of the world such as it is. Here, by seeking how it
is that man is both at once, Merleau-Ponty resumes the
task, which is that of *The Structure of Behavior,* of revealing who man is. Inasmuch as it is being-for-itself that is
proper to man alone, whereas being-in-the-world refers to
the situation formed by man and phenomena found in his

world, the question as to who man is focuses in particular on the nature of the act by which man brings about the existence of the world such as it is. The nature of the linguistic act is included. Just as it is the failure to affirm man's being-in-the-world prior to theoretical objectification that leads to the assumption that language is ontologically distinct from other phenomena found in man's world and thus cannot possibly be involved in processes of mutual determination with other dimensions of man's life, it is the failure to affirm that man acts so as to bring about the existence of the world such as it is that leads to the assumption that, whereas speaking is an activity of man, perception, including hearing, is a purely passive state of man. Once set in opposition to the act involved in perceiving, the linguistic act itself is misunderstood.

By considering three traditional strongholds of the concept of a subject portrayed as apart from the world—the *Cogito*, temporality, and freedom—Merleau-Ponty reveals the full ontological import of the concept of being-in-the-world. The source of man's acts that bring about the existence of the world such as it is is not a subject portrayed as apart from the world but rather is in-the-world. Subjectism falls along with the subject-object dualism. The philosopher will have to turn aside from the point of view of a subject as perceiver and begin at the point, so to speak, where the structure perceiver-perceived comes into being. Merleau-Ponty's study of language in the chapter of *Phenomenology of Perception* entitled "The Body as Expression, and Speech" emphasized language as a current of man's being-in-the-world. Spoken language was disclosed as originating in man's precognitive bodily intentionality specifically directed toward words as phenomena. This current of man's being-in-the-world was disclosed as involved in processes of mutual determination with the other currents of man's being-in-the-world, and words were disclosed as involved in such processes with other phenomena found in man's world. It may seem to be the case from this account of language that the task of the philosopher who wishes to lay bare what is would be to bring to light words as phenomena and in so doing shed light on the other phenomena with which words are involved in processes of mutual determination. In effect, this task would be that described by Merleau-Ponty when he spoke of the possibility of disregarding in any language restrictions imposed by the mechanical laws of phonetics and historical accidents that befall a language, and thereby discovering in that language "a way for the human body to sing the world's praises and in the last resort to live it." But this can no longer be the case once it is affirmed that the philosopher has to turn aside from the point of view of a subject as perceiver and begin at the point, so to speak, where the structure perceiver-perceived comes into being. The philosophical act of doing this would be precisely that act of originary speaking to which Merleau-Ponty referred in the chapter devoted to the body as expression, and speech, an act of speaking that allows words to be what they are, that is, that allows them to have the meanings they have in the sense already described by Merleau-Ponty, rather than using words as though they were objects that can be manipulated at will. Precisely because such an act of speaking does not involve the habitual use of words as complete objects, the meanings of which are assumed to be available to everyone and manipulable at will, such an act of speaking marks the coming into being of new meaning, the ontogenesis of language. It is such an act itself, rather than the attempt to turn away from language and represent it in theoretical metalinguistic constructs, that makes manifest what language is. Because this act of philosophical speaking begins at the point, so to speak, where the structure perceiver-perceived comes into being, it in no way involves the prejudice of an already-complete world of objects. This act lets phenomena other than words be what they are, rather than covering them over with unwarranted objectifications. The fact that both the radically dynamic process of ontogenesis and phenomena, including words, as what they are, will be disclosed in and by this act is a paradox that cannot be skirted methodologically at the outset but must be faced by engaging in the task at hand. The things themselves demand this. The question is: How is this act accomplished?

A. The Overcoming of Subjectism

1. *The Cogito*

Part three of *Phenomenology of Perception* opens with a discussion of the *Cogito* in which Merleau-Ponty demonstrates that this grasp of self by the self that Descartes made explicit is not evidence of an innermost subjectivity set apart from a would-be external reality but rather can only be understood if one acknowledges that man is thoroughly in-the-world. In other words, man is both being-for-itself and being-in-the-world.

First, Merleau-Ponty points out the truth contained in the philosophical step taken by Descartes away from realism, according to which that which comprises known reality is transcendent to the subject and affects the subject in such a way as to bring about knowledge as a sort of by-product. What this position overlooks, and what Descartes brought to light, is that the claim that things exist transcendent to the subject that then affect the subject is unfounded. Reality that is fully transcendent would be entirely unknown, hence a contradiction. As soon as one speaks of reality, one is speaking of thought-of-reality. To be conscious of something is simultaneously to be conscious of one's consciousness of that thing, to be conscious of one's consciousness. This self-consciousness is not a stage reached subsequent to one's original consciousness of a thing. If the original consciousness of the thing preceded consciousness of that consciousness, the former would be fully transcendent, unknowable, and thus the claim to be conscious of it would again be contradictory.

Descartes's position may lead to the conclusion that the "I" is only the name given to a collection of psychological events or is the hypothetical cause of these events. This conclusion is unsatisfactory because all is reduced to momentary experiences of both self and world, psychological events transcendent to each other, thus again making it impossible to know anything—either the self or the world. This position is tantamount to that empiricist theory which reduces all to atomistic sense data and can offer no means of accounting for experience of things, of the world, or of the self.

Descartes's position may lead to the conclusion that the subject is essentially a consciousness that grasps itself once and for all time, outside the limitations of the temporal flow of psychological events. Merleau-Ponty points out the difficulty in accepting this position. Positing the subject outside of time theoretically removes the subject from all limitations, from all effects that a world experienced in time could possibly have on the subject, and thus poses the subject as infinite, as coincident with God. The finite self is lost in the Absolute. The original Cartesian project of grounding consciousness of things in a grasp of the self takes a different turn when the finite self is posited as coincident with the Absolute, because then it could no longer be grasped by human consciousness. Man's original situation in the world, man's being-in-the-world, is ignored. This is the situation of a finite self. According to the above-described conclusion drawn from Descartes's position, the subject is coincident with the Absolute.

How then is the truth involved in Descartes's original move beyond realism to be sustained? Merleau-Ponty draws on his study of perception. Perception does not involve an automatic process, one that yields sense data that are only subsequently organized by consciousness into that which is known. Rather, the original content of perception is meaningful. When one perceives a thing, one is certain of perceiving that thing, and not, as Descartes claimed, only of the thought of perceiving that thing. Here Merleau-Ponty reasserts one of the foundational tenets of Husserlian phenomenology: consciousness is consciousness of something. In keeping with his interpretation of Husserl, Merleau-

Ponty again asserts the impossibility of separating essence from existence. Consciousness is consciousness not only of essences, but of a meaningful structure, a perceptual field, that exists. What one perceives is neither the product of a pure consciousness, nor the instantiation, in some unexplained manner, of an ideal system of meaning. This is not to say that every perception yields truth. When one claims that one's perception is "correct," one is essentially claiming that further experience will not demonstrate that the world affirmed as the real world at that moment is incompatible with one's original situation in the world. But the possibility persists that this will be the case and that on this basis I will "correct" my perception.[3] Merleau-Ponty sustains Descartes's opposition to realism which claims that knowledge comes about as the result of mechanical workings on a subject of external reality without accounting for how it is that this process can be known despite the claim that this external reality is at first unknown. However, Merleau-Ponty maintains that knowledge of the explicitly perceived world is founded upon the perceiver's original situation in the world and thus involves knowledge of that situation even though, and at the same time precisely inasmuch as, the possibility persists that further experience will reveal what one claims to be "correct" perception to be incompatible with one's original situation in the world. This is not knowledge of exhaustively determinate essences, divorced from radically dynamic existent meaning, and completely grasped by the knower. Merleau-Ponty is speaking of knowledge of the world founded upon man's being-in-the-world, not upon the immanence of thought-of-reality within a self-contained subject.

Merleau-Ponty considers two modes of consciousness, which at first glance seem to involve a complete grasp of self by the self, namely, consciousness of "psychic facts" such as will and feeling on the one hand, and "pure thought" such as consciousness of mathematical entities on the other, and demonstrates that one can give a better account of these modes of consciousness in terms of being-in-the-world than in terms of a self-contained subject outside the world. At first glance it seems as though when one loves it is impossible to doubt the fact that one loves and thus it seems as though there is a complete grasp of self in such an experience. However, Merleau-Ponty points out that it is possible to distinguish false love from true love. By false love Merleau-Ponty means neither a simple misinterpretation of a situation that could be cleared up by a better-thought-out interpretation, nor instances in which a person merely acts out the role expected of a lover although no commitment was actually felt in the situation. Merleau-Ponty is referring to situations in which a person is committed to the feeling but does not grasp the full situation, which during the course of the love remains in the background but eventually becomes evident in such a manner as to reveal the love as incompatible with it. For example, a person may love only certain qualities of the beloved, in which case other qualities of the beloved which at first remain in the background may eventually become evident and disclose the love as a false love. Similarly, areas of the life of the person who loves that are not committed to the love may at first remain in the background of the situation and eventually become evident in such a manner as to disclose the love as a false love. In such instances the person does love, but in a way that must be distinguished from true love. In instances of true love, in which a person's life, including areas of the person's life that are not explicitly grasped by the person, is thoroughly committed to the love, it is precisely that fact which does not allow one to say that there is in such a case a complete grasp of self by the self. Merleau-Ponty compares the lover with the dreamer. As was noted in the discussion of the body in its sexual being, the sexual content of a dream is not grasped by the dreamer as an abstract system of meaning that later can be used to interpret the actual content of the dream. Rather, sexuality coincides with that content. Similarly, the lover does not grasp an abstract meaning of love that can be used to interpret his life. Rather, love coincides with the person's being-in-the-world. Thus love must be understood in terms of man's being-in-the-world—an original situation that is not completely given in the world of which man is explicitly conscious—rather than in terms of complete grasp of self by the self. Although Merleau-Ponty does not provide the analysis, the same can be said of the will. At first glance it may seem as though when one wills something there can be no doubt concerning this fact and therefore a complete grasp of self by the self is involved. However, instances of false will may be discerned that are not simple misinterpretations that could be cleared up by better interpretations or cases of a person lying to himself. Instances of false will include those in which a person wills certain aspects of a situation that are accompanied, when they obtain, by other aspects of that situation of which the person was not explicitly conscious and that the person does not will to obtain. Other instances of false will are those in which certain areas of a person's life that remain in the background are not committed to that which the person wills and eventually become evident in such a way as to disclose the will of the person as a false will. In instances of true will, a person is thoroughly committed to the extent that even areas of the person's life of which he is not explicitly conscious are directed toward establishing that which is willed. The person's will coincides with the person's situation in the world, which is not completely given as a totality in explicit consciousness. Thus will must be understood in terms of man's being-in-the-world rather than in terms of a complete grasp of self by the self.

The other mode of consciousness that at first glance seems to involve a complete grasp of self by the self is so-called pure thought. Merleau-Ponty considers what is involved in executing a geometrical proof. According to one interpretation, in order to move from the premises of a proof concerning a geometrical figure to the conclusion, it must be the case that consciousness grasps the unchanging essence of that figure. Thus in such cases there would be a complete grasp of self by the self, consciousness of the consciousness of an eternal essence, unaffected by what occurs in the world in time. But Merleau-Ponty points out that the original premises of a geometrical proof never do contain all that is and can be derived from them and that the formalization of the foundational propositions of geometry to include explicitly or implicitly all that may be derived can only occur after the actual processes of mathematical thinking are accomplished. Here Merleau-Ponty approaches Kant's argument for the synthetic character of mathematics. However, according to Merleau-Ponty, the possibility of beginning with given premises concerning a geometrical figure and arriving at a conclusion concerning that figure does not derive from a complete spatial system that the mind employs in ordering all experience, but rather from the body's intentionality directed toward the geometrical figure, a grasp of the geometrical figure that is dynamic in such a manner as to allow the generation of new geometrical constructions disclosing new properties of the same figure. If the claim is made that all the properties of the geometrical figure were contained in a complete spatial system according to which the mind always orders experience, the actual process of thinking involved in geometrical proofs would be inexplicable, because it would have to be the case that all properties of the figure are known immediately. The thinking involved in geometry must be understood in terms of man's being-in-the-world rather than in terms of a complete grasp of self by the self.

Descartes's step beyond realism is to be sustained neither in terms of an "I" as the name of, or hypothetical cause of, a collection of psychological events, nor in terms of a self outside the world that changes in time. The truth involved in Descartes's surpassing of realism is to be sustained in terms of man's being-in-the-world. Man's original situation in the world is never taken up as a completed totality into the world as explicitly perceived. The world as explicitly perceived may later be proved incompatible with the perceiver's original situation in the world. What then becomes of Descartes's intention to establish certainty of knowledge, in particular of the self, on the basis of his step beyond realism? According to Descartes, thought of reality is more easily known than reality itself. The mind, which contains this thought, is more easily known than external reality. It is certain that the mind exists. Even if one doubts that this is the case, doubting is a mode of thinking and thus again affirms the existence of the mind. Thus Descartes states: I think, therefore I exist. I exist as, at least, a thinking thing, a mind.

According to Merleau-Ponty, it is not only thought about reality that is known; it is reality itself. Man's existence in the world is always already a perceiving of the world, a consciousness of the world, a thought of the world. Therefore, an affirmation of the fact that I think is ipso facto an affirmation of the fact that I exist. I do not exist as a thinking thing, a mind, outside the world. I am in-the-world.

> In the proposition: "I think, I am," the two assertions are to be equated with each other, otherwise there would be no *cogito*. Nevertheless we must be clear about the meaning of this equivalence: it is not the "I am" which is pre-eminently contained in the "I think," not my existence which is brought down to the consciousness which I have of it, but conversely the "I think," which is re-integrated into the transcending process of the "I am," and consciousness into existence.[4]

This account extends to "inner perceptions" as well as "outer perceptions." It is not thought about feeling that is known, but feeling itself that is directed toward people and things found in man's world rather than toward thought about objects. True, the world as explicitly perceived now may later prove to be incompatible with one's original situation in the world, and in this sense, false. Nevertheless, there is a certainty of perception. When one perceives a thing, one is certain of perceiving that thing, and not another. Even if one's perception should later be proved to have been false in the sense just described, it is still certain that I originally did perceive what I perceived. For example, if I perceive a person and it is later proved that I mistook the person I perceived for another, it is still certain that at the time of the original perception, I perceived the person-as-another and not that I perceived the person later proved to have been there and simply made a mistake in judging the identity of the person. The certainty of perception lies in the act of perceiving, an act initiated by the perceiver. This certainty is not a judgment subsequent to perception. The act of perceiving involves a grasp of that which is perceived, an affirmation of the perceived, and itself contributes the quality of certainty. Even if one truly doubts what one perceives, this doubt is certain because the perceiver initiates the act of doubting and what is perceived is certain as that-which-is-perceived-as-doubtful. If perception did not involve an act initiated by the perceiver, that which is perceived would evolve as a mere spectacle, and thus certainty would not be involved as a quality of the experience.

> There can therefore be no doubt at all that I think. I am not sure that there is over there an ash-tray or a pipe, but I am sure that I think I see an ash-tray or a pipe. Now is it in fact as easy as is generally thought to dissociate these two assertions and hold, independently of any judgment concerning the thing seen, the evident certainty of my "thought about seeing"? On the contrary, it is impossible. Perception is precisely that kind of act in which there can be no question of setting the act itself apart from the end to which it is directed. Perception and the percept necessarily have the same existential modality, since perception is inseparable from the consciousness which it has, or rather is, of reaching the thing itself. Any contention that the perception is indubitable, whereas the thing perceived is not, must be ruled out. If I see an ash-tray, *in the full sense of the word see,* there must be an ash-tray there, and I cannot forego this assertion. To see is to see something. To see red, is actively to see red in existence.[5]

Extending this account of the quality of certainty as derived from the act of perceiving to "inner perceptions," Merleau-Ponty writes:

It is true neither that my existence is in full possession of itself, nor that it is entirely estranged from itself, because it is action or doing, and because action is, by definition, the violent transition from what I have to what I am to have, from what I am to what I intend to be. I can effect the *cogito* and be assured of genuinely willing, loving, or believing, provided that in the first place I actually do will, love or believe, and thus fulfil my own existence. If this were not so, an ineradicable doubt would spread over the world, and equally over my own thoughts. I should be for ever wondering whether my "tastes," "volitions," "desires" and "ventures" were really mine, for they would always seem artificial, unreal, and unfulfilled. But then this doubt, not being an actual doubt, could no longer even manage to confer the absolute certainty of doubting. The only way out and into "sincerity," is through the silencing of such scruples and taking a blind plunge into "doing." Hence it is not *because* I think that I am that I am certain of my existence; on the contrary the certainty I enjoy concerning my thoughts stem from their genuine existence. My love, hatred and will are not certain as mere thoughts about loving, hating and willing; on the contrary the whole certainty of these thoughts is owed to that of the acts of love, hatred or will of which I am quite sure because I *perform* them.[6]

At this point the nature of man's acts, by which man brings about the existence of the world such as it is, is precised. It is not the case that a subject outside the world acts upon a world external to that subject. Rather, this action is inherent in man's very being-in-the-world. This is not to reduce being-for-itself to being-in-the-world. Man initiates these acts. Rather, it is to affirm that man must be understood as both simultaneously. Inasmuch as the affirmation of being-in-the-world disallows the theoretical separation of subject and object, and inasmuch as it is man who is the source of these actions that bring about the existence of the world such as it is, it may be said that this acting is the contribution, made by man, to what is. That is, this acting is the completion of the world, which is not to say the totalizing of the world, because the world is not an objective totality. There is no self-enclosed self that remains behind these actions. Correlatively, there is no world in-itself that remains behind the world as explicitly perceived, untouched by man's actions. Man's acts contribute to the structuralization of his original situation in the world. True, this original situation is precognitive. It precedes all conscious representation. But it does not escape consciousness. Man's original situation in the world is the source of the world as explicitly perceived. In instances where the world as explicitly perceived later proves to be incompatible with the perceiver's original situation in the world, it is on the grounds of that original situation that perception is "corrected" by the perceiver. The "resistance" of the perceiver's original situation in the world to being taken up as a completed totality into the world as explicitly perceived is experienced in perceiving. Man's original situation in the world accounts for the perceiver's access to the world and for the transcendence of the world as perceived. Man's original situation in the world does not escape consciousness. Man is conscious of his original situation in the world, man perceives it, which is to say that man's acts contribute to bringing about its existence such as it is.

> The consciousness I have of seeing . . . is the actual effecting of vision. I reassure myself that I see by seeing this or that, or at lest by bringing to life around me a visual surrounding, a visible world which is ultimately vouched for only by the sight of a particular thing. Vision is an action, not, that is, an eternal operation (which is a contradiction in terms) but an operation which fulfils more than it promises, which constantly outruns its premises and is inwardly prepared only by my primordial opening upon a field of transcendence, that is, once again, by an *ek-stase*. Sight is achieved and fulfils itself in the thing seen. It is of its essence to take a hold upon itself, and indeed if it did not do so it would not be the sight of anything, but it is none the less of its essence to take a hold upon itself in a kind of ambiguous and ob-

scure way, since it is not in possession of itself and indeed escapes from itself into the thing seen. What I discover and recognize through the *cogito* . . . is the deepseated momentum of transcendence which is my very being, the simultaneous contact with my own being and with the world's being.[7]

It is true that Merleau-Ponty's study of perception disclosed that being-in-the-world is inherently radically dynamic, that it is structured from within, that it is not thoroughly within man's grasp or control. This is indeed why man's situation in the world has been called an "original situation," prior to any act on man's part. Neither this inherent dynamism, nor man's actions that bring about the existence of the world such as it is can be overlooked. The task at hand is to understand how both obtain simultaneously.

From Merleau-Ponty's point of view, what becomes of the self, which for Descartes was the mind, the thinking thing, the existence of which is certain because I cannot doubt that I think? According to Merleau-Ponty, the self is one pole, so to speak, of this "momentum of transcendence which is the simultaneous contact with my own being and with the world's being." The self is never grasped as a complete totality. Rather, the self is invoked, as an open, indefinite unity, in each act performed by man. Just as man's being-in-the-world is the source of the world as explicitly perceived and the source of the resistance the world offers to the perceiver, in short, of the "worldness" of the world, so it may be said that man's being-in-the-world is the souce of the "I" as known explicitly in each of man's actions and of the resistance of the "I" to ever being completely grasped, that is, of the "I-ness of the I."

There must be, corresponding to this adumbration of being which appears through the concordant aspects of my own experience, or of the experience I share with others—experience which I presume capable of being consummated through indefinite horizons, from the sole fact that my phenomena congeal into a thing, and display, as they occur, a certain consistency of style—there must be, then, corresponding to this open unity of the world, an open and indefinite unity of subjectivity. Like the world's unity, that of the *I* is invoked rather than experienced each time I perform an act of perception, each time I reach a self-evident truth, and the universal *I* is the background against which these effulgent forms stand out: it is through one present thought that I achieve the unity of all my thoughts. What remains, on the hither side of my particular thoughts, to constitute the tacit *cogito* and the original project towards the world, and what, ultimately, am I in so far as I can catch a glimpse of myself independently of any particular act? I am a field, an experience.[8]

2. Temporality

Having demonstrated that the truth of Descartes's *cogito* can only be sustained in terms of man's being-in-the-world, Merleau-Ponty now takes another step into the subect, so to speak. Once again he finds the world, that is, once again affirms man as simultaneously being-for-itself and being-in-the-world. Temporality is the feature of man and world that now concerns Merleau-Ponty. In terms of temporality, the issue at hand may be posed in this manner: given the fact that man acts so as to bring about the existence of the world such as it is, is it the case that this determining action on man's part is one of actually assigning temporal durations to the contents of perception, failing which no structure would endure and thus ultimately there would be no world? And furthermore, is it the case that these individual acts on man's part and the structures they bring about are unified by temporality itself as the endurance of the subject from moment to moment and thus as the innermost identity of a subject outside the world?

Before arriving at the point at which these questions may be posed, Merleau-Ponty reveals the inadequacy of the traditional concept of time, according to which time is the passage of one instantaneous now to the next instantaneous now, with no contribution made by a subject. The passage of time is known only by the occurrence of change in the world and the occurrence of change is known only by a subject who is conscious of this change. Can it therefore be said that the passage of time is a succession of instantaneous nows comprising the content of consciousness? This account is also inadequate. There would be nothing in these instantaneous moments that would mark some of them as now being in the past or that would mark some of them as now being in the future, and consequently there would be no means of distinguishing a now or present. In short, there would be no time. It must be the case that the subject already has an experience of the past-present-future quality of time.

What is the nature of this experience? If past, present, and future cannot be read, so to speak, in time portrayed as instantaneous nows comprising the content of consciousness, must it be concluded that consciousness itself contributes these qualities to that of which it is consciousness, or in other words that consciousness "unfolds or constitutes time," and that the endurance of this past-present-future structure of time marks the endurance of a constituting consciousness that exists apart from that which it constitutes? Merleau-Ponty observes that this account of the past-present-future structure of time as an ideal structure imparted by consciousness to its content is inadequate because, once again, it portrays past, present, and future as always present as ideal determinants and thus actually destroys any intrinsic distinctions between past, present, and future. Once again, the result is to render time impossible. It must be the case that past, present, and future differ essentially.

> Time as the immanent object of a consciousness is time brought down to one uniform level, in other words it is no longer time at all. There can be time only if it is not completely deployed, only provided that past, present and future do not all three have their being in the same sense.[9]

This indicates that although temporality requires a subject who is conscious of changes in the world, of the passage of time, temporality is not a quality imparted to the world by a pure consciousness portrayed as apart from the world, but rather it must be said that time exists. Time passes. That is, time is never a completed structure fully graspable by man. The theoretical portrayal of time in terms of a series of instantaneous nows is derived from existing time.

> It is of the essence of time to be in process of self-production, and not to be; never, that is, to be completely constituted. Constituted time, the series of possible relations in terms of before and after, is not time itself, but the ultimate recording of time, the result of its *passage,* which objective thinking always presupposes yet never manages to fasten on to.[10]

Thus time, like space, is neither an objective characteristic of a world portrayed in accord with realism, nor is it a quality imparted to the world by a pure consciousness portrayed as apart from an external world. Time, like space, is an existent structure contributing to man's being-in-the-world.

> We must therefore avoid saying that our body is *in* space, or *in* time. It *inhabits* space and time.[11]

And again:

> I am not in space and time, nor do I conceive space and time; I belong to them, my body combines with them and includes them.[12]

Merleau-Ponty describes the temporal structure of man's being-in-the-world, relying on Husserl's account of temporality to do so. One's past is not a series of moments that one constructs or represents by an intellectual act in the present. Rather one still has a grasp on the past. That is, one is open to the past as past, "in its own domain,"[13] through a

mode of intentionality that Husserl called "retention." As
time passes, a present moment slips into the past and one
grasps it no longer precisely as it was, but in terms of what
Husserl called an *Abschattung,* an adumbration. As time
continues to pass, a past moment continues to alter in one's
grasp and a series of *Abschattungen* comes about, in terms
of which one grasps the past moment, which is receding.
Similarly, one's future is not a series of moments that one
constructs or represents by an intellectual act, but rather
exists as the future, again "in its own domain," and is
grasped through a mode of intentionality that Husserl called
"protention." One does not grasp a moment in the future in
precisely the same manner as it will be lived through as
present, but rather through a series of *Abschattungen* that
accompany the moments that intervene between the present and the remote future. As time passes, the remote future approaches and is known through progressively fewer
Abschattungen.

This description leaves open one last possibility to assert
that temporality is a structure imparted to the world by a
pure consciousness that resides apart from the world. Is it
not the case that an intellectual synthesis must be made by
the subject of each series of *Abschattungen* plus the moment that is grasped in terms of those *Abschattungen* such
that ultimately consciousness has a continuous grasp of the
moment in question precisely as it was or will be experienced as present, in order that the series of *Abschattungen*
in question may be linked with that moment? Just as did
previously considered attempts to attribute temporality to
an ideal structure imparted by the subject to the world, so
this one destroys the past-present-future structure of temporality. Each moment would always be grasped as a present moment. Thus no recession into the past or approach
from the future would be displayed by these moments. With
both an experience of past and an experience of future lack-
ing, the present would not be distinguishable and hence
time would be impossible. There is a synthesis of *Abschattungen* plus the past or future grasped in terms of these

Abschattungen, but it is not an intellectual synthesis. Rather, the linkage of past and future moments in terms of their respective *Abschattungen* resides in the intentional grasp of past and future itself. Specifically, one neither continuously grasps a moment in time as the same moment as it was or will be lived through and thus identify *Abschattungen* with that moment, nor does one recontruct a past moment or construct a future moment on the basis of intellectual analysis of *Abschattungen.* Rather, one is open to the past and to the future through the respective *Abschattungen,* which is to say that one continuously grasps the moments in question, but in a manner that changes as those moments recede into the past or approach from the future.

One possible objection to this account of temporality is that Merleau-Ponty is still portraying each present, past, and future, in addition to each *Abschattung,* as a moment of time, thus implying a continuous grasp of each as the same individual temporal element, and that he is thus ultimately portraying time as an ideal structure—which is tantamount, as has been shown, to making time impossible. Merleau-Ponty provides a more thorough account of the nature of these moments that answers the criticism. These moments must be distinguishable in some sense, because if they were not, the structure past-present-future would collapse. There would be no time. However, each moment is distinguishable in terms of what occurs to the other moments as it approaches from the future, becomes present, and recedes into the past. For example, the becoming present of one moment is the receding into the past of others and the approach from the future of others. The occurrence of a present is not the instantaneous appearance of a self-enclosed moment which, so to speak, pushes previous self-enclosed moments farther into the past and pulls other self-enclosed moments closer from the future.

There is, then, not a multiplicity of linked phenomena, but one single phenomenon of lapse. Time is the one single movement appropriate to itself in all its parts, as a gesture includes all the muscular contractions necessary for its execution.[14]

When a present becomes past it does not disintegrate but is still grasped by consciousness at present because it has always involved in itself its becoming past and the arrival of a new present. The future is grasped by consciousness at present because the present has always involved in itself the arriving of that future. There is an analogy between this account of temporality and Merleau-Ponty's preceding account of perception in general, and this comes as no surprise inasmuch as temporality has been affirmed as an existent structure contributing to man's being-in-the-world. In the case of the experience of seeing a thing at a distance, for example, Merleau-Ponty points out that one does not interpret particular aspects of that perceptual experience and conclude that one is seeing the same thing that was seen at close range. Rather, one actually sees that same thing-as-seen-at-a-distance.[15] Similarly, one does not intellectually reconstruct a past and construct a future on the basis of the present. Rather, one experiences a present as a present that always has been, and continues to be, announced by the past, and always has announced, and continues to announce, the future.

> There is a temporal style of the world, and time remains the same because the past is a former future and a recent present, the present an impending past and a recent future, the future a present and even a past to come; because, that is, each dimension of time is treated or aimed at *as* something other than itself and because, finally, there is at the core of time a gaze, or, as Heidegger puts it, an *Augen-blick, someone* through whom the word *as* can have a meaning.[16]

Just as it is man who acts so as to affirm that thing-as-seen-at-a-distance as an element of the explicitly perceived world, so it is man who acts so as to affirm the present as the present, specifically as the present that always has been and continues to be announced by the past and that always has announced and continues to announce the future. Man does not find temporality as an objective feature of a world as portrayed by realism, nor does man, conceived of as a pure consciousness apart from the world, impart to the world an ideal temporal structure; man acts so as to bring about the existence of the temporal structure of the world such as it is.

> The passage of one present to the next is not a thing which I conceive, nor do I see it as an onlooker, I perform it.[17]

As he did in the discussion of the *Cogito,* Merleau-Ponty determines further the nature of this act on man's part that brings about the existence of the world such as it is—in this case specifically, the existence of the temporal structure of the world such as it is. In no manner is it a question of a subject outside the world acting upon the world portrayed as external to that subject. Rather, this acting is inherent in man's very being-in-the-world. Merleau-Ponty now affirms this in a passage that makes quite evident his struggle to present man as simultaneously being-in-the-world and being-for-itself, while reducing neither to the other:

> We are not saying that time is *for* someone, which would once more be a case of arraying it out, and immobilizing it. We are saying that time *is* someone, or that temporal dimensions, in so far as they perpetually overlap, bear each other out and ever confine themselves to making explicit what was implied in each, being collectively expressive of that one single explosion or thrust which is subjectivity itself. We must understand time as the subject and the subject as time. . . . We are forced to recognize the existence of "a consciousness having behind it no consciousness to be conscious of it"[18] which, consequently, is not arrayed out in time, and in which its "being coincides with its being for itself."[19] We may say that ultimate consciousness is "timeless" *(zeitlose)* in the

sense that it is not intratemporal.[20] "In" my present, if I grasp it while it is still living and with all that it implies, there is an *ek-stase* towards the future and towards the past which reveals the dimensions of time not as conflicting, but as inseparable: to be at present is to be always and for ever. Subjectivity is not in time because it takes up or lives through time, and merges with the cohesion of a life.[21]

This "ultimate consciousness" that is "timeless" is not an eternal subject outside the world. It is timeless only in the sense that it is not arrayed out in time but rather is the very act that brings about the existence of the temporal structure of the world such as it is. Furthermore, Merleau-Ponty emphasizes that there is a priority of the present that rules out an eternal subject. It is through the present that one is conscious of the past and the future. Moreover, the lapse of time, the occurring of a present as a receding of other moments into the past and as an approach of other moments from the future, requires an act on man's part, inherent in man's being-in-the-world, that is performed at the present moment. It is only by becoming present that a moment becomes timeless (not eternal), because it is the moment at which the existing temporal structure of the world such as it is comes into being. If the subject were eternal, there would be no priority of present, past, or future. There would be only a hypothetical eternal identity that is to be sought but that could never be found, because each act of attempting to grasp it would be one that is performed at present and thus would distort my consciousness of its eternal nature by giving it the quality of being present, as opposed to being past or future. This dynamism that Merleau-Ponty refers to as the lapse of time is both the dynamism of man's action to bring about the existing temporal structure of the world such as it is and the inherent dynamism of man's being-in-the-world.

We said above that we need to arrive at a consciousness with no other behind it, which grasps its own being, and in which, in short, being and being conscious are one and the same thing. This ultimate consciousness is not an eternal subject perceiving itself in absolute transparency, for any such subject would be utterly incapable of making its descent into time, and would, therefore have nothing in common with our experience: it is the consciousness of the present. In the present and in perception, my being and my consciousness are at one, not that my being is reducible to the knowledge I have of it or that it is clearly set out before me—on the contrary perception is opaque, for it brings into play, beneath what I know, my sensory fields which are my primitive alliance with the world—but because "to be conscious" is here nothing but "to belong to," and because my consciousness of existing merges into the actual gesture of "ex-sistence."[22]

Whether or not these lapses of time, these "burstings forth" of time,[23] cohere to form what may be called History, and if so in what manner, is a question or questions left open here by Merleau-Ponty.

This discussion of temporality fully affirms the fundamental tenet of Merleau-Ponty's thought that "there is the world." Each present does not become meaningless by being annulled by a succeeding moment nor is it rendered trivial by a would-be eternal reality untouched by the passage of time. Nor can it be said that the present is "less meaningful" than a present that has passed by or a present that is approaching from the future. Each present is a "timeless moment" that is meaningful because it is the moment at which the existing temporal structure of the world comes into being as it is. Merleau-Ponty writes: "What does not elapse in time is the lapse of time itself."[24] So it may be said at each moment that despite the inherent radical dynamism of the world, there is the world. To be fully conscious of all that is implicit in the statement that what does not elapse in time is the lapse of time itself would be to act in such a manner as to live the "synthesis" of one's life as a "synthesis" of "timeless moments" at which the existing temporal structure of the world comes into being as it is. Merleau-Ponty writes:

[T]ime's "synthesis" [the fact that the past is the past of the present and the future is the future of the present, or, in short, the fact that time is] is a transitional synthesis [as opposed to an intellectual synthesis accomplished by a would-be pure consciousness on the basis of an ideal past-present-future structure], *the action of a life which unfolds, and there is no way of bringing it about other than by living that life.*[25]

To be fully conscious of all that is implicit in the statement that, despite the inherent radical dynamism of the world, there is the world, would be to lay bare what is. How is this to be accomplished? We must await Merleau-Ponty's work after *Phenomenology of Perception* for an attempt to answer this question.

3. Freedom

The final chapter of *Phenomenology of Perception* begins with a presentation of the argument in favor of the position that man's freedom is unlimited, absolute freedom. When I turn to myself in order to describe myself, what I find is an apparently anonymous consciousness that is not qualified by any of the qualifications, such as physical features, occupation, ethnic background, and the like, by which I am known to others. This freedom from objective qualification is a freedom from causation from without. If I were qualified objectively, I would be an object, a thing, and only things can be affected by causal action. Thus my actions are absolutely free. Furthermore, all of my actions must be absolutely free, because if I were ever an object acted upon by causal factors, if I were ever reduced to a thing, it is inconceivable that my freedom could ever be rekindled. It is also impossible that my freedom could ever be attenuated. For example, if motives are, in the ultimate analysis, what compel me to perform an act, then I am not free at all. But if I am free, then it is only my free decision that gives motives any force. One is misled into thinking that motives attenuate freedom by the process of deliberation that some-times accompanies decisions. In reality it is the decision that precedes the deliberation, because it is only on the basis of what has been decided that motives can acquire any weight in the process of deliberation.

From all this it would seem as though the only qualifica-tions I must accept are those which derive from how others see me. However, here too it may be argued that, in the ultimate analysis, it is I who freely choose to take others into consideration at all.

One argument that may be advanced against this notion of absolute freedom is the fact that even though I may will myself to be a particular type of human being—a warrior and a seducer are the examples Merleau-Ponty uses—I may not be capable of converting myself, and thus I would be left constantly trying to be a warrior or seducer. Here it may be argued that it is not the capacity to convert myself that is failing, but rather that the original decision was never truly made. I am deceiving myself. One other argument that may be advanced against this notion of absolute freedom is that there are objective obstacles that freedom cannot over-come. For example, although I may wish to climb a moun-tain, there can be physical features of the mountain that simply make this impossible. In this instance it may be argued that such obstacles are not objective but rather be-come obstacles only in virtue of the endeavor that I con-ceived. Consequently, it may be said that the only conceiv-able limits to freedom are limits that are contrived freely and hence are not really limits at all.

But there is a fatal flaw in this notion of absolute free-dom. If one maintains that all acts are absolutely free acts, one is forced into the contradictory position of being unable to distinguish free acts from a background provided by one's life, from which free acts should stand out if they are distinguishable. In short, freedom would not be at all identi-fiable and there would be no warrant for speaking of it. In order that freedom be identifiable, it must make its mark, so to speak, in the world. That is, free acts must be identified by their role in bringing about situations in which freedom thrives. This being the case, given a free act, once committed, other free acts will be directed toward a situation in such a manner as to preserve and expand the freedom manifest in the situation. Freedom is inseparable from a situation. This is not to say that the structure of a situation causes a free act. It is to say that there can be no freedom that resides outside a world that it constructs; there can only be a freedom that resides in the world and stands out as freedom to act by taking up the structure of a situation and transforming it.

Merleau-Ponty describes three types of situations in which the structure of the situation provides the path of freedom, so to speak. The first type is one in which a task is to be performed involving things found in the world. If, for example, I wish to climb a mountain, certain physical features of the mountain will present obstacles. It may be argued that these obstacles are the result of my freely chosen project of climbing the mountain and therefore are not real limitations of my absolute freedom. However, prior to my express decision to climb the mountain, I grasped the mountain, so to speak, through my bodily intentionality, and it is this precognitive situation that is the source of my conscious identification of obstacles. I decide that the mountain's height presents an obstacle, not because I am aware of an objective spatial scale that obtains in the world, nor because as a pure consciousness I contrive a spatial scale of the world, but rather on the basis of my bodily intentional grasp of the mountain. If I attempt to climb the mountain, this original situation in the world will be the source of my decisions as to how to proceed step-by-step. If at some point I decide that the mountain is unclimbable, the decision will be on the basis of this bodily intentional grasp, which was elaborated if I did make attempts to climb it, and not because I freely created an obstacle to my absolute freedom.

The second type of situation that Merleau-Ponty describes is one in which obstacles to carrying out a project arise from within myself. Fatigue may, for example, present an obstacle to continuing a journey. Eventually, I may halt because of fatigue. It may be argued that this obstacle is the result of my own freely chosen project and not a real limit to my absolute freedom. However, once again, before an express decision is made as to whether or not to continue my journey, I am in-the-world in a particular way, which will be the source of my decision as to whether or not I find fatigue tolerable. Here Merleau-Ponty again speaks of what he calls "sedimentation." Sedimentation has been identified previously in terms of the contribution to the phenomenal body made by habitual acts, and inasmuch as the phenomenal body is the vehicle of man's being-in-the-world, the contribution made by habitual acts to the structuralization of man's being-in-the-world.[26] Here, the sedimentation spoken of is that of an "attitude towards the world, [which] when it has received frequent confirmation, acquires a favored status for us."[27] If fatigue halts my journey, the source of my decision that the fatigue is intolerable may lie in such a sedimented attitude, in my way of being-in-the-world, rather than in an obstacle to my absolute freedom, namely fatigue, which I have created by freely choosing to make the journey.

Sedimentation can be identified as the source as well of certain decisions made in situations of the type described previously, situations in which a task is to be performed involving things found in the world. For example, I may have attempted a certain bodily task repeatedly in the past and failed. The movements I repeatedly made that were inadequate to the task have restructured my phenomenal body such that, when confronted with the task again, I decide that I cannot perform it. This decision is not made on the basis of an intellectual consideration of the situation. Rather, the source of this decision is my precognitive being-in-the-world through my phenomenal body, which here stands between me and the task, so to speak.

The final type of situation that Merleau-Ponty describes is a situation involving one's relations with others, a situation of historical dimensions. Why is it that a worker decides that in order to achieve his desired economic situation he will be a member of the proletarian class by taking up the side of that class in revolution? It is not simply because of objectively identifiable aspects of his life. Such factors do not cause this decision. Consciousness is not causally determined. Merleau-Ponty notes that there was exploitation long before there were revolutionaries. Nor is this decision a gratuitous act. The source of the decision lies in a certain way of being-in-the-world, of dealing with the world and with others, which has built up through one's life and precedes the express decision to be a member of the proletarian class by engaging in revolution.

> What makes me a proletarian is not the economic system or society considered as systems of impersonal forces, but these institutions as I carry them within me and experience them; nor is it an intellectual operation devoid of motive, but my way of being in the world within this institutional framework.[28]

Once again, sedimentation contributes to the situation. The manner of being-in-the-world, which is the source of the express decision to be a member of the proletarian class by engaging in revolution, is built up in the course of the worker's life. This notion of sedimentation calls for further investigation. Sedimentation is involved in the structuralization of man's being-in-the-world. But the notion of being-in-the-world refers to man's situation prior to any acts on his part. What is the distinction between being-in-the-world and sedimentation, and precisely how does sedimentation enter into the structuralization of man's being-in-the-world? Precisely how is sedimentation sustained within man's being-in-the-world?

Merleau-Ponty's descriptions of these three types of situations do make evident how it is that freedom is inseparable from a situation. Freedom stands out from the background of a situation that provides the path of freedom, so to speak.

There is, therefore, never determinism and never absolute choice, I am never a thing and never bare consciousness. In fact, even our own pieces of initiative, even the situations which we have chosen, bear us on, once they have been entered upon by virtue of a state rather than an act. The generality of the "role" and of the situation comes to the aid of decision, and in this exchange between the situation and the person who takes it up, it is impossible to determine precisely the "share contributed by the situation" and the "share contributed by freedom."[29]

Once again, Merleau-Ponty determines further the nature of the acts on man's part that bring about the existence of the world such as it is. There is no self-contained subject who comes to the world from outside in order to act upon it. Man's actions which bring about the existence of the world such as it is are inherent to man's being-in-the-world. Speaking of man's being-in-the-world specifically as the structure of a situation that provides the path of freedom, the path of those acts which bring about the existence of the world such as it is, Merleau-Ponty writes:

There is an autochthonous meaning of the world that is constituted in the dealings that our incarnate existence has with it, and that forms the ground of every deliberate *Sinngebung.*[30]

This "autochthonous meaning" comprises man's original being-in-the-world and yet it is constituted in man's "dealings" with the world. Merleau-Ponty's language is again ambiguous here, and the reason is that the point of view adopted in *Phenomenology of Perception,* that of perceiver perceiving a world constituted in perception, will not allow a response to the question to which the study of perception has led, namely: how is it that man is situated in the world prior to any act on man's part, and yet man acts so as to bring about the existence of the world such as it is? However, by disclosing the nature of man's acts that bring about the existence of the world such as it is, by determining that

these acts are inherent in man's being-in-the-world, which
does not reduce being-for-itself to being-in-the-world but
fully affirms man as both simultaneously, Merleau-Ponty
points toward the manner in which the question will henceforth have to be approached. What has been affirmed is the
full ontological import of the notion of being-in-the-world.
Inasmuch as the affirmation of man's being-in-the-world
disallows the positing of a subject apart from the world, the
question may arise as to how it is possible to speak of man.
That is, why is not the identity of man, as differentiated
from the world in which he is, simply declared an illusion?
This is disallowed by the fact that a unique contribution
made by man to the world has been identified, and that
contribution is specifically those acts which bring about the
existence of the world such as it is. The question as to
whether it is possible to speak of a "Self" as initiator of
these acts is not resolved in *Phenomenology of Perception*.
But if the source and nature of these acts is to be understood, one must not search for a faculty within a hypostatized subject theoretically set apart from the world.
Rather, one must look within the world now affirmed as
subsuming man.

> Far from its being the case that my freedom is always
> unattended, it is never without an accomplice, and its
> power of perpetually tearing itself away finds its fulcrum
> in my universal commitment in the world. My actual free-
> dom is not on the hither side of my being, but before me,
> in things.[31]

Man is not causally determined, but neither is man absolutely free. Freedom is freedom in a situation. This being
the case, it is not possible to speak of a quantity of freedom
that would remain constant and that man would bring to
every situation. The freedom manifest in each situation
does vary in degree.

> Taken concretely, freedom is always a meeting of the
> inner and the outer—even the prehuman and prehistoric

freedom with which we began—and it shrinks without ever disappearing altogether in direct proportion to the lessening of the *tolerance* allowed by the bodily and institutional data of our lives.[32]

There are acts performed in situations in which there is little tolerance, in which case freedom does not carry the act far toward transforming one's situation. It is only by being fully who I am that I can possibly contribute to the coming about of a new situation. Only by actively taking up my situation-in-the-world as it is can it possibly be transformed.

It is by being unrestrictedly and unreservedly what I am at present that I have a chance of moving forward; it is by living my time that I am able to understand other times, by plunging into the present and the world, by taking on deliberately what I am fortuitously, by willing what I will and doing what I do, that I can go further.[33]

Such an act would be an act in the fullest sense, an act initiated by man as in-the-world that could not be curtailed by man's original situation in the world because it would take up that situation as it is and transform it. How is such an act to be performed? Merleau-Ponty poses the question on the last page of *Phenomenology of Perception:*

Just as reflection borrows its wish for absolute sufficiency from the perception which causes a thing to appear, and as in this way idealism tacitly uses that "primary opinion" which it would like to destroy as opinion, so freedom flounders in the contradictions of commitment, and fails to realize that without the roots which it thrusts into the world, it would not be freedom at all. Shall I make this promise? Shall I risk my life for so little? Shall I give up my liberty in order to save liberty? There is no theoretical reply to these questions. But there are these *things* which stand, irrefutable, there is before you this person whom you love, there are these men whose existence around you is that of slaves, and *your* freedom

cannot be willed without leaving behind its singular rele-
vance, and without willing freedom *for all*. Whether it is a
question of things or of historical situations, philosophy
has no function other than to teach us once more to see
them clearly, and it is true to say that it comes into being
by destroying itself as separate philosophy. But what is
here required is silence, for only the hero lives out his
relation to men and the world.[34]

But silence that ignores the dilemma is an act of turning
away from it. The type of act called for is not an act that is
an attempt to step outside man's situation in the world, but
rather is an act that takes up man's situation in the world as
it is and transforms it, an act in the fullest sense.[35] The
philosophic act of speaking, which is to begin at that point,
so to speak, where the perceiver-perceived structure comes
into being, would be just such an act. After *Phenomenology
of Perception* Merleau-Ponty's efforts will alternate between an attempt to determine how the philosopher is to
speak in the fullest sense and an attempt to do so.

B. The Philosophic Act of Speaking

Language arises both from the dynamism inherent in
man's being-in-the-world, in particular that strain or current of intentionality directed toward words, and from acts
on man's part. Language is not the province of a faculty of
mind distinct from would-be faculties of the mind involved
in perception. The task that language presents is to determine precisely what the nature of this dynamism is, how it
can be that man is situated in the world prior to any acts on
man's part and yet is the one who acts so as to bring about
the existence of the world such as it is. This much was
revealed by Merleau-Ponty's study of the body as expression, and speech.

In the course of his study of the *cogito*, Merleau-Ponty
explicitly confirms the fact that the task of understanding
perception of things and other people and the task of under-

standing language both involve this fundamental question as to how man is simultaneously situated in the world prior to any acts on man's part and yet is the one who acts so as to bring about the existence of the world such as it is. Having affirmed the truth of Descartes's *cogito* as a step beyond realism, Merleau-Ponty pointed out the obstacles to basing the *cogito* on either a conception of the "I" as a name given to independent psychological events or a conception of the "I" as an eternal "I" unaffected by an external world. Instead, the truth of the *cogito* must be based on man's being-in-the-world. Intentionality accedes directly to that which is perceived. Consciousness is always consciousness of something. The quality of certainty in the perception derives from the perceiver's act of perceiving, which brings about the existence of the world such as it is. This act is not by any means one performed by a subject apart from the world. This act is inherent in man's being-in-the-world. This poses the following question:

> The problem is how I can be the constituting agent of my thought in general, failing which it would not be thought by anybody, would pass unnoticed and would therefore not be thought at all—without ever being that agent of my particular thoughts, since I never see them come into being in the full light of day but merely know myself through them. The question is how subjectivity can be both dependent yet irremovable.[36]

In order to illustrate why neither being-in-the-world nor being-for-itself can be understood apart from the other, Merleau-Ponty chooses the example of language rather than the perception of things or other people. The fundamental issue is the same. The basics of the analysis provided here in the discussion of the *cogito* are already familiar from the study of the body as expression, and speech. Language arises from man's being-in-the-world, from original intentionality, in this case directed in particular toward words.

The word "sleet," when it is known to me, is not an object which I recognize through any identificatory synthesis, but a certain use made of my phonatory equipment, a certain modulation of my body as a being in the world. Its generality is not that of the idea, but that of a behavioral style "understood" by my body in so far as the latter is a behavior-producing power, in this case a phoneme-producing one. One day I "caught on" to the word "sleet," much as one imitates a gesture, not, that is, by analyzing it and performing an articulatory or phonetic action corresponding to each part of the word as heard, but by hearing it as a single modulation of the world of sound, and because this acoustic entity presents itself as "something to pronounce" in virtue of the all-embracing correspondence existing between my perceptual potentialities and my motor ones, which are elements of my indivisible and open existence. The word has never been inspected, analyzed, known and constituted, but caught and taken up by a power of speech and, in the last analysis, by a motor power given to me along with the first experience I have of my body and its perceptual and practical fields.[37]

The dynamism that brings about language combines that dynamism inherent in man's being-in-the-world and an act initiated by man. Thus Merleau-Ponty writes that my body "understands" the "behavioral style" of the word, a description that emphasizes man's receptivity—or rather, the inherent dynamism of being-in-the-world—as the source of language, but quickly qualifies this by adding that this process of understanding my body is one that is affected by my body as a "behavior-producing power," a description that emphasizes the act initiated by man that contributes to the genesis of language.

In a manner in keeping with the affirmation in part three of *Phenomenology of Perception* of the full ontological import of the notion of being-in-the-world, Merleau-Ponty describes the nature of this act initiated by man that is involved in the genesis of language. In no way is it an act performed by a subject residing outside the world. The source and nature of these acts are to be found in the world now understood as subsuming man. Thus Merleau-Ponty writes that the "power of speech" and, in the last analysis, the "motor power" that contributes to the genesis of language, are "given to me along with the first experience I have of my body and its perceptual and practical fields." And again:

> Silent consciousness grasps itself only as a generalized "I think" in face of a confused world "to be thought about." Any particular seizure, even the recovery of this generalized project by philosophy, demands that *the subject bring into action powers which are a closed book to him and, in particular, that he should become a speaking subject.*[38]

Man initiates these acts that contribute to the genesis of language, but the "powers" that man brings into action are a closed book to him; they are given to man. Being-for-itself and being-in-the-world are inseparable. Man must be understood as both simultaneously. If the nature and source of these acts are to be disclosed, the philosopher must not search for a faculty possessed by a would-be subject apart from an external world, but must rather seek the nature and source of these acts in the world now understood as subsuming man.

Merleau-Ponty's study of temporality called attention to a certain priority of the present, which is declared by the tenet "there is the world." How is the philosopher to arrive at the appropriate language for making explicit all that is contained in the word *the* as it appears in this statement? That is, how is the philosopher to lay bare what is? Language is, in a sense, past. What language we have at our disposal has been spoken toward various ends in situations that no longer obtain. On the other hand, language is not complete. The future that is approaching holds possibilities of new meaning in language. How is something to be said, in the fullest sense, at present? It appears as though the philosopher can only remain silent. But it is through the present that one is conscious of the past and the future. The act on man's part that contributes to the lapse of time as the occurring of a present precisely as a receding of other moments into the past and the approach of other moments from the future, is an act performed at the present moment. One is conscious of the inadequacy of past language for saying something in the fullest sense at present, and one is conscious of the possibility of new meaning in language in the future that seems to threaten the attempt to say something in the fullest sense at present, precisely because there is something to be said in the fullest sense at present. There is the world, and the silence at which the philosopher arrives in the face of the inadequacies of past language and the possibilities of new meaning in language in the future is not a mute silence, but one that is the language appropriate for laying bare what is. Just as it may be said that what does not elapse in time is the lapse of time itself, and that despite the inherent radical dynamism of the world, there is *the* world, so may it be said that the silence at which the philosopher arrives in engaging in the task of saying something in the fullest sense, in engaging in the task of laying bare what is, does not become mute. What is called for is an act of speaking that does not break this silence, that does not turn away from that which is to be said in the fullest sense at present, either by relapsing into the use of past language under the assumption that language was completed in the past so that possibilities for new meaning in language in the future, which is now present, were closed, or by attempting to focus on the future of language as though the future were not the future of the present. How is the philosopher to utter this language that does not break the silence, that is appropriate to the task of laying bare what is?

Merleau-Ponty's discussion of freedom called attention to the fact that it is only by being fully who he is, by actively taking up his situation-in-the-world as it is, that man can possibly contribute to the coming about of a new situation.

If man turns away from the task of uttering that language which is appropriate to the task of laying bare what is— either by relapsing into the use of past language under the assumption that language was completed in the past, or by refusing to speak and awaiting a future when presumably language will no longer appear inadequate to saying something in the fullest sense because of its past usage and because of possibilities of new meaning in language in the future—then man turns away from the task of being fully who he is, of actively taking up his situation-in-the-world as it is. Uttering this language that does not break the silence at which the philosopher arrives in engaging in the task of saying something in the fullest sense, requires an act in the fullest sense initiated by man. This particular act, the philosophic act, would lay bare what is and thus facilitate other acts in the fullest sense which, in taking up man's situation-in-the-world as it is, may transform that situation.

Conclusion

With each step into the subject so to speak, Merleau-Ponty has discovered the world. In order to give an account of each of three traditional strongholds for the concept of a subject portrayed as apart from the world—the *cogito,* temporality, and freedom—man's being-in-the-world has to be fully affirmed. This is not to say that a theoretical synthesis of subject and world has been found or need be found. There is no justification for beginning with the two theoretically apart from one another.

Subjectism falls along with the subject-object dualism. The theoretical point of view of a subject describing the world must be totally abandoned. No longer will it be possible to maintain the point of view of a perceiver describing the content of perception. In order to lay bare what is, what is called for is that the philosopher begin at that point, so to speak, where the structure perceiver-perceived comes into being. This is precisely what Merleau-Ponty refers to when he writes in *Phenomenology of Perception,* at the conclusion of his study of the world as perceived:

> These descriptions need to provide us with an opportunity of defining a variety of comprehension and reflection altogether more radical than objective thought. To phenomenology understood as direct description needs to be added a phenomenology of phenomenology.[39]

To begin at the point where the structure perceiver-perceived comes into existence would be to fully acknowledge the radically dynamic nature of existence. Thus to understand fully the constancy of the perceiver-perceived structure promises to shed light on an issue left unresolved by the analyses in *Phenomenology of Perception:* precisely how is the affirmation "there is the world" cotenable with the acknowledgment of the radically dynamic nature of existence?

What is called for is that the philosopher begin with that milieu which Merleau-Ponty continues, in part three of *Phenomenology of Perception,* to call existence.

> In so far as, when I reflect on the essence of subjectivity, I find it bound up with that of the body and that of the world, this is because my existence as subjectivity is merely one with my existence as a body and with the existence of the world, and because the subject that I am, when taken concretely, is inseparable from this body and this world. The ontological world and body which we find at the core of the subject are not the world or body as idea, but on the one hand the world itself contracted into a comprehensive grasp, and on the other the body itself as a knowing-body.[40]

And again:

> The synthesis of *in itself* and *for itself* which brings Hegelian freedom into being has, however, its truth. In a

sense, it is the very definition of existence, since it is effected at every moment before our eyes in the phenomenon of presence, only to be quickly re-enacted, since it does not conjure away our finitude.[41]

Existence will reappear in *The Visible and the Invisible* as Being. Phenomenology becomes ontology.[42] Merleau-Ponty's effort to overcome the subject-object dualism, which began with the recognition of the body as man's opening onto the world and extended through the recognition of things as correlates, within man's being-in-the-world, of the body, of man's opening onto the world, and the recognition of other people as in-the-world with me, allows him to resume the task in which he first engaged in *The Structure of Behavior,* the task of finding man's place in the world, by beginning not with the traditionally prior attempt to determine an innermost nature of a subject seeking his place in the world, but by beginning from Being.

Abandoning the subject-object dualism puts an end to the attempt to determine man's place in the world by theoretically dividing man's dealings with the world into the workings of separate faculties possessed by a subject. In particular, it can no longer be claimed that certain faculties at work in perception of objects are surmounted in a subject by an intellectual faculty or faculties that would be responsible for language. Merleau-Ponty has uncovered one fundamental issue at the root of both the perception of things and other people, and the speaking of language: how is it that man is situated in the world prior to any acts on man's part and yet is the one who acts so as to bring about the existence of the world such as it is?

Abandoning subjectism puts an end to the attempt to ascertain, from the point of view of a subject as external observer, an ontologically homogeneous metaphysical structure of reality as prerequisite to philosophical treatment of any particular problematic. Consequently, the philosopher may now begin with any area of man's dealings with the world, any current of man's being-in-the-world, or

as we may now say, any dimension of existence. This is not
to say that dimensions of existence are independent of each
other. Merleau-Ponty's study of various currents of man's
being-in-the-world reveals that they are both unique and
mutually determining. But the only path open toward understanding precisely how dimensions of existence are mutually determining is to lay bare what each dimension is.
That the philosopher may now begin with any dimension of
existence does not in any way mean that the act of philosophizing is gratuitous. Philosophic problems are not puzzles
spontaneously conceived by the philosopher. It is precisely
by overcoming the traditional concept of perception, according to which an automatic process is at work that provides data for a subsequent intervention by intellectual faculties of a subject—that is, precisely by affirming man's
being-in-the-world and thereby discrediting subjectism—
that Merleau-Ponty has affirmed that there is *the* world.
The philosophic act of laying bare what is, the act of speaking in the fullest sense, requires that the philosopher take
up his situation in the world as it is.

Merleau-Ponty's insistence that the structures employed
in theories intended to explain man and the world derive
from perception, and that therefore the prior task is one of
revealing the original content of perception, has not resulted in confining the philosopher to a single dimension of
man's existence, but has on the contrary opened the way
toward understanding how all dimensions of man's existence are lived by man. The contrary procedure—that of
constructing a theoretical hierarchy of faculties, each one
intended to account for dimensions of life unaccounted for
by those which it surmounts, of searching for one faculty
that integrates all others and completes the theoretical portrayal of the subject precisely because it is free from the
contingencies of life and marks the pure coincidence of self
with self—is doomed, because the act of bringing this
would-be faculty to explicit consciousness is one that
would always be performed at present and thus would distort the assumed eternality of this sought-after refuge of

pure subjectivity by giving it the quality of being present, as opposed to being past or future. This procedure, unrealizable by its very nature, belies the fact that life is indeed lived, and withdraws from the responsibility that faces man when he affirms that his acts bring about the existence of the world such as it is. In "The Primacy of Perception," which is a summary and defense before the Société française de philosophie of the central thesis of *Phenomenology of Perception* shortly after its publication, Merleau-Ponty said of the various dimensions of existence:

> By these words, the "primacy of perception," we mean that the experience of perception is our presence at the moment when things, truths, values are constituted for us; that perception is a nascent *logos;* that it teaches us, outside all dogmatism, the true conditions of objectivity itself; that it summons us to the tasks of knowledge and action. It is not a question of reducing human knowledge to sensation, but of assisting at the birth of this knowledge, to make it as sensible as the sensible, to recover the consciousness of rationality. This experience of rationality is lost when we take it for granted as self-evident, but is, on the contrary, rediscovered when it is made to appear against the background of non-human nature.
>
> The work [*Phenomenology of Perception*] which was the occasion for this paper is still, in this respect, only a preliminary study, since it hardly speaks of culture or of history. On the basis of perception—taken as a privileged realm of experience, since the perceived object is by definition present and living—this book attempts to define a method for getting closer to present and living reality, and which must then be applied to the relation of man to man in language, in knowledge, in society and religion, as it was applied in this work to man's relation to perceptible reality and with respect to man's relation to others on the level of perceptual experience. We call this level of experience "primordial"—not to assert that everything else derives from it by transformations and evolution (we have expressly said that man perceives in a way different from any animal) but rather that it reveals to us the per-

manent data of the problem which culture attempts to resolve. If we have not tied the subject to the determinism of an external nature and have only replaced it in the bed of the perceptible, which it transforms without ever quitting it, much less will we submit the subject to some impersonal history. History is other people; it is the interrelationships we establish with them, outside of which the realm of the ideal appears as an alibi.[43]

Language is that dimension of existence which suggests itself for immediate attention because the act of philosophizing itself is an act of speaking. Merleau-Ponty faces the task of laying bare what language is, a task that in itself requires that he speak in the fullest sense. His work after *Phenomenology of Perception* will increasingly be devoted to this task. The problematic nature of the philosophical act itself poses an issue that eminently merits attention. One may contend that the philosopher must begin somewhere and then proceed to engage in the dialogue concerning questions worthy of philosophic attention with the goal of following a circular path which, although circular, nevertheless traces a circle large enough to touch all issues worthy of philosophic attention before returning to the beginning. But there are two dangers. One is that philosophy will fail to fully affirm man's situation in the world prior to any act on man's part, will overlook that there is *the* world, and thus will not lay bare what is in a manner that could facilitate other acts in the fullest sense. The other is that philosophy will become a self-contained perpetuation of a tradition for its own sake and thus will fail to say something in the fullest sense. *Phenomenology of Perception* brings Merleau-Ponty to a position at which he is fully aware of these dangers and can proceed only while avoiding them.

Notes

1. "Language" (from *On the Way to Language*) in *Poetry, Language, Thought,* trans. Albert Hofstadter (New York: Harper and Row, 1971), p. 208.

2. The question is first raised with the original overturning of traditional intellectualist and empiricist theories of perception and the acknowledgment of the original content of perception as the structure of man's being-in-the-world, man's original situation in the world, and as the yield of man's acts of perceiving. (See above, chapter 1A.)

The question is raised again by Merleau-Ponty's study of motility: "We must therefore avoid saying that our body is *in* space, or *in* time. It *inhabits* space and time. . . . In so far as I have a body through which I act in the world, space and time are not, for me, a collection of adjacent points nor are they a limitless number of relations synthesized by my consciousness, and into which it draws my body. I am not in space and time, nor do I conceive space and time; I belong to them, my body combines with them and includes them. The scope of this inclusion is the measure of that of my existence; but in any case it can never be all-embracing. The space and time which I inhabit are always in their different ways indeterminate horizons which contain other points of view. The synthesis of both time and space is a task that always has to be performed afresh" (*Phenomenology of Perception,* pp. 139–40).

And again the question is raised by Merleau-Ponty's study of the body in its sexual being, where the inadequacy of the standard notion of necessity and contingency, of which we took note, is asserted: "Sexuality cannot, any more than the body in general, be regarded as a fortuitous content of our experience. Existence has no fortuitous attributes, no content which does not contribute to giving it its form; it does not admit in itself any pure fact because it is the movement by which the facts are taken up and assimilated. . . . Everything is necessary in man. . . . Everything is contingency in man in the sense that this human manner of existing is not guaranteed to each human child through some essence that the child would have received at birth, and in the sense that this human manner of existing must constantly be remade in him through the hazards encountered by the objective body. Man is a historical idea and not a natural species. In other words, there is in human existence no unconditioned possession and, nevertheless, no fortuitous attribute. Human existence will force us to revise our usual notion of necessity and contingency, because it is the changing of contingency into necessity by the act of taking up again. All that we are, we are on the basis of a de facto situation that we make ours and that we transform ceaselessly through a sort of *escape* that is never unconditioned liberty. There is no explanation of sexuality that reduces it to anything other than itself, because it is already something other than itself, and if one likes, our entire being. Sexuality, it is said, is dramatic *because* we commit our whole personal life to it. But just why do we do it? Why is our body, for us, the mirror of our being, if not because it is a *natural self,* a current of given existence, such that we never know if the forces that carry us on are its or ours—or rather such that they are never entirely its or ours." ("La sexualité, pas plus que le corps en général, ne doit donc être tenue pour un contenu fortuit de notre expérience. L'existence n'a pas d'atrributs fortuits, pas de contenu qui ne contribue à lui donner sa forme, elle n'admet pas en elle-même de pur fait parce qu'elle est le mouvement par lequel les faits sont assumés. . . .

Tout est nécessité dans l'homme. . . .Tout est contingence dans l'homme en ce sens que cette manière d'exister n'est pas garantie à tout enfant humain par quelque essence qu'il aurait reçue à sa naissance et qu'elle doit constamment se refaire en lui à travers les hasards du corps objectif. L'homme est une idée historique et non pas une espèce naturelle. En d'autres termes il n'y a dans l'existence humaine aucune possession inconditionée et pourtant aucun attribut fortuit. L'existence humaine nous obligera à reviser notre notion usuelle de la nécessité et de la contingence, parce qu'elle est le changement de la contingence en nécessité par l'acte de reprise. Tout ce que nous sommes, nous le sommes sur la base d'une situation de fait que nous faisons nôtre et que nous transformons sans cesse par une sorte *d'échappement* qui n'est jamais une liberté inconditionée. Il n'y a pas d'explication de la sexualité qui la réduise à autre chose qu'elle même, car elle était déjà autre chose qu'elle-même, et si l'on veut, notre être entier. La sexualité, dit-on, est dramatique *parce que* nous y engageons toute notre vie personnelle. Mais justement pourquoi le faisons-nous? Pourquoi notre corps est-il pour nous le miroir de notre être, sinon parce qu'il est un *moi naturel,* un courant d'existence donnée, de sorte que nous ne savons jamais si les forces qui nous portent sont les siennes ou les nôtres—ou plûtot qu'elles ne sont jamais ni siennes ni nôtres entièrement" [*Phénoménologie de la perception,* pp. 197-99; my translation]).

And again by Merleau-Ponty's study of sense experience and the world as perceived: ". . . The subject of sensation is neither a thinker who takes note of a quality, nor an inert setting which is affected or changed by it, *it is a power which is born into, and simultaneously with, a certain existential environment, or is synchronized with it.* The relations of sentient to sensible are comparable with those of the sleeper to his slumber: sleep comes when a certain voluntary attitude suddenly receives from outside the confirmation for which it was waiting. *I* am breathing deeply and slowly in order to summon sleep, and suddenly it is as if my mouth were connected to some great lung outside myself which alternately calls forth and forces back my breath. A certain rhythm of respiration, which a moment ago I voluntarily maintained, now becomes my very being, and sleep, until now aimed at as a significance, suddenly becomes a situation. In the same way I give ear, or look, in the expectation of a sensation, and suddenly the sensible takes possession of my ear or my gaze, and I surrender a part of my body, even my whole body, to this particular manner of vibrating and filling space known as blue or red. Just as the sacrament not only symbolizes, in sensible species, an operation of Grace, but is also the real presence of God, which it causes to occupy a fragment of space and communicates to those who eat of the consecrated bread, provided that they are inwardly prepared, in the same way the sensible has not only a motor and vital significance, but is nothing other than a certain way of being in the world suggested to us from some point in space, and seized and acted upon by our body, provided that it is capable of doing so, so that sensation is literally a form of communion" (*Phenomenology of Perception,* pp. 211-12; emphasis added).

In the concluding passages to the study of the world as perceived, Merleau-Ponty writes: "The problem of the existential modality of the social is here at one with all problems of transcendence. Whether we are concerned with my body, the natural world, the past, birth or death, the question is always how I can be open to phenomena which transcend me, and which nevertheless exist only to the extent that I take them up and live them; *how the presence to myself (Urpräsenz) which establishes my own limits and conditions every alien presence is at the same time depresentation (Entgegenwärtigung)* (Husserl, *Die Krisis der europäischen Wissenschaften und die transzendentale Phänomenologie,* III [unpublished]. [Merleau-Ponty's note] *and throws me outside myself" (Phenomenology of Perception,* p. 363).

3. "Perceiving is pinning one's faith, at a stroke, in a whole future of experiences, and doing so in a present which never strictly guarantees the future; it is placing one's belief in a world. It is this opening upon a world which makes possible perceptual truth and the actual effecting of a *Wahr-Nehmung,* thus enabling us to 'cross out' the previous illusion and regard it as null and void. Seeing, some distance away in the margin of my visual field, a large moving shadow, I look in that direction and the phantasm shrinks and takes up its due place; it was simply a fly near my eye. *I was conscious of seeing a shadow and now I am conscious of having seen nothing more than a fly.* My adherence to the world enables me to allow for the variations in the *cogito,* to favor one *cogito* at the expense of another and to catch up with the truth of my thinking beyond its appearances. In the very moment of illusion this possibility of correction was presented to me, because illusion too makes use of this belief in the world and is dependent upon it while contracting into a solid appearance, and because in this way, always being open upon a horizon of possible verifications, it does not cut me off from truth. But, for the same reason, I am not immune from error, since the world which I seek to achieve through each appearance, and which endows that appearance, rightly or wrongly, with the weight of truth, never necessarily requires this particular appearance" (*Phenomenology of Perception,* p. 297).

4. *Phenomenology of Perception,* p. 383.

5. Ibid., p. 374.

6. Ibid., pp. 382–83.

7. Ibid., pp. 376–77.

8. Ibid., p. 406.

9. Ibid., p. 415.

10. Ibid.

11. Ibid., p. 139.

12. Ibid., p. 140.

13. Ibid., p. 413.

14. Ibid., p. 419.

15. Ibid., p. 261.

16. Ibid., p. 422.

17. Ibid., p. 421.

18. Edmund Husserl, "Vorlesungen zur Phänomenologie des inneren Zeitbewusstseins," *Jahrbuch für Philosophie und Phänomenologische Forschung* 9 (1928): 442; Merleau-Ponty's note.

19. Ibid., p. 471; Merleau-Ponty's note.

20. Ibid., p. 464; Merleau-Ponty's note.

21. *Phenomenology of Perception,* p. 422.

22. Martin Heidegger, *Qu'est-ce que la Métaphysique,* trans. H. Corbin (Paris: Gallimard, 1938), p. 14; Merleau-Ponty's note. *Phenomenology of Perception,* p. 424.

23. Ibid., p. 419.

24. Ibid., p. 423.

25. Ibid., p. 423; emphasis added.

26. "The body is our general medium for having a world. Sometimes it is restricted to the actions necessary for the conservation of life, and accordingly it posits around us a biological world; at other times, elaborating upon these primary actions and moving from their literal to a figurative meaning, it manifests through them a core of new significance: this is true of motor habits such as dancing. Sometimes, finally, the meaning aimed at cannot be achieved by the body's natural means; it must then build an instrument, and it projects thereby around itself a cultural world. At all levels it performs the same function which is to endow the instantaneous expressions of spontaneity with a 'little renewable action and independent existence.' [Valéry, *Introduction à la méthode de Léonard de Vinci, Variété*, p. 177; Merleau-Ponty's note.] Habit is merely a form of this fundamental power. We say that the body has understood, and habit has been cultivated when it has absorbed a new meaning, and assimilated a fresh core of significance" (*Phenomenology of Perception*, p. 146).

27. *Phenomenology of Perception*, p. 441.

28. Ibid., p. 443.

29. Ibid., p. 453.

30. "Il y a un sens autochtone du monde qui se constitue dans le commerce avec lui de notre existence incarnée et qui forme le sol de toute *Sinngebung* décisoire" (*Phénoménologie de la perception*, p. 503; my translation).

31. *Phenomenology of Perception*, p. 452.

32. Ibid., p. 454.

33. Ibid., pp. 455–56.

34. Ibid., p. 456.

35. The question as to whether man can act in the fullest sense is fundamental to Merleau-Ponty's work. In his first book, *The Structure of Behavior*, Merleau-Ponty writes that "[what] defines man is not the capacity to create a second nature—economic, social or cultural— beyond biological nature; it is rather the capacity of going beyond created structures in order to create others" (*The Structure of Behavior*, p. 175). And in the conclusion to that work, in comparing the implications of the notion of "structure" as developed there with Freudian and sociological accounts of the process that brings about change in man and his world, Merleau-Ponty writes: ". . . it will be necessary to distinguish in development an ideal liberation, on the one hand, which does not transform us in our being and changes only the consciousness which we have of ourselves, and, on the other, a real liberation. . . . It is easy to argue in the same way, in opposition to the sociologist, that the structures of consciousness which he relates to a certain economic structure are in reality the consciousness of certain structures. This argument hints at a liberty very close to mind, capable by reflection of grasping itself as spontaneous source, and naturizing from below the contingent forms with which it has clothed itself in a certain milieu. Like Freud's complex, the economic structure is only one of the objects of a transcendental consciousness. But 'transcendental consciousness,' the full consciousness of self is not ready made; it is to be achieved, that is, realized in existence" (Ibid., p. 221). It is precisely acting in the fullest sense that Merleau-Ponty has in mind when in *The Visible and the Invisible* he speaks of the philosophical act of speaking as one that is to be a return to "brute or wild" being, neither the world as constituted in man's perception nor unformed, undifferentiated being, the Sartrean *en-soi*. (See *The Visible and the Invisible*, pp. 102–3.)

This question as to whether man can act in the fullest sense does link Merleau-

Ponty's work to that of Sartre and also contrasts his work with that of Heidegger. In the conclusion to his *Being and Nothingness*, Sartre states that the problematic of action involves the "elucidation of the transcendent efficacity of consciousness," action that brings about modification in the very being of that which is, and he poses the question as to whether or not, if man recognizes the futility of the constant attempts to define an essence of man and then coincide with it, man would then be in a position to act in the fullest sense. (See *Being and Nothingness: An Essay on Phenomenological Ontology,* trans. Hazel E. Barnes [New York: Philosophical Library, 1956], pp. 617–28.) Sartre, after *Being and Nothingness*, philosophically acted on the political level by espousing marxism down to its instantiation in the Soviet state. But events, in particular the Soviet suppression of the Hungarian revolt in 1956, demonstrated a discrepancy between the political structure of the time, at least as conceived by Sartre, and history. Soviet marxism could no longer be mistaken as the locus of free human action. Deciding how action in the fullest sense is constituted, if indeed such action is possible, is the prior task. In presenting the discussion of the problematic of action contained in *Being and Nothingness,* Sartre makes a point of criticizing Heidegger for totally neglecting the problematic. Whether or not the criticism is fully justified, it perhaps marks the divergence of Sartre and Merleau-Ponty from Heidegger, to the extent that the two French philosophers share this concern, which after digesting Heidegger's work they decide for their own reasons is unsatisfactorily treated by Heidegger. Merleau-Ponty for his part demonstrates his dissatisfaction with Heidegger on these grounds when, in the course of the discussion of temporality in *Phenomenology of Perception,* he takes issue with Heidegger's emphasis on the future dimension of time. Merleau-Ponty emphasizes the present, in which man as being-in-the-world, already situated temporally as well as spatially, nevertheless acts and in so doing temporalizes his being-in-the-world. (See *Phenomenology of Perception,* pp. 426–28.)

Merleau-Ponty's concern with the issue of man's ability to act in the fullest sense situates his work historically. Since Nietzsche, this question has been critical. The significance of the question in Nietzsche's thought merits an extensive study of its own. Here we can but note the crucial themes of the *Übermensch* and the eternal return. Nietzsche sought to point the way toward the *Übermensch,* man who would act in the fullest sense, not merely react to the world as it stands with its established values and purposes. The *Übermensch* would will the eternal return of the same because only then would this act remain uncontaminated by preestablished goals. Hence the *Übermensch* would will that he will the same, eternally. Willing the same eternally is the complement of an act uncontaminated by established norms. Or, in other words, man's already being-in-the-world prior to any action is the complement of man as the one who acts so as to bring about the world such as it is. Willing to will the eternal return of the same is the key to acting in the fullest sense. Nietzsche's question is, What is this will to will the same? Merleau-Ponty's is, What is action in the fullest sense? (This theme in Nietzsche's work is focused in Heidegger's discussion of Nietzsche in *What Is Called Thinking?,* trans. Fred D. Wieck and J. Glenn Gray, *Religious Perspectives* [New York: Harper & Row, 1968], pp. 28–110. Heidegger notes that Nietzsche was first to ask the question concerning whether or not man is ready to assume the dominion over the earth that is at hand. Nietzsche's reply is No. Man must first transform himself into the *Übermensch.* The way is indicated by Nietzsche in part two of *Thus Spake Zarathustra,* in the section "On the Tarantulas": *"For that man be delivered from revenge:* that is the bridge to the highest hope for me and a rainbow after long storms." What does Nietzsche mean by revenge? "This, yes, this alone is *revenge* itself: the will's revulsion against time and its 'It was!' " [*Thus Spake Zarathustra,* pt. 2, "On Deliverance."]

How is revenge to be overcome? How is this "It was" removed? Heidegger observes that this does not occur at the point when passing away ceases, because for us men it is not possible that time be removed. Instead, Heidegger writes: ". . . what is revolting to the will fades away when the past does not freeze in the mere 'It was,' to confront willing in fixed rigidity. What is revolting vanishes when the passing is not just a letting-pass in which the past sinks away into the mere 'It was.' The will becomes free from what revolts it when it becomes free as will, that is, free for the going in the passing away—but the kind of going that does not get away from the will, but comes back, bringing back what is gone. The will becomes free from its revulsion against time, against time's mere past, when it steadily wills the going and coming, this going and coming back, of everything. The will becomes free from what is revolting in the 'It was' when it wills the constant recurrence of every 'It was.' The will is delivered from revulsion when it wills the constant recurrence of the same. Then the will wills the eternity of what is willed. The will wills its own eternity." [*What Is Called Thinking?,* p. 104.] With Merleau-Ponty, acting in the fullest sense would require taking up man's original situation-in-the-world, man's being-in-the-world, as it is, including the sedimentation of man's being-in-the-world, as it is, that is as itself consisting of originary acts, acts that mark the coming into being of new, meaningful structuralizations of man's being-in-the-world, the ontogenesis of man's situation-in-the-world.)

36. *Phenomenology of Perception,* p. 400.

37. Ibid., p. 403.

38. Ibid., p. 404; emphasis added.

39. Ibid., p. 365.

40. Ibid., p. 408.

41. Ibid., p. 455.

42. Merleau-Ponty writes in a working note for *The Visible and the Invisible:* "Kant's or Descartes's analysis: the world is neither finite nor infinite, it is indefinite—i.e. it is to be thought as *human* experience—of a finite understanding faced with an infinite Being (or: Kant: with an *abyss* of human thought)   This is not at all what Husserl's *Offenheit* or Heidegger's *Verborgenheit* means: the ontological milieu is not thought of as an order of 'human representation' in contrast with an order of the in itself—It is a matter of understanding that truth itself has no meaning outside the relation of transcendence, outside of the *Ueberstieg* toward the horizon—that the 'subjectivity' and the 'object' are one sole whole, that the subjective 'lived experiences' count in the world, are part of the *Weltlichkeit* of the 'mind,' are entered in the 'register' which is Being, that the object is nothing else than the *tuft* of these *Abschattungen.* . . . It is not we who perceive, it is the thing that perceives itself yonder—it is not we who speak, it is truth that speaks itself at the depths of speech—" (*The Visible and the Invisible,* p. 185).

43. *The Primacy of Perception and Other Essays,* p. 25.

3   Living Language

If we must, therefore, seek the speaking of language in what is spoken, we shall do well to find something that is spoken purely rather than to pick just any spoken material at random. What is spoken purely is that in which the completion of the speaking that is proper to what is spoken is, in its turn, an original.[1]

—Heidegger

"ON the Phenomenology of Language," a paper presented by Merleau-Ponty on April 13, 1951, before the first International Phenomenology Colloquium at Brussels, gathers together those disclosures made in *Phenomenology of Perception* which bear directly on the problematic of language and which must be kept in mind in order to penetrate further the problematic of language now that the abandonment of subjectism has indicated a new point of departure. In addition, "On the Phenomenology of Language" contains certain new disclosures concerning what language is that have important implications for the philosophical act of speaking called for in order to say fully what language is.

Merleau-Ponty begins by situating language in what in *Phenomenology of Perception* was called the phenomenal field, the existing, structured field in which man is situated prior to any objectification by man of the original content of perception. Traditionally, two aspects of language have been juxtaposed. First, there is the scientific view of language as an objective system developed historically and open to objective analysis. Second, there is the account of what occurs when language is spoken, when available language somehow comes together in such a manner that something is said. The scientific view cannot account for how it is that something may be said in the fullest sense, that is, for how it is that the historical development of language can be brought together to express what is at present, that new meaning may come about in language. But when the two aspects of language are simply juxtaposed, it appears as though the account of spoken language may only add to the other account details of the psychological process involved in using available language. In keeping with the general effort in *Phenomenology of Perception* to displace objective characteristics of the content of perception from an unwarranted dominating role, Merleau-Ponty proceeds to demonstrate that aspects of language revealed by these approaches point toward a level other than that of objective linguistics or pure psychology on which language must be philosophically scrutinized.

Acknowledgment of the meaningfulness of language for a subject who speaks and who may in speaking bring about new meaning in language leads to the recognition that language existed in this manner in the past as well. That is, rather than conceive of language as an objective system built up by fortuitous objective processes in history, language must be conceived of as a system that has been and is meaningful for a speaker, and that undergoes change with the advent of new meaning in the language as spoken. Language must be conceived of as what Merleau-Ponty calls a "moving equilibrium." The scientific view of language, according to which the past of language is a frozen sequence of moments in which language was altered by completed objectively analyzable changes, can no longer stand on its own because, viewing language in history from the present, one must acknowledge it as at all times a meaningful structure open to the advent of new meaning—which is its mode of existence at present. In other words, the past of language is still present and, correlatively, the present of language cannot be conceived of as the latest moment in a succession of moments of which those which have past are now frozen.

On the other hand, acknowledgment of the contingency of language throughout its history leads to the recognition that this "moving equilibrium" is never a totalized system but rather "always involves latent or incubating changes."[2] Inasmuch as the past of language is still present, the contingency of past language invades even present language and ultimately it must be acknowledged that the advent of new meaning in language is never the simple addition of a further part to a complete system but rather a restructuralization throughout language. Language must be understood on this level of meaningful structure, which is however, never totalized, which is indeed radically contingent, rather than in terms of an objective system to which is appended a psychological account of a speaking subject's experience of this system.

Language conceived of in this manner, which Merleau-Ponty calls "living language," is to be found within the context of a speaker's or hearer's being-in-the-world, that is within the context of bodily intentionality directed toward the world. Briefly, Merleau-Ponty notes evidence to this effect. First, following the linguist Fernand de Saussure, he points out that each element of an instance of language does not contain an element of meaning from which the meaning of the whole is constructed as a "verbal chain." On the contrary, each element derives its role in the whole instance of language from its relationships to the other elements. The elements of language do not stand in a one-to-one correspondence with an ideal system of meaning, which is thus instantiated in each occurrence of language. Since all instances of language contain only "differences of signification," that is, relationships between the various elements, meaning cannot be found contained in the instances of language but must lie elsewhere and be grasped in a manner different from the intellectual representation of an objective meaning structure that would correspond to the linguistic structure of a particular instance of language.

The reason why a language finally intends to say and does say something is not that each sign is the vehicle for a signification which allegedly belongs to it, but that all the signs together allude to a signification which is always in abeyance when they are considered singly, and which I go beyond them toward without their ever containing it.[3]

This meaning of language, which is not known by intellectual representation but which nevertheless is expressed in spoken language, is precisely meaning as described by Merleau-Ponty in *Phenomenology of Perception*—that is, existent structure that is grasped by the speaker and the hearer of language through bodily intentionality.

Additional evidence to the effect that what Merleau-Ponty has described as "living language" lies within the context of a speaker's or hearer's being-in-the-world is found in the fact that in the very act of speaking, one does not intellectually compare thoughts of what is to be said with available language but rather utters language that is precognitively available. This precognitive contribution to speaking can be isolated, so to speak, if one recognizes that the sum of morphological, syntactical, and lexical meanings of a language is neither necessary nor sufficient to provide a child, who is learning a language, with the ability to speak. This ability presupposes that meaning in language is structured for the speaker prior to any intellectual act. Once again, this is precisely meaning as described by Merleau-Ponty in *Phenomenology of Perception,* that is, existent structure that is grasped by the speaker and the hearer of language through bodily intentionality. It is "languagely meaning."[4] Here Merleau-Ponty confirms what was disclosed in the chapter in *Phenomenology of Perception* on the body as expression, and speech, to the effect that the structure of meaningful language for the speaker or hearer is to be understood in terms of man's being-in-the-world and not on the level of pure psychology in terms of an intellectual understanding of represented theoretical structures.

As for the dynamism of "living language," Merleau-Ponty confirms here what was learned in *Phenomenology of Per-*

ception in the chapter on the body as expression, and speech, to the effect that spoken language is in a sense the resolution of strains or tensions within man's being-in-the-world, although, as was emphasized in that earlier discussion of language, it must be kept in mind that an act of speech does not render being-in-the-world a static objectivistic system, that the strains or tensions persist as the source for future acts of speech.

> Speech is comparable to a gesture because what it is charged with expressing will be in the same relation to it as the goal is to the gesture which intends it, and our remarks about the functioning of the signifying apparatus will already involve a certain theory of the significations expressed by speech. My corporeal intending of the objects of my surroundings is implicit and presupposes no thematization or "representation" of my body or milieu. Signification arouses speech as the world arouses my body—by a mute presence which awakens my intentions without deploying itself before them. In me as well as in the listener who finds it in hearing me, the significative intention (even if it is subsequently to fructify in "thoughts") is at the moment no more than a *determinate gap* to be filled by words—the excess of what I intend to say over what is being said or has already been said.[5]

This account of "living language" in terms of man's being-in-the-world suggests that no instance of language is complete, because each arises from a precognitive situation in the world that is never totally expressed. But the very characterization of instances of language as incomplete may suggest that there is a thematized structure of meaning of which the speaker is not conscious but that nevertheless subsists independently of instances of language. This is an indemonstrable assumption. Consequently, Merleau-Ponty rejects the categories of complete and incomplete in this regard.

So let us not say that every expression is imperfect because it leaves things understood. Let us say that every expression is perfect to the extent it is unequivocally understood, and admit as a fundamental fact of expression *a surpassing of the signifying by the signified which it is the very virtue of the signifying to make possible.*[6]

This is to say that, although meaning is not contained in instances of language in the sense that an objective analysis of the morphological, syntactical, and lexical characteristics of an instance of language would yield its meaning, instances of language do nevertheless bear their meanings. It is the unwarranted dominance of objective characteristics in the traditional conception of language and the complementary assumption that language is amenable only to objectivistic, scientific analysis that causes difficulty in recognizing the meaningfulness of instances of language. In effect Merleau-Ponty affirms here a finding in *Phenomenology of Perception,* where it was disclosed that meaning is coincident with the original content of perception, in this case with language as involved in the original content of perception. Furthermore, this account of the meaningfulness of instances of language serves to affirm what was disclosed in part three of *Phenomenology of Perception,* "Being-for-Itself and Being-in-the-World," to the effect that in no manner could the world as explicitly perceived be conceived of as divorced from man's original situation in the world and that, indeed, it must be acknowledged that the acts on man's part that bring about the world as explicitly perceived contribute to the structuralization of man's original situation in the world. In the present discussion of language, what is called the "signifying" is what is explicitly perceived, and what is called the "signified" constitutes the speaker's or hearer's original linguistic situation. Instances of language, particular acts of speech, mark the genesis of meaning. Thus Merleau-Ponty affirms here what was disclosed in *Phenomenology of Perception* to the effect that the genesis of meaning is coincident with the process of ontogenesis, in this case, with the ontogenesis of language.

Merleau-Ponty dwells on this last conclusion drawn from the account of the meaningfulness of language because it requires that the notion of an objectivistic ideal language that would be instantiated in particular instances of language be abandoned in favor of the concept of "living language." At first glance it may appear as though the new meaning comes about primarily through the reordering of existent language, the components of which contain fixed meanings. But existent language must be understood as in origin arising from acts of speech in which new meaning comes about, and not from the arbitrary construction of linguistic symbols to which ideal meanings would be assigned. It is true that the lexical meanings of words may have been changed from one point in history to another, but such alterations are founded upon the original fecundity of the words. This feature of language is precisely that toward which Merleau-Ponty was pointing when, in opposing "living language" to the summation of a scientific historical view of language and a psychological view of language, he described how it is that the past of language is still present, how the advent of new meaning is an event that occurs throughout language, and how the contingency of the linguistic past invades even the present of language. Thus, in pursuing the genesis of meaning in language, we always arrive at originary acts of speaking and not at an objectivistic ideal language that would be instantiated in particular occurrences of language.

Available language, as Merleau-Ponty has referred to it in this account of living language, is an example of what is called, in *Phenomenology of Perception,* sedimentation. In that work the examples of sedimentation that were described were the contribution made to the phenomenal body by habitual acts, and, inasmuch as the phenomenal body is the vehicle of man's being-in-the-world, the contribution made by habitual acts to the structuralization of

man's being-in-the-world, in addition to attitudes toward
the world that acquire favored status through frequent confirmation. Now Merleau-Ponty develops this concept in
terms of sedimentation in language.

> The significative intention gives itself a body and knows
> itself by looking for an equivalent in the system of avail-
> able significations represented by the language I speak
> and the whole of the writings and culture I inherit. For
> that speechless want, the significative intention, it is a
> matter of realizing a certain arrangement of already sig-
> nifying instruments or already speaking significations
> (morphological, syntactical, and lexical instruments, lit-
> erary *genres,* types of narrative, modes of presenting
> events, etc.) which arouses in the hearer the presenti-
> ment of a new and different signification, and which in-
> versely (in the speaker or the writer) manages to anchor
> this original signification in the already available ones.
> But why, how, and in what sense are they available?
> They became such when, in their time, they were *estab-
> lished* as significations I can have recourse to—that I
> *have*—through the same sort of expressive operation.[7]

Questions concerning sedimentation that remained unanswered in *Phenomenology of Perception* are not resolved
here. Sedimentation is involved in the structuralization of
man's being-in-the-world. But the notion of being-in-the-
world refers to man's situation prior to any acts on his part.
What is the precise relationship between sedimentation and
being-in-the-world? Precisely how is sedimentation sustained within man's being-in-the-world? What is learned
here is that the problematic of language offers a vehicle for
precising the notion of sedimentation and answering these
questions.

Abandonment of the notion of an ideal language that
would be instantiated in particular occurrences of language
in favor of living language makes evident the possibility of
originary acts of speech, of saying something in the fullest
sense. Merleau-Ponty now describes such an act:

I understand or think I understand the words and forms of French; I have a certain experience of the literary and philosophical modes of expression offered me by the given culture. I express when, utilizing all these already speaking instruments, I make them say something they have never said. We begin reading a philosopher by giving the words he makes use of their "common" meaning; and little by little, through what is at first an imperceptible reversal, his speech comes to dominate his language, and it is his use of words which ends up assigning them a new and characteristic signification. At this moment he has made himself understood and his signification has come to dwell in me.[8]

The problematic of language offers a vehicle for determining precisely how man is to perform those acts to which Merleau-Ponty called attention in the concluding chapter of *Phenomenology of Perception,* acts in the fullest sense, which involve being fully who one is, taking up one's original situation in the world, including sedimentation brought about by previous originary acts, and transforming it.

At this point Merleau-Ponty asks about the broader philosophical import of the foregoing account of language. Is it the case, despite the rejection of an ideal language that subsists in some way independently of particular instances of language, that the account of living language is to terminate in the determination of universal structures that would serve as organizing principles of living language? Given that language has been identified as a mode of bodily intentionality, is it the case that certain universal structures of bodily intentionality serve as such principles? *Phenomenology of Perception* has made evident the need to abandon the subject-object dualism as an underlying assumption, to subject the very notions of phenomenon and perceiver to phenomenological scrutiny, or in short, to do what was called in *Phenomenology of Perception* a phenomenology of phenomenology. Merleau-Ponty now affirms this:

The reason why the return to the *Lebenswelt* (and par-

ticularly the return from objectified language to speech) is
considered absolutely necessary is that philosophy must
reflect upon the object's mode of presence to the subject—upon the conception of the object and of the subject
as they appear to the phenomenological revelation—instead of replacing them by the object's relationship to the
subject as an idealistic philosophy of total reflection con-
ceives of it. From this point on, phenomenology envelops
philosophy, which cannot be purely and simply added on
to it.[9]

Consequently, philosophy of language is not to terminate in
the determination of universal structures of bodily intentionality that would serve as organizing principles of living
language. Rather, what is called for is an act of taking up
this philosophical situation as it is in order to transform it,
an act of speaking in the fullest sense. Once it is affirmed
that even the objectification inherent in the notions of perceiver and phenomenon must be subjected to phenomenological scrutiny, it must be acknowledged that philosophy is
not to terminate in the determination of objectivistic structures about which reality would be organized in some
sense. The fact that the act of philosophy is an act of speech
does not mean that all philosophical issues are reducible to
linguistic issues that would dissolve once universal linguistic structures are identified; rather, it calls for the effort of
determining precisely how the philosopher is to say something in the fullest sense, take up his situation as it is in
order to transform it. The primary importance of the particular problematic of language, as it was already antici-
pated at the close of *Phenomenology of Perception,* is now
explicitly confirmed by Merleau-Ponty.

More clearly than any other, this problem [the problem of
language] requires us to make a decision concerning the
relationships between phenomenology and philosophy or
metaphysics. For more clearly than any other it takes the
form of both a special problem and a problem which contains all the others, including the problem of philosophy.

If speech is what we have said it is, how could there possibly be an ideation which allows us to dominate this *praxis*? How could the phenomenology of speech possibly help being a philosophy of speech as well? And how could there possibly be any place for a subsequent elucidation of a higher degree? It is absolutely necessary to underline the *philosophical* import of the return to speech.[10]

As *Phenomenology of Perception* revealed, this so-called phenomenology of phenomenology requires that the philosopher abandon the viewpoint of a subject and begin at that point, so to speak, where perceiver and perceived come into being, that is, begin with that dynamic medium which Merleau-Ponty has called existence. The task is that of doing ontology. At this point, Merleau-Ponty does explicitly confirm that his interest with the particular dimension of existence in question, namely language, is a concern with the being of language. Inasmuch as the dimensions of existence are involved in processes of mutual determination, and this much is disclosed in *Phenomenology of Perception,* this concern extends to that of the general task of ontology. When the issue is first raised as to whether or not language can be thought of as an objectivistic system, historically accumulated, to which the psychological experience of speaking is appended, Merleau-Ponty writes:

But then we might think that phenomenology is distinguished from linguistics only as psychology is distinguished from the science of language. Phenomenology would add our inner experience of a language to our linguistic knowledge of it as pedagogy adds to our knowledge of mathematical concepts the experience of what they become in the minds of those who learn them. *Our experience of speech would then have nothing to teach us about the being of language; it would have no ontological bearing.*[11]

But after demonstrating that the account of language in terms of the summation of the objectivistic historical view

and a psychological view must be replaced by an account of
what he calls living language, Merleau-Ponty writes:

> What the phenomenology of language teaches me is not
> just a psychological curiosity—the language observed by
> linguistics experienced in me and bearing my particular
> additions to it. It teaches me a new conception of the
> being of language, which is now logic in contingency—an
> oriented system which nevertheless always elaborates
> random factors, taking what was fortuitous up again into
> a meaningful whole—incarnate logic.[12]

With the rejection of the notion of an ideal language that
would be instantiated in particular occurrences of language
in favor of the concept of living language, which is to be
understood in terms of man's being-in-the-world, the question arises as to whether or not one has fallen into psychl-
ogism. This question may again be raised with the radic-
zation of phenomenology, so to speak, the abandonmer*
the point of view of the subject and the attempt to beg
philosophizing at the point at which the structure perceive
perceived comes into being. Is it the case that according t
the concept of living language, meaning in language ca
only be understood on a private psychological level?
Merleau-Ponty points out that this is impossible, because
spoken or living language is an eminent case of a current c.
man's being-in-the-world through which one is aware of the
presence of other persons. This cannot be accounted for oi
the purely psychological level. The attempt to so account
for it comes up against an insurmountable obstacle. I am
aware that language that I speak and hear is being constituted within another person's field of consciousness at
the same time as it is being constituted within my field of
consciousness. If the entire process were confined to my
private psychological field, the insupportable claim would
have to be made that I constitute the other as constituting,
indeed as constituting with respect to the act through which

I constitute the other. Being-in-the-world, and in particular the current of being-in-the-world under consideration here, namely language, cannot be relegated to the private psychological field but, on the contrary, must be acknowledged as disclosed in *Phenomenology of Perception,* that is, as meaningful and existent, not a complete objectivistic system within the grasp of a pure consciousness, but contingent. An attempt to overcome psychologism by positing an ideal system of meaning that would be known by myself and another person would raise the question as to how it is possible for myself and the other to ascertain that we both know this ideal system. The use of language would be required, thus simply pushing the issue back a step and leading to an infinite regress. Only by affirming that the genesis of meaning is coincident with the ontogenesis of living language in the context of man's being-in-the-world is there a possibility of giving an account of one's experience, through language, of the presence of another person. This does not in any way rule out the contribution to originary instances of language made by acts on man's part, and Merleau-Ponty reiterates the fact that acts by man are involved:

> If the central phenomenon of language is in fact *the common act of the signifying and the signified,* we would deprive it of its distinctive characteristic by realizing the result of expressive operations in advance in a heaven of ideas; we would lose sight of the *leap* these operations take from already available significations to those we are in the process of *constructing* and acquiring. And the intelligible substitute we would try to base them on would not exempt us from understanding how our knowing apparatus expands to the point of understanding what it does not contain. We would not husband our transcendence by prescribing it to a factual transcendent. In any case the place of truth would still be that anticipation *(Vorhabe)* through which each spoken word or acquired truth opens a field of understanding, *and the symmetrical*

recovery (Nachvollzug) through which we bring this ad-
vent of understanding or this commerce with others to a
conclusion and contract them into a new view.[13]

Once again, the problematic of language appears as a vehicle for arriving at a philosophical account of man as simultaneously situated in the world prior to any act on man's
part and as the one who acts so as to bring about the existence of the world such as it is.

Finally, with the affirmation of the full ontological bearing of the concept of being-in-the-world, the abandonment
of the point of view of the subject and the turn toward the
issue of the being of language and the being of the other
dimensions of existence, one begins at the point, so to
speak, where the structure myself-other comes into existence and thus the possibility of psychologism does not
arise. In *Phenomenology of Perception,* Merleau-Ponty
acknowledged that his extended treatment there of the issue of intersubjectivity does not fully resolve it. Nor is the
issue fully resolved here. But the discussion in *Phenomenology of Perception* did make evident the fact that the
very question of whether or not I can know the other as an
other arises from the experience of the other that I do have,
from my being-in-the-world with the other, and it is on this
basis that psychologism is disposed of here.

The abandonment of the notion of an ideal language that
would be instantiated in particular occurrences of language
and the affirmation of living language is not a lapse into
psychologism. It also disallows dogmatism. The originary
philosophical act of speech is one that takes up other philosophical acts of speech as what they are—that is, as themselves originary acts of speech and not as instances of language composed of elements that would contain objectivistic meanings. Although an originary instance of language
marks the genesis of meaning and thus is a transformation
that occurs throughout living language, it does not involve
going beyond other originary instances of language to
meaning that would be henceforth imposed on them, but

rather simultaneously allows them to be what they are. Hence the full affirmation of the coincidence of meaning with living language. Merleau-Ponty borrows the phrase *coherent deformation* from Malraux in an attempt to portray this process:

> I say that a signification is acquired and henceforth available when I have succeeded in making it dwell in a speech apparatus which was not originally destined for it. Of course the elements of this expressive apparatus did not really contain it—the French language did not, from the moment it was established, contain French literature; I had to throw them off center and recenter them in order to make them signify what I intended. It is just this "coherent deformation" (Malraux) of available significations which arranges them in a new sense and takes not only the hearers *but the speaking subject as well* through a decisive *step*.[14]

Here Merleau-Ponty is approaching the process of ontogenesis in language and the general process of ontogenesis that was first glimpsed as early as the accounts of motility and language in *Phenomenology of Perception,* when it was affirmed that actual bodily motion and speech are in a sense the resolution of strains or tensions within man's being-in-the-world but that these strains or tensions persist as the grounds for future motion and speech. These strains or tensions now appear as the dynamism by which originary acts bring about a transformation throughout that which is while simultaneously allowing that which is to be what it is.

The philosophical act of speaking in the fullest sense is not one that involves the attempt to annul other originary acts of speech, but involves allowing other such acts to be what they are. As for the originary instances of language themselves, involved in the process just described, although each of them marks a thorough transformation of the others, each must be completely affirmed in its specificity. At the close of the essay "On the Phenomenology of Language" Merleau-Ponty writes:

The ultimate philosophical step is to recognize what
Kant calls the "transcendental affinity" of moments of
time and temporalities. This is undoubtedly what Husserl
is trying to do when he takes up the finalist vocabulary of
various metaphysics again, speaking of "monads," "en-
telechies," and "teleology." But these words are often
put in quotations in order to indicate that he does not
intend to introduce along with them some agent who
would then assure externally the connection of the related terms. Finality in a dogmatic sense would be a com-
promise; it would leave the terms to be connected and
their connecting principle unconnected. Now it is at the
heart of my present that I find the meaning of those presents which preceded it, and that I find the means of
understanding others' presence at the same world; and it
is in the actual practice of speaking that I learn to understand.[15]

These moments of time are those "timeless" moments of
which Merleau-Ponty spoke in the account of temporality
in *Phenomenology of Perception*. They are not eternal, but
rather "timeless" moments in the sense that they are not
arrayed out in time but rather are moments at which the
temporal structure of existence comes into being. To understand the "transcendental affinity" of these moments would
be to understand how it is that, while each marks the thorough transformation of the others, each must be completely
affirmed in its specificity. A full account of living language
should provide a clue to understanding how it is that the
various currents of man's being-in-the-world as disclosed in
Phenomenology of Perception are indeed as they were disclosed, specifically that is, as involved in processes of mutual determination and yet such that the specificity of each
is thoroughly maintained. In addition, when the account of
man's bodily intentionality is extended into the world as
perceived, as was done in *Phenomenology of Perception,*
this clue should also help clarify how it is that prior to any
objectification that covers over this feature of the original
content of perception, the qualities of phenomena found in

the original content of perception are likewise mutually determining and yet thoroughly specific. Here we are on grounds that can be glimpsed as early as Merleau-Ponty's first book, *The Structure of Behavior,* where Merleau-Ponty reveals the inadequacy of theories such as materialism or mentalism that portray all sectors and dimensions of man's behavior as ultimately derivative of one substrate or order. The structures that comprise the orders integrated within man, the physical, the vital, and the human orders, are disclosed as "forms," as "global" structures in which each component influences every other and is in turn influenced by every other component, and in which these components are "total parts," "parts" (not in the sense of objective parts as portrayed by realism) that thoroughly maintain their specificity in the midst of the "global" order. We are coming up against that which, according to Merleau-Ponty, Husserl had already come up against—the back side of phenomena, that aspect of phenomena which demonstrates that they are known prior to any perceptual perspectives precisely because it is prior awareness of a phenomenon that enables one to affirm that perceptual perspectives are perceptual perspectives of the same phenomenon.[16] We are approaching an understanding of how it is that, despite the radical dynamism of existence, it must be fully affirmed that there is the world. We are approaching what Merleau-Ponty will come to call Wild Being.

What has been learned concerning language bears directly on the task of determining how the philosophical act of speaking in the fullest sense—which is to lay bare what is, which would make manifest what language is—is to be performed. Originary instances of language are such that, while marking the genesis of meaning and a transformation throughout language, each allows the other originary instances of language to be what they are. The transformation that occurs throughout language does not involve going beyond existent language to an ideal system of meaning, which would supposedly be instantiated in a confused manner in existent language, and henceforth only employing existent language in keeping with such an ideal system of meaning. Thus the philosophical act of speaking, which is to be an act of originary speaking, must allow existent instances of language to be what they are.

This characterization of the philosophical act of speaking in the fullest sense indicates that such an act is not to be performed by first representing the problematic of other philosophical acts and then responding to that represented problematic as though other responses are confused attempts to give an account of that problematic. Merleau-Ponty's work in *The Structure of Behavior* and in *Phenomenology of Perception* exemplifies the intentional avoidance of such a methodological procedure. In those works the intent is not to demonstrate that traditional accounts of man and the world fail because they do not adequately correspond to what is objectively given, but rather to reveal dimensions of man and the world that are bypassed by traditional accounts and that are not amenable to objectivistic categories. *The Structure of Behavior* demonstrates that objectivistic categories are derived from the content of perception, and thus makes evident the necessity to return to the content of perception in order to reveal what is. In order to reveal what he refers to at the outset of *Phenomenology of Perception* as the phenomenal field, Merleau-Ponty finds it necessary to effect a transformation of perception that would displace objectivistic characteristics of perception from a dominating role. Thus in no manner is his effort that of replacing traditional accounts with an account that would correspond more thoroughly with what would supposedly be objectively given and confusedly portrayed by traditional accounts. At the close of *Phenomenology of Perception* it is evident that in order to lay bare what is, a philosophical act of speaking in the fullest sense is required, one that would take up the philosophical situation as it is and transform it—in particular, turning aside from the underlying assumption of a subject-object dualism. It is also evident that this effort is not to involve correcting the portrayal, in *Phenomenology of Perception,* of perceiver and perceived phenomenon. Indeed, this effort is to begin at the point, so to speak, where the perceiver-perceived structure comes into being. There is no question of correcting the portrayal of perceiver and perceived phenomenon, because subjectivism has also been undermined. Thus the point of view of a subject who would represent to itself perceiver and perceived and attempt to clarify these representations as though the efforts in *Phenomenology of Perception* were a confused attempt to give an account of the problematic, is untenable. The philosophical act of speaking in the fullest sense is not to be accomplished by a subject clarifying representations of the philosophical situation. This is confirmed by what was learned in part three of *Phenomenology of Perception,* with the affirmation of the full ontological significance of the concept of man's being-in-the-world, to the effect that not even the source of those acts by which man brings about the existence of the world such as it is is to be found in a subject portrayed as apart from the world but must be sought in the world now understood as subsuming man. The philosophical act of speaking in the fullest sense is not a response to representations of a philosophical problematic. The act originates in the world. Nevertheless, an originary act is initiated by man.

Merleau-Ponty's reflections on the scope of the work of other philosophers provide assistance in focusing what is at issue here in this attempt to precise the nature of a philosophical act of speaking in the fullest sense. In the essay "The Philosopher and His Shadow," Merleau-Ponty describes Husserl's endeavor as one that pushes the "picture of a well-behaved world left to us by classical philosophy" to its limits only to come up against the world that thoroughly resists the objectivistic categories of classical philosophy and that is precisely the world of beings that are mutually determining and yet transcendent to one another of which Merleau-Ponty speaks in the essay "On the Phenomenology of Language." Husserl's endeavor initially was directed toward the possession in consciousness of essences, which are what make things be what they are. The goal was philosophy as a rigorous science, more rigorously scientific than the empirical sciences of Husserl's day and more rigorously scientific than philosophies that had preceded his own. But according to Merleau-Ponty the demand for rigor led to a point at which scientific objectivism would have to be discarded. Thus Husserl set out to develop a philosophy that, notwithstanding its exclusive attention to consciousness and the content of consciousness, would be more objective than other objectivistic philosophical and scientific accounts, and he reached a point at which he could no longer proceed by responding to his representation of the central problematic of classical philosophy. At this point what was required, according to Merleau-Ponty, in order to enter that world which thoroughly resists the categorial structure of classical philosophy, was a philosophical act in the fullest sense—an act that would thoroughly transform the philosophical situation while simultaneously allowing other instances of philosophical speaking to be what they are, rather than seeking to discredit them as confused attempts to give an account of a philosophical concern.[17]

One additional example comes from Merleau-Ponty's discussion, in his inaugural lecture at the Collège de France on January 15, 1953, entitled "In Praise of Philosophy,"[18] of the work of one of his predecessors, Henri Bergson. First, Merleau-Ponty presents Bergson's initial position. Philosophy is to be intuition as coincidence or contact with that which is, intuition to which Bergson refers as "fusion" with things or "inscription," "recording," "impression" of things in us. But then Merleau-Ponty proceeds to identify this initial position of Bergson's with a response to the philosophical problematic posed by the tradition that Bergson ultimately sought to transform thoroughly.

> This [Bergson's initial position] is an aspect of Bergsonism which is the easiest to see. But it is not the only one, nor the most valid. For these formulas express less

what Bergson had to say than his break with received doctrine at the time he began his research. It is said that he restored intuition against the intellect and logic, spirit against matter, life against mechanism. This is how both his friends and his adversaries understood him when his studies appeared. But his adversaries have missed the point. Perhaps it is time to look in Bergson for something more than the antithesis to their abandoned theses. In spite of the paradox, the wholly positive Bergson is a polemic writer, and as the negative begins to reappear in his philosophy, it is progressively affirmed. It would perhaps show more attention to his writings if we were to look in them for his views of the living and difficult relations of the spirit with the body and the world, rather than for the critique of Taine and Spencer; to look for the interior movement which animates his intentions, which ties them to one another, and which frequently reverses their initial relationships, rather than for successive assertions. In this way Bergson would be truly delivered from his adversaries, delivered also from his "friends" who, as Péguy has already said, understood him no better.[19]

In this instance, we hear in Bergson's own words what is required of the philosopher instead of polemic:

Bergson wanted to be finished with traditional problems, not to eliminate the problematic of philosophy but to revivify it. He saw so clearly that all philosophy must be in the words of Le Roy, a new philosophy, that it is so little the discovery of a solution inscribed in being which satisfies our curiosity, that he demands of it not only the invention of solutions but the invention of its own problems. In 1935 he wrote: "I call an *amateur* in philosophy anyone who accepts the terms of a usual problem as they are . . . doing philosophy authentically would consist in *creating* the framework of the problem and of *creating* the solution."[20]

This creative act would be a philosophical act of speaking in the fullest sense. It would not be polemic. The philosopher would not represent to himself the problematic of other philosophic efforts and respond to that represented problematic as though other efforts were confused attempts to give an account of that problematic.

The philosophical act of speaking in the fullest sense, while marking the genesis of meaning and a transformation throughout language, must allow other instances of philosophical speaking to be what they are. Herein lies the dynamics of authentic philosophic dialogue. Representing the problematic of other philosophical efforts and then responding to that representation does not constitute authentic philosophic dialogue. Merleau-Ponty speaks of the dynamics of such dialogue at the opening of his essay concerning Husserl, "The Philosopher and His Shadow":

> I borrow myself from others; I create others from my own thoughts. This is no failure to perceive others; it is the perception of others. . . . [They are there for us to begin with.] Not to be sure with the frontal evidence of a thing, but installed athwart our thought and, like different selves of our own, occupying a region which belongs to no one else but them. Between an "objective" history of philosophy (which would rob the great philosophers of what they have given others to think about) and a meditation disguised as a dialogue (in which we would ask the questions and give the answers) there must be a middle-ground on which the philosopher we are speaking about and the philosopher who is speaking are present together, although it is not possible even in principle to decide at any given moment just what belongs to each.[21]

Thus far we have considered the nature of an originary philosophical act of speaking in terms of its relationships with other instances of philosophical speech. An originary philosophical act of speaking may also be considered in terms of its specificity. While each originary instance of language marks the thorough transformation of other originary instances of language, each must also be completely affirmed in its specificity. A philosophical act of speaking in the fullest sense would be one that fully takes up the philosopher's situation as it is. This act would transform this situation, not replace it with another situation. This much was learned in the discussion of freedom in *Phenomenology of Perception*. Freedom cannot be conceived of as absolute freedom, but rather can only be discerned as freedom in a situation. Consequently, the situation is not a hindrance to a philosophical act of speaking in the fullest sense, but rather guides this act, so to speak, and frees the philosopher from the burden of a universality which, precisely because it would demand that philosophy account for every situation, would not permit the philosopher to account for any situation, and would thus render the philosopher incapable of philosophizing. The philosophical act of speaking in the fullest sense would not involve responding to that which is by determining universally applicable categories. The intent to philosophically act in the fullest sense underlies the attempt to determine such categories, but it is misled by the unwarranted assumption that this act can only be accomplished by contriving a response free of the contamination of any situation and thus applicable to all situations. Merleau-Ponty affirms this in an essay entitled "The Metaphysical in Man." He writes:

> Metaphysics is not a construction of concepts by which we try to make our paradoxes less noticeable but is the experience we have of these paradoxes in all situations of personal and collective history and the actions which, by assuming them, transform them into reason. One cannot conceive of a response which would eliminate such an inquiry; one thinks only of resolute actions which carry it further. Metaphysics is not a knowledge come to complete the edifice of knowledges but is lucid familiarity with whatever threatens these fields of knowledge and the acute awareness of their worth. The contingency of all that exists and all that has value is not a little truth for

which we have somehow or other to make room in some nook or cranny of the system: it is the condition of a metaphysical view of the world.[22]

The philosophical act of speaking in the fullest sense would contribute to the philosopher's situation in the world rather than be the contrivance of a response to that which is. Once again, this characterization of the philosophical act of speaking in the fullest sense confirms what was learned in part three of *Phenomenology of Perception,* with the affirmation of man's being-in-the-world, to the effect that the nature and source of those acts by which man brings about the existence of the world such as it is are not to be found in a subject portrayed as apart from the world, a subject who would respond to the world, but must be sought in the world now understood as subsuming man.

The significance of this characterization of a philosophical act in the fullest sense can be gauged by a comparison with philosophical knowing in a Hegelian sense. At particular moments in the Hegelian dialectic the process proceeds in terms of particular dimensions of man's life, such as art and religion. Philosophical efforts appropriate to particular moments of the dialectic are efforts concerned with these dimensions of man's life. But these efforts are necessarily provisional inasmuch as these dimensions of man's life will only be known fully when the philosopher thinks the *Absolute Concept,* which is universal knowledge of that which is. Thus does Hegel situate the work of his predecessors in the philosophical tradition in the context of the dialectic. Their work was by no means inappropriate to the moment of the dialectic that obtained when they lived but it was provisional. In contrast, the nature of the philosophical act of speaking in the fullest sense sought by Merleau-Ponty would be such that it would be an act in a situation, but it would not be merely provisional in comparison with a future absolute knowledge. The freedom of philosophically speaking in the fullest sense need not await transparent self-consciousness, which allegedly would be at the same time universal knowledge of that which is.

The specificity of originary philosophical acts of speech is not defined solely vis-à-vis other such acts but is also defined vis-à-vis dimensions of existence other than language. Once again, the significance of this characterization can be gauged by a comparison with philosophical knowing in a Hegelian sense. The freedom of philosophically speaking in the fullest sense, which is man's freedom to initiate an act that need not be conceived of as playing a role in the historical march of Absolute Spirit, need not await the establishment of a particular political state, and need not await the moment when artistic and religious traditions are to be overcome. The philosophical act is an act of speaking. It is neither necessitated by man's activities in other dimensions of life nor can it claim to be the task of reforming those activities. Nevertheless, inasmuch as it is an act in the fullest sense, the philosophical act could shed light on acts in the fullest sense appropriate to other dimensions by means that will be comprehended only when the philosophical act opens that order cohabited by structuralizations of existence that are transcendent to one another, that order which Merleau-Ponty will come to call Wild Being. Merleau-Ponty affirms this characterization of the philosophical act in his introduction to *Signs:*

> Disclosing fundamental meaning-structures through all its many fissures, our age calls for a philosophical interpretation. Our times have not swallowed up philosophy; philosophy does not loom over our times. It is neither history's servant nor its master. The relationship between philosophy and history is less simple than was believed. It is in a strict sense an *action at a distance,* each from the depths of its difference requiring intermingling and promiscuity. We have yet to learn the proper uses of this encroachment. Above all, we have not yet learned a philosophy which is all the less tied down by political responsibilities to the extent it has its own, and

all the more free to enter everywhere to the extent it does not take anyone's place (does not *play* at passions, politics, and life, or reconstruct them in imagination) but discloses exactly the Being we inhabit.[23]

In a preliminary description of the situation of philosophy with respect to history, which appears in his inaugural address to the Collège de France, Merleau-Ponty observes that it is impossible to theoretically set up a one-to-one correspondence between historical events and instances of philosophical speech. Philosophy and history do transcend one another. Yet, at the same time, philosophy is in history and the very affirmation of historical events whereby the efforts of individual persons are to be measured is a philosophical affirmation. Thus the relationship between an instance of philosophical speech and historical events does appear to be analogous to that between originary instances of speech, each of which transforms the other, and yet each of which is transcendent to the other. The full relationship between an instance of philosophical speech and historical events may be learned via an originary philosophical act, one that returns the philosopher to that order of structuralizations of existence of which each is a thorough transformation of the other structuralizations of existence that nevertheless allows the others to be what they are—that order which Merleau-Ponty will come to call Wild Being— and sustains him there in order that he may lay it bare.

Philosophy turns towards the anonymous symbolic activity from which we emerge, and towards the personal discourse which develops in us, and which, indeed, we are. It scrutinizes this power of expression which the other forms of symbolism exercise only in a limited way. In touch with every kind of fact and experience, it tries rigorously to grasp those fecund moments in which a meaning takes possession of itself. It recovers this meaning, and also pushes beyond all limits the becoming of truth, which presupposes and brings it about that there is only one history and one world.[24]

Conclusion

In order to give an account of language the philosopher must turn away from the notion of an ideal language that would be instantiated in particular occurrences of language and must turn toward spoken language. Spoken language is precisely particular instances of language spoken by particular speakers and heard by particular hearers. The question may be asked as to whether this turn to spoken language is a critical threat to what has been regarded as an essential characteristic of philosophy, namely, the universality of the philosophic endeavor. One may reply that what has traditionally been conceived of as universal must not be used as an excuse for abandoning the task of philosophically responding appropriately to particular situations at hand. The choice between universality that in some way transcends particulars and relativism is not necessarily exhaustive. Merleau-Ponty indicates this in the essay "On the Phenomenology of Language":

> Far from particular languages appearing as the "confused" realization of certain ideal and universal forms of signification, the possibility of such a synthesis becomes problematical. If universality is attained, it will not be through a universal language which would go back prior to the diversity of languages to provide us with the foundations of all possible languages. It will be through an oblique passage from a given language that I speak and that initiates me into the phenomenon of expression, to another given language that I learn to speak and that effects the act of expression according to a completely different style—the two languages (and ultimately all given languages) being contingently comparable only at the outcome of this passage and only as signifying wholes, without our being able to recognize in them the common elements of one single categorial structure.[25]

But if the notion of an ideal system of meaning that subsists independently of the contingencies of individual lives is rejected, what then becomes of truth as goal of philosophy? It must be recalled that each originary instance of language is not annulled by other originary instances of language. Once it occurs, an originary instance of language must be contended with in all originary instances of language. It is the task of seeking how the philosophical act of speaking in the fullest sense, which effects a transformation throughout language but which allows originary instances of language to be what they are, is to be performed, rather than guaranteeing the success of the philosophic endeavor in advance by positing an ideal system of meaning, which holds open the possibility of becoming fully aware of the inexhaustibility of that which is called truth and thus of drawing that much closer to it.

The return to spoken language is not simply a turn away from the proper concern of comparative linguistics to the actual discourse that is the source of those structures which comprise the theoretical body of knowledge of the science of linguistics. It is a return to what Merleau-Ponty calls living language, that order of originary instances of language, each of which marks a transformation throughout language and yet allows the others to be what they are. The philosophical act of speaking, which will make manifest what language is, is to be an act in the fullest sense that effects a transformation throughout the meaningful structure of existence. This is why Merleau-Ponty speaks of the "power of speech," which can only be understood by returning to living language,[26] and writes:

> Speech, as distinguished from language, is that moment when the significative intention (still silent and wholly in act) proves itself capable of incorporating itself into my culture and the culture of others—of shaping me and others by transforming the meaning of cultural instruments.[27]

At the same time, the philosophical act of speaking in the fullest sense is to allow other structuralizations of existence to be what they are. It is to be a return to that order of beings which transcend each other and yet cohabit existence, a return to what Merleau-Ponty will come to call Wild Being and to which he refers at this point as an order of "instructive spontaneity."

> That order of instructive spontaneity—the body's "I am able to," the "intentional transgression" which gives us others, the "speech" which gives us the idea of an ideal or absolute signification—cannot be subsequently placed under the jurisdiction of an acosmic and a pancosmic consciousness without becoming meaningless again. It must teach me to comprehend what no constituting consciousness can know—my involvement in a "pre-constituted" world.[28]

And again:

> Thus the proper function of a phenomenological philosophy seems to us to be to establish itself definitively in the order of instructive spontaneity that is inaccessible to psychologism and historicism no less than to dogmatic metaphysics. The phenomenology of speech is among all others best suited to reveal this order to us. When I speak or understand, I experience that presence of others in myself or of myself in others which is the stumbling-block of the theory of intersubjectivity, I experience that presence of what is represented which is the stumbling-block of the theory of time, and I finally understand what is meant by Husserl's enigmatic statement, "Transcendental subjectivity is intersubjectivity." To the extent that what I say has meaning, I am a different "other" for myself when I am speaking; and to the extent that I understand, I no longer know who is speaking and who is listening.[29]

In particular, as the philosophical act of speaking, this act is to lay bare what is.

Certain characteristics of such an act have emerged. It is nonpolemical. It is not a response to represented problematics of other philosophical acts. It originates in the world although it is initiated by man, and the freedom to initiate it need not await transparent self-consciousness and the determination of universal theoretical categories. The specificity of such an act has emerged. The freedom to initiate the act is not an absolute freedom. The act is an act in a situation, and it involves fully taking up that situation as it is. To acknowledge the specificity of this act is to acknowledge that it is an act with limits but, inasmuch as it is specific by nature, these limits are not constraints. It could be said of limits that they are constraints only if they contained that which by nature would expand if its container were removed. To fully acknowledge the situational nature of the philosophical act is to affirm that there is *the* world, and to affirm that the act of saying something in the fullest sense, which would lay bare what is, must be a specific act. Situationality must be understood here in this radical sense, rather than conceiving of a situation as a segment of the world to which the philosopher is limited and which could be added to other situations to form an infinity of possible situations in which the philosopher could possibly find himself. The philosophical act of saying something in the fullest sense, of laying bare what is, cannot involve an effort at performing an act proper to a dimension of existence other than language. Only in this manner can the philosophical act avoid transforming what is into philosophy and covering over that which is with theoretical objectifications. Only in this manner can the act of speaking maintain the silence at which the philosopher arrives when the philosopher seeks to lay bare what is.

These characteristics of the philosophical act of speaking in the fullest sense will help clarify Merleau-Ponty's concern with art during the period after *Phenomenology of Perception* up to and including his final work.

Notes

1. "Language" (from *On the Way to Language*) in *Poetry, Language, Thought,* trans. Albert Hofstadter (New York: Harper and Row, 1971), p. 194.
2. *Signs,* p. 87.
3. Ibid., p. 88.
4. See above, chapter 1A.
5. *Signs,* p. 89.
6. Ibid., p. 90.
7. Ibid.
8. Ibid., p. 91.
9. Ibid., pp. 92–93.
10. Ibid., p. 93.
11. Ibid., p. 86; emphasis added.
12. Ibid., pp. 87–88.
13. Ibid., p. 95; last two emphases added.
14. Ibid., p. 91.
15. Ibid., p. 97.
16. "Originally a project to gain intellectual possession of the world, constitution becomes increasingly, as Husserl's thought matures, the means of unveiling a back side of things that we have not constituted. This senseless effort to submit everything to the properties of 'consciousness' (to the limpid play of its attitudes, intentions, and impositions of meaning) was necessary—the picture of a well-behaved world left to us by classical philosophy had to be pushed to the limit—in order to reveal all that was left over: these beings beneath our idealizations and objectifications which secretly nourish them and in which we have difficulty recognizing noema. . . .

"Willy-nilly, against his plans and according to his essential audacity, Husserl awakens a wild-flowering world and mind. Things are no longer there simply according to their projective appearances and the requirements of the panorama, as in Renaissance perspective; but on the contrary upright, insistent, flaying our glance with their edges, each thing claiming an absolute presence which is not compossible with the absolute presence of the other things, and which they nevertheless have all together by virtue of a configurational meaning which is in no way indicated by its "theoretical meaning." Other persons are there too (they were already there along with the simultaneity of things). To begin with they are not there as minds, or even as 'psychisms,' but such for example as we face them in anger or love—faces, gestures, spoken words to which our own respond without thoughts intervening to the point that we sometimes turn their words back upon them even before they have reached us, as surely as, more surely than, if we had understood—each one of us pregnant with the others and confirmed by them in his body. This baroque world is not a concession of mind to nature; for although meaning is everywhere figurative, it is meaning which is at issue everywhere. This renewal of the world is also mind's renewal, a rediscovery of that brute mind which, untamed by any culture, is asked to create culture anew. From then on the irrelative is not nature in itself, nor the system of absolute consciousness' apprehensions, nor man either, but that 'teleology' Husserl speaks about which is written and thought about in parentheses—that jointing and framing of Being which is being realized through man" (*Signs,* pp. 180–81).

17. See also Merleau-Ponty's interpretation of phenomenology in the preface to *Phenomenology of Perception*. Here Merleau-Ponty suggests that, by engaging in phenomenology itself, one has ultimately become engaged in the task of performing an act that is not an attempt to discredit other instances of philosophical speaking as confused attempts to give an account of a reality that is given, but rather is an originary act.

18. *In Praise of Philosophy,* trans. John Wild and James M. Edie, Northwestern University Studies in Phenomenology and Existential Philosophy (Evanston, Ill.: Northwestern University Press, 1963).

19. *In Praise of Philosophy,* pp. 12–13.

20. Ibid., p. 14.

21. *Signs,* p. 159.

22. "The Metaphysical in Man" in *Sense and Non-Sense,* trans. Hubert L. Dreyfus and Patricia Allen Dreyfus, Northwestern Studies in Phenomenology and Existential Philosophy (Evanston, Ill.: Northwestern University Press, 1964), pp. 95–96.

23. *Signs,* p. 13.

24. *In Praise of Philosophy,* pp. 57–58.

25. *Signs,* p. 87.

26. Ibid., pp. 90–91.

27. Ibid., p. 92.

28. Ibid., pp. 94–95.

29. Ibid., p. 97.

4 Toward an Originary Act of Speaking

A. Art

As does the philosopher, the artist engages in an originary effort. Merleau-Ponty describes this effort:

> There is thus no art for pleasure's sake alone. One can invent pleasurable objects by linking old ideas in a new way and by presenting forms that have been seen before. This way of painting or speaking at second hand is what is generally meant by culture. Cézanne's or Balzac's artist [the character Frenhofer in Balzac's *Le Chef-d'oeuvre inconnu*] is not satisfied to be a cultural animal but assimilates the culture down to its very foundations and gives it a new structure: he speaks as the first man spoke and paints as if no one had ever painted before. What he expresses cannot, therefore, be the translation of a clearly defined thought, since such clear thoughts are those which have already been uttered by ourselves or by others. "Conception" cannot precede "execution." There is nothing but a vague fever before the act of artistic expression, and only the work itself, completed and understood, is proof that there was *something* rather than *nothing* to be said. Because he returns to the source of silent and solitary experience on which culture and the exchange of ideas have been built in order to know it, the artist launches his work just as a man once launched the first word, not knowing whether it will be anything more than a shout, whether it can detach itself from the flow of individual life in which it originates and give the independent existence of an identifiable meaning either to the

181

future of the same individual life or to the monads coexisting with it or to the open community of future monads. The meaning of what the artist is going to say *does not exist* anywhere—not in things, which as yet have no meaning, nor in the artist himself, in his unformulated life. It summons one away from the already constituted reason in which "cultured men" are content to shut themselves, toward a reason which contains its own origins.[1]

The artist's act displays those characteristics which have emerged from Merleau-Ponty's study of language as characteristics of a philosophical act of speaking in the fullest sense. The artist's act is nonpolemical. It makes no sense to speak of one work of art as disproving another work of art. Even those works of art involving explicit references to other works are not efforts to disclose those works as confused attempts to create what should be created. To impose upon art the categories proper to describing the dynamics of conflicting theories is to distort those relationships among works of art which allow us to speak of a History of Art.

Art preeminently exhibits the other characteristic of a philosophical act of speaking in the fullest sense that has emerged from Merleau-Ponty's study of language, namely, its specificity. This is why Merleau-Ponty can describe a painting as "sufficient unto itself and closed in upon its intimate signification."[2] It makes no sense to speak of a work of art as an effort to universally present all possible situations. The artist's freedom to perform an originary act is freedom in a situation. Art presents Merleau-Ponty with an opportunity to refocus a fundamental problem that remained at the conclusion of *Phenomenology of Perception,* that is, how to give an account of man who acts so as to bring about the existence of the world such as it is and yet who simultaneously is situated in the world prior to any act on his part to the extent that even those acts by which man brings about the existence of the world such as it is originate in the world. As early as 1945, the year in which *Phenomenology of Perception* was published, Merleau-Ponty affirms this in his essay "Cézanne's Doubt":

The meaning Cézanne gave to objects and faces in his paintings presented itself to him in the world as it appeared to him. Cézanne simply released this meaning: it was the objects and faces themselves as he saw them which demanded to be painted, and Cézanne simply expressed what they *wanted* to say. How, then, can any freedom be involved? . . . If we experience no external constraints, it is because we are our whole exterior. That eternal Cézanne whom we first saw emerge and who then brought upon the human Cézanne the events and influences which seemed *exterior* to him and who planned all that happened to him—that attitude toward men and toward the world which was not chosen through deliberation—free as it is from external causes, is it free in respect to itself? . . . If I am a certain project from birth, the given and the created are indistinguishable in me. . . . If there is a true liberty, it can only come about in the course of our life by our going beyond our original situation and yet not ceasing to be the same: this is the problem. Two things are certain about freedom: that we are never determined and yet that we never change, since, looking back on what we were, we can always find hints of what we have become. It is up to us to understand both these things simultaneously, as well as the way freedom dawns in us without breaking our bonds with the world.[3]

The specificity of a work of art is not defined solely vis-à-vis other works of art, but is also defined vis-à-vis domains of man's cultural life other than art. The work of art is neither necessitated by other domains of man's cultural life nor does it reform them. How then can the artist perform originary acts free of the demands of the other cultural domains, and yet, by means of these very acts, awaken in people echoes of their freedom to engage in all dimensions of life in such a way that their endeavors allow them to be who they are? Merleau-Ponty poses the question in his essay "Eye and Mind":

Only the painter is entitled to look at everything without being obliged to appraise what he sees. For the painter, we might say, the watchwords of knowledge and action lose their meaning and force. Political regimes which denounce "degenerate" painting rarely destroy paintings. They hide them, and one senses here an element of "one never knows" amounting almost to a recognition. The reproach of escapism is seldom aimed at the painter; we do not hold it against Cézanne that he lived hidden away at Estaque during the war of 1870. And we recall with respect his "C'est effrayant, la vie," even when the lowliest student, ever since Nietzsche, would flatly reject philosophy if it did not teach how to live fully. It is as if in the painter's calling there were some urgency above all other claims on him. Strong or frail in life, he is incontestably sovereign in his own rumination of the world. With no other technique than what his eyes and hands discover in seeing and painting, he persists, in drawing from this world, with its din of history's glories and scandals, *canvases* which will hardly add to the angers or the hopes of man—and no one complains.

What then, is this secret science which he has or which he seeks? That dimension which lets Van Gogh say he must go "further on"? What is this fundamental of painting, perhaps of all culture?[4]

The artist engages in an originary effort. The artist's act exhibits certain characteristics that have emerged as characteristics of the philosophical act of speaking. Finally, art exhibits a structural kinship with that dimension of existence in and through which the philosophical act is performed, namely, language. The components of spoken or written language derive their significance from their context. In this context there are only relationships among signs. Meaning is not contained within the "verbal chain." Each sign does not contain a meaning such that the meaning of an instance of language would be the result of the summation of individual signs. Nor is the meaning of an instance of language the result of a one-to-one correspondence between the signs and an ideal system of meaning conceived of as preexisting the instance of language. The genesis of meaning in language, or as Merleau-Ponty called it in "On the Phenomenology of Language," "languagely meaning," is coincident with the ontogenesis of language.

Meaning in a work of art is not reducible to the summation of the components of the work, such as pigment on a canvas. Nor does each component correspond to an ideal meaning that must be known by the intellect before the meaning of the work can be discerned. The genesis of the meaning of a work of art is coincident with the ontogenesis of the work.

Art presents itself as a domain that, if properly understood, could shed light on the nature of a philosophical act of speaking in the fullest sense. During the period after *Phenomenology of Perception* up to and including his final work, Merleau-Ponty focused his attention on the art of painting in the three essays: "Cézanne's Doubt," "Indirect Language and the Voices of Silence," and "Eye and Mind," which was the last work he saw published. Merleau-Ponty's study of art will first enable us to comprehend how art is language and how the question concerning an originary act comes to be posed in the field in which an act of art is performed. In section B of this chapter, "The Flesh," and in section C, "The Visible and the Invisible," our attention will focus on discoveries made in the course of Merleau-Ponty's study of art that shed light on the nature of a philosophical act of speaking in the fullest sense, and here we shall see how those discoveries are presented in the text on which Merleau-Ponty was working when he died in 1961, the text which has been published as *The Visible and the Invisible,* a title suggested by working notes for the project.

1. Art as Language

The occasion for Merleau-Ponty's essay "Indirect Language and the Voices of Silence" is Malraux's account of art. Merleau-Ponty finds that Malraux's analysis can help to determine the nature of originary acts if that analysis is detached from what Merleau-Ponty calls "the philosophy of the individual or of death which, with its nostalgic inclination toward civilizations based upon the sacred, is at the forefront of his thought."[5]

First, Merleau-Ponty takes issue with Malraux's description of modern painting as a turn away from the objectivity of classical painting, the representation of the world as seen objectively, toward subjectivity. As was made clear by *Phenomenology of Perception,* there simply is no objective spatial scale given in perception.[6] The perspective of classical painting represents a decisive act by the painters. Only "that which could be seen from a certain 'vanishing point' of a certain 'vanishing line'" is allowed to appear on the canvas.[7] If classical painting is "subjective" to this extent, there is no reason for interpreting modern painting as a "passage to the subjective and a ceremony glorifying the individual."[8]

If a particular painter's works, those of a classical painter or a modern painter, can be identified on sight, it is because the painter puts his style in his works. This style is not a procedure for painting that the painter carries within him and that in bursts of spontaneity ends up on canvases. Rather, a painter's style is a "system of equivalences" of the elements of the painter's works, which emerges in the course of a painter's development, and which permits the painter to make visible the system of equivalences of perspectival views of his world, which are seen precisely as perspectival views of the same world.[9] Although Merleau-Ponty does not do so, the claim can be made that this process by which the painter's style permits the making visible of this system of equivalences of perspectival views has itself become the "object" of contemporary "nonrepresentational" art.

On a broader scale, similarities and divergences of styles through the ages need not be attributed to the intervention, at certain points in history, of styles that define all painting by necessity and that are discerned at work in the history of painting by the authority of the Museum. Similarities and divergences of style through the ages originate in the fact that each painting is a gesture by the human body and each painting alters the field of painting as an instance of originary language alters the language, such that future paintings will have to contend with that painting. This is not to say that each painting necessarily bears formal relationships to every other painting because each is painted by an artist whose body is basically structured identically to the bodies of all other artists. Merleau-Ponty notes that in everyday experience we find a manifestation of the constancy of style found in the works of a particular artist, regardless of the scale of the works, such as miniature or full-scale painting. Our handwriting is recognizable whether we write on paper or on a blackboard. In each case there are different physiological paths at work, and no cognitive process intervenes to direct these physiological paths in such a manner that the results are analogous. This experience can only be understood in terms of the phenomenal body, which was described in *Phenomenology of Perception* as the locus of intentional threads that link man to the world and as one "pole" of man's being-in-the-world. "[The] hand with which we write is a phenomenon-hand which possesses, in the formula of a movement, something like the effectual law of the particular cases in which it may have to realize itself."[10] Despite the radical dynamism of man's being-in-the-world, we have to fully affirm that there is *the* world, and there is *the* body, and writing on a blackboard or on paper, works in miniature or full-scale paintings—even the world one focuses from the things competing to engulf one's perception—all bear the stamp of the body.

We must therefore recognize that what is designated by the terms "glance," "hand," and in general "body" is a system of systems devoted to the inspection of a world and capable of leaping over distances, piercing the perceptual future, and outlining hollows and reliefs, distances and deviations—a meaning—in the inconceivable flatness of being. The movement of the artist tracing his arabesque in infinite matter amplifies, but also prolongs, the simple marvel of oriented locomotion or grasping movements.[11]

Similarities and divergences of style that allow us to speak of a History of Painting reflect the kinship of these systems of systems, human bodies, as they perform acts of expression.

Finally, we can speak of the field of painting, speak of painting as though we were claiming that every painting that has been accomplished and will be accomplished has been taken into account, not because we have access to a universal essence of painting that contains an infinitude of possible paintings, for we do not, but rather because a painting is not only created on canvas by an artist but is also seen, and when our seeing does participate in the same gesture that has permitted the artist to make his world visible, we actually see the kinship of a painting with all paintings that have been accomplished, the modification this painting makes in the field of painting, and what this painting establishes that future painting must take into account.

In comparison with painting, spoken or written language more actively solicits our confirmation of its meaning. Merleau-Ponty describes this difference:

> A painting makes its charm dwell from the start in a dreaming eternity where we easily join it many centuries later, even without knowing the history of the dress, furnishings, utensils, and civilization whose stamp it bears. Writing, on the contrary, relinquishes its most enduring meaning to us only through a precise history which we must have some knowledge of.[12]

It would seem as though an originary instance of spoken or written language would be one that made thoroughly explicit its kinship with all originary instances of spoken or written language that have been accomplished, the modification that it makes itself in language, and what it establishes that future originary instances of language must take into account. However, for it to do so would amount to making use of other originary instances of language as though they were completed facts with assumed meanings

and thus would not be a taking up of other originary instances of language as what they are. An originary instance
of language must not break the silence that allows other
originary instances of language to be what they are.
Whereas an originary instance of language is one that
speaks without breaking this silence, painting remains silent without ceasing to speak: "language speaks, and the
voices of painting are the voices of silence."[13]

2. *Interrogation*

In "Eye and Mind" Merleau-Ponty describes the painter's vision as an "interrogation" of the world, and discloses
how the painter's "interrogation" suggests a means of precising the nature of a philosophical act of speaking in the
fullest sense. He describes this interrogation of a mountain:

> What exactly does he ask of it? To unveil the means,
> visible and not otherwise, by which it makes a mountain
> before our eyes. Light, lighting, shadows, reflections,
> color, all the objects of his quest are not altogether real
> objects; like ghosts, they have only visual existence. In
> fact they exist only at the threshold of profane vision;
> they are not seen by everyone. The painter's gaze asks
> them what they do to suddenly cause something to be *this*
> thing, what they do to compose this worldly talisman and
> to make us see the visible.[14]

In seeing an object, "profane vision" does not see the
light, the lighting, the shadows, the reflections, the color,
the factors that compose a particular thing, each of which
competes for one's vision in a sense, each of which is "incompossible and yet together."[15] "The visible in the profane sense forgets its premises. . . ."[16] The painter's effort
is that of recreating a "total visibility"[17] that is the visibility
of a thing that is there even as it is composed by "incompossible" factors. In doing so, the painter makes visible dynamic relations among these factors that compose the

thing: he "liberates the phantoms captive in [profane vision]."[18]

Can the philosopher, in an effort to determine what is, bypass these factors that are "incompossible and yet together," and that the painter's interrogating vision does see? One line of thinking that emerges from Descartes's work attempts to do precisely this. According to Descartes's *Dioptric,* vision is a thinking that deciphers signs given within the body, signs that arise there as a result of the action by contact, the mechanistic causal action of light upon the body. Although one's vision does exhibit a dimensionality according to which objects hide each other and yet in which this hiding is itself hidden, that is, a dimensionality in which objects must be described as "incompossible and yet together," one does not actually see this dimensionality. Rather, one sees relationships of height and width and thinks a third dimension, namely, depth, according to which what one sees is arranged such that objects appear to be one behind the other. According to this account, from a viewpoint outside all bodies one would be able to see that things are located at particular places in space, and that each point in space is where it is and is not where any other point is. Merleau-Ponty describes this concept of space:

> this space without hiding places which in each of its points is only what it is, neither more nor less. . . . Space is in-itself; rather, it is the in-itself *par excellence.* Its definition is *to be* in itself. Every point of space is and is thought to be right where it is—one here, another there; space is the evidence of the "where." Orientation, polarity, envelopment are, in space, derived phenomena inextricably bound to my presence. *Space* remains absolutely in itself, everywhere equal to itself, homogeneous; its dimensions, for example, are interchangeable.[19]

Merleau-Ponty recalls that despite this account of the spatial arrangement of things, Descartes did affirm that vision does not involve a thinking that is a spontaneous activity of the soul but rather a thinking that deciphers signs given within the body, and it would seem possible on this basis to ask what signs occasion that thinking which, according to Descartes, arranges things in depth. The process by which the soul deciphers the signs given within the body must contain the key to the ultimate affirmation of a particular arrangement of things seen. For Descartes, however, this pact that unites soul and body can be affirmed but ultimately cannot be thought, precisely because it is a union of the body and the soul. But perhaps the alternatives are not limited to silence on the one hand, and attempts to explain away enigmas on the other. "We are the compound of soul and body, and so there must be a thought of it."[20] If thinking is not limited by definition to the construction of devices, such as the thought derivation of depth from height and width, in order to explain away enigmas—in this case the dimensionality exhibited in vision in which objects hide one another and yet in which this hiding is hidden—perhaps a way of thinking is available analogous to the painter's vision, which interrogates the world that is there even as it emerges from factors that are incompossible yet together. Perhaps as this vision permits the painter to liberate dynamic relationships among these factors which are incompossible yet together, this way of thinking would allow the philosopher to speak so as to lay bare what is.

No more is it a question of speaking of space and light; the question is to make space and light, which are *there,* speak to us. There is no end to this question, since the vision to which it addresses itself is itself a question. The inquiries we believed closed have been reopened.

What is depth, what is light, τί τὸ 'όν ? What are they—not for the mind that cuts itself off from the body but for the mind Descartes says is suffused throughout the body? And what are they, finally, not only for the mind but for themselves, since they pass through us and surround us?

Yet this philosophy still to be done is that which animates the painter—not when he expresses his opinions about the world but in that instant when his vision becomes gesture, when, in Cézanne's words, he "thinks in painting."[21]

What can be found in the artist's act that would help us to understand how the philosopher can say something in the fullest sense?

3. The Artistic Gesture

In the essay "Cézanne's Doubt" Merleau-Ponty indicates the field in which the artist acts. Cézanne's paintings present objects that are there, that we do perceive, and yet that are never given as transparent completed objects but are always emerging in perspectives. Merleau-Ponty describes the painter's act as one that makes the world, as it emerges in perception prior to being overlaid by a cultural stock of perceptual habits, visible. This must be understood literally. The painter's act is not confined to the physical application of paint to a canvas and the painter's effort cannot be divided into a seeing of the world and a subsequent painting of a representation of what is seen. Through the act of painting something is done to the world—it is made visible. In the essay "Indirect Language and the Voices of Silence" Merleau-Ponty comes closer to delimiting the field in which the artist acts. While speaking of the source of similarities and divergences of style in the history of art, Merleau-Ponty points out that the similarity between one's handwriting on paper and one's handwriting on a blackboard can only be understood if it is affirmed that it is a "phenomenon-hand" that writes, a "phenomenon-hand which possesses, in the formula of a movement, something like the effectual law of the particular cases in which it may have to realize itself." Merleau-Ponty goes on to make the point that an analogous process is at work in one's glance that focuses things emerging from the aspects of these things that compete to engulf one's vision. Completing the analogy, it may be said that one sees with phenomena-eyes, which possess, in the formula of a glance, something like the effectual law of the particular cases in which it may have to realize itself. Finally, it is the artist's body that performs the gesture of painting—the artist's body understood as "a system of systems devoted to the inspection of a world and capable of leaping over distances, piercing the perceptual future, and outlining hollows and reliefs, distances and deviations—a meaning—in the inconceivable flatness of being." This system of systems does not involve an apparatus for seeing and an apparatus for movement of the hand that are totally isolated. Once again, the painter's effort cannot be divided into a seeing of the world and a subsequent painting of a representation of what is seen. The gesture of painting made by the body, understood as this "system of systems," is a gesture that simultaneously involves vision as well as movement. How is this to be understood?

In "Eye and Mind" Merleau-Ponty provides the key. My visual field and the field of my motor projects overlap. The structure of the field of this overlap can be traced at both poles, so to speak, of this field, my body and the world. My body:

> I have only to see something to know how to reach and deal with it, even if I do not know how this happens in the nervous machine. My mobile body makes a difference in the visible world, being a part of it; that is why I can steer it through the visible. Conversely, it is just as true that vision is attached to movement. We see only what we look at. What would vision be without eye movement? And how could the movement of the eyes bring things together if the movement were blind? If it were only a reflex? If it did not have its antennae, its clairvoyance? If vision were not prefigured in it?[22]

The world:

> In principle all my changes of place figure in a corner of my landscape; they are recorded on the map of the visible. Everything I see is in principle within my reach, at least within reach of my sight, and is marked upon the

map of the "I can." Each of the two maps is complete. The visible world and the world of my motor projects are each total parts of the same Being.[23]

Inasmuch as the field of my motor projects is profoundly intermingled with my visual field, it may be said that there is a reciprocation of my seeing by the objects, which are movable and moved in the field of my motor projects. This is not an anthropomorphism. Thus Merleau-Ponty describes the total process by saying that it is my vision that involves both a seeing and a being seen.

The enigma is that my body simultaneously sees and is seen. That which looks at all things can also look at itself and recognize, in what it sees, the "other side" of its power of looking.[24]

This seeing and being seen is not to be understood in terms of two acts, one the act of looking at the world and the other the act of looking at myself. Seeing and being seen occur simultaneously in my vision.

This field of overlap of vision and movement is the field in which the act of painting is performed. Now Merleau-Ponty can describe a painting in and through which this act is performed. The reciprocation of my seeing awakens an echo in my body. " 'Nature is on the inside,' says Cézanne. Quality, light, color, depth, which are there before us, are there only because they awaken an echo in our body and because the body welcomes them."[25] In return the body may "awaken an echo" in the world, one in which anyone may recognize the structure of this field of overlap of vision and movement. A painting is such an "echo."

Things have an internal equivalent in me; they arouse in me a carnal formula of their presence. Why shouldn't these in their turn give rise to some visible shape in which anyone else would recognize those motifs which support his own inspection of the world? Thus there appears a "visible" of the second power, a carnal essence or icon of the first. It is not a faded copy, a *trompe-l'oeil,* or another *thing.* The animals painted on the walls of Lascaux are not there in the same way as the fissures and limestone formations. But they are not *elsewhere.* Pushed forward here, held back there, held up by the wall's mass they use so adroitly, they spread around the wall without ever breaking from their elusive moorings in it. I would be at great pains to say *where* is the painting I am looking at. For I do not look at it as I do at a thing; I do not fix it in its place. My gaze wanders in it as in the halos of Being. It is more accurate to say that I see according to it, or with it, than that I *see it.*[26]

B. The Flesh

In revealing the field in which the act of painting is performed, Merleau-Ponty has discovered a path toward the point at which the philosophic act of speaking in the fullest sense is to begin. We recall that such an act, required in order to resolve issues posed by *Phenomenology of Perception,* must begin at that point at which perceiver and perceived come into being. It must begin with that medium which, in *Phenomenology of Perception,* Merleau-Ponty called "existence." Indeed, the source and nature of this act were not to be sought in a subject set apart from the world who would act upon that world, but rather were to be sought in the world understood as subsuming man. The path toward the point at which the philosophic act of speaking in the fullest sense is to begin is the simultaneity in vision of seeing and being seen, a realm that is found neither inside a subject nor outside a subject, but is that place at which perceiver and perceived come into being. What was called the point at which perceiver and perceived come into being has opened up and engulfed both man, who does act so as to bring about the existence of the world such as it is, and the world, in which man is situated prior to any act on man's part. It is now called Being, and Merleau-Ponty's concern is now with what appeared in *Phenomenology of*

Perception as currents of man's being-in-the-world, such as vision and motility, inasmuch as they are "each total parts of the same Being." The path may be broadened:

> This initial paradox cannot but produce others. Visible and mobile, my body is a thing among things; it is caught in the fabric of the world, and its cohesion is that of a thing. But because it moves itself and sees, it holds things in a circle around itself. Things are an annex or prolongation of itself; they are incrusted into its flesh, they are part of its full definition; the world is made of the same stuff as the body. This way of turning things around, these antinomies, are different ways of saying that vision happens among, or is caught in, things—in that place where something visible undertakes to see, becomes visible for itself by virtue of the sight of things; in that place where there persists, like the mother water in crystal, the undividedness of the sensing and the sensed. . . .
>
> The body's animation is not the assemblage or juxtaposition of its parts. Nor is it a question of a mind or spirit coming down from somewhere else into an automaton; this would still suppose that the body itself is without an inside and without a "self." There is a human body when, between the seeing and the seen, between touching and the touched, between one eye and the other, between hand and hand, a blending of some sort takes place—when the spark is lit between sensing and sensible, lighting the fire that will not stop burning until some accident of the body will undo what no accident would have sufficed to do.[27]

It is this discovery of a realm that lies neither inside a subject nor outside a subject, but is that place at which perceiver and perceived come into being, that place at which the philosophic act of speaking in the fullest sense is to begin, that is presented in the segment of *The Visible and the Invisible* entitled "The Intertwining—The Chiasm." After extensive discussions of certain methodologies, the philosophical methodology called reflection and its companion, the modern scientific method, the methodology of dialectic, and the methodology of intuition—discussions that are of interest not only because of the foci of the dialogues with those thinkers in whose works these methodologies reach fruition, Kant, Sartre, Hegel, Husserl, and Bergson, but also because of the implicit philosophy of the history of philosophy developed as Merleau-Ponty makes explicit some of the process of fully taking up the philosophical situation in which he found himself in order to transform that situation through an act of philosophically speaking in the fullest sense—Merleau-Ponty takes his bearings in "The Intertwining—the Chiasm" as he commences what evidently was to have been a work of major proportions.[28]

At the very outset of "The Intertwining—The Chiasm" Merleau-Ponty does indeed assert that his project will not involve responding to a representation of a problematic that has been "worked over" in other philosophical efforts:

> If it is true that as soon as philosophy declares itself to be reflection or coincidence it prejudges what it will find, then once again it must recommence everything, reject the instruments reflection and intuition had provided themselves, and install itself in a locus where they have not yet been distinguished, in experiences that have not yet been "worked over," that offer us all at once, pell-mell, both "subject" and "object," both existence and essence, and hence give philosophy resources to redefine them. Seeing, speaking, even thinking (with certain reservations, for as soon as we distinguish thought from speaking absolutely we are already in the order of reflection), are experiences of this kind, both irrecusable and enigmatic. They have a name in all languages, but a name which in all of them also conveys significations in tufts, thickets of proper meanings and figurative meanings, so that, unlike those of science, not one of these names clarifies by attributing to what is named a circumscribed signification. Rather, they are the repeated index, the insistent reminder of a mystery as familiar as it is unexplained, of a light which, illuminating the rest, remains at

its source in obscurity. If we could rediscover within the exercise of seeing and speaking some of the living references that assign them such a destiny in a language, perhaps they would teach us how to form our new instruments, and first of all to understand our research, our interrogation, themselves.[29]

What Merleau-Ponty rediscovers in "The Intertwining—The Chiasm" is the flesh. Once again, this realm is affirmed once it is recognized that vision simultaneously involves seeing and being seen.

As soon as I see, it is necessary that the vision (as is so well indicated by the double meaning of the word) be doubled with a complementary vision or with another vision: myself seen from without, such as another would see me, installed in the midst of the visible, occupied in considering it from a certain spot.[30]

Likewise, feeling that which is tangible simultaneously involves touching and being touched:

How does it happen that I give to my hands, in particular, that degree, that rate, and that direction of movement that are capable of making me feel the texture of the sleek and the rough? Between the exploration and what it will teach me, between my movements and what I touch, there must exist some relationship by principle, some kinship, according to which they are not only, like the pseudopods of the amoeba, vague and ephemeral deformations of the corporeal space, but the initiation to and the opening upon a tactile world. This can happen only if my hand, while it is felt from within, is also accessible from without, itself tangible, for my other hand, for example, if it takes its place among the things it touches, is in a sense one of them, opens finally upon a tangible being of which it is also a part. Through this crisscrossing within it of the touching and the tangible, its own movements incorporate themselves into the universe they interrogate, are recorded on the same map as it; the two

systems are applied upon one another, as the two halves
of an orange. . . . [I]n the "touch" we have just found three
distinct experiences which subtend one another, three
dimensions which overlap but are distinct: a touching of
the sleek and of the rough, a touching of the things—a
passive sentiment of the body and of its space—and finally a veritable touching of the touch, when my right
hand touches my left hand while it is palpating the things,
where the "touching subject" passes over to the rank of
the touched, descends into the things, such that the touch
is formed in the midst of the world and as it were in the
things.[31]

The realm that opens here for investigation is not only to be
found in vision and touch, but rather extends throughout
one's bodily commerce with the world.[32]

This realm, the flesh, holds open the possibility of precisely determining the nature of the genesis of man's original meaningful situation in the world, the source, as was
learned in *Phenomenology of Perception,* of both man's
access to the world and the opacity of the world, in short, of
the "worldness of the world."

We understand then why we see the things themselves,
in their places, where they are, according to their being
which is indeed more than their being-perceived—and
why at the same time we are separated from them by all
the thickness of the look and of the body; it is that this
distance is not the contrary of this proximity, it is deeply
consonant with it, it is synonymous with it. It is that the
thickness of flesh between the seer and the thing is constitutive for the thing of its visibility as for the seer of his
corporeity; it is not an obstacle between them, it is their
means of communication.[33]

Here it is not a question of the genesis of the world as
explicitly perceived in perceptual consciousness but rather
of the genesis of the original meaningful man-world structure from which the content of explicit perceptual consciousness arises.

[The flesh is not] a fact or a sum of facts, and yet adherent to *location* and to the *now*. Much more: the inauguration of the *where* and the *when,* the possibility and exigency for the fact; in a word: facticity, what makes the fact be a fact. And, at the same time, what makes the facts have meaning, makes the fragmentary facts dispose themselves about "something." For if there is flesh, that is, if the hidden face of the cube radiates forth somewhere as well as does the face I have under my eyes, and coexists with it, and if I who see the cube also belong to the visible, I am visible from elsewhere, and if I and the cube are together caught up in one same "element" (should we say of the seer, or of the visible?), this cohesion, this visibility by principle, prevails over every momentary discordance. In advance every vision or very partial visible that would here definitively come to naught is not nullified (which would leave a gap in its place), but, what is better, it is replaced by a more exact vision and a more exact visible, according to the principle of visibility, which, as though through a sort of abhorrence of a vacuum, already invokes the true vision and the true visible, not only as substitutes for their errors, but also as their explanation, their relative justification, so that they are, as Husserl says so aptly, not erased, but "crossed out."[34]

In *Phenomenology of Perception* the process by which man's original situation in the world comes about was described as involving both the inherent radical dynamism of existence and acts initiated by man. The structure of the body and the structure of the world in which the body is situated were revealed as inherently radically dynamic and, at the same time, the structuralization of the body and the structuralization of the world in which the body is situated were revealed as involving acts initiated by man. Each of these factors is sustained in the following description by Merleau-Ponty of that which was to command so much attention in the studies to follow "The Intertwining—The Chiasm," that is, the flesh:

The body interposed is not a thing, an interstitial matter, a connective tissue, but a *sensible for itself,* which means, not that absurdity: color that sees itself, surface that touches itself—but this paradox [?][35]: a set of colors and surfaces inhabited by a touch, a vision, hence an *exemplar sensible,* which offers to him who inhabits it and senses it the wherewithal to sense everything that resembles himself on the outside, such that, caught up in the tissue of the things, it draws it entirely to itself, incorporates it, and with the same movement, communicates to the things upon which it closes over that identity without superposition, that difference without contradiction, that divergence between the within and the without that constitutes its natal secret.[36] The body unites us directly with the things through its own ontogenesis, by welding to one another the two outlines of which it is made, its two laps: the sensible mass it is and the mass of the sensible wherein it is born by segregation and upon which, as seer, it remains open. It is the body and it alone, because it is a two-dimensional being, that can bring us to the things themselves, which are themselves not flat beings but beings in depth, inaccessible to a subject that would survey them from above, open to him alone that, if it be possible, would coexist with them in the same world. When we speak of the flesh of the visible, we do not mean to do anthropology, to describe a world covered over with all our own projections, leaving aside what it can be under the human mask. Rather, we mean that carnal being, as a being of depths, of several leaves or several faces, a being in latency, and a presentation of a certain absence, is a prototype of Being, of which our body, the sensible sentient, is a very remarkable variant, but whose constitutive paradox already lies in every visible. For already the cube assembles within itself incompossible *visibilia,* as my body is at once phenomenal body and objective body, and if finally it is, it, like my body, is by a tour de force. What we call a visible is, we said, quality pregnant with a texture, the surface of a depth, a cross section upon a massive being, a grain or corpuscle borne by a wave of Being. Since the total visible is always behind, or after, or between the aspects we see of it, there is access to it only through an experience which, like it, is wholly outside of itself. It is thus, and not as the bearer of a knowing subject, that our body commands the visible for us, but it does not explain it, does not clarify it, it only concentrates the mystery of its scattered visibility; and it is indeed a paradox of Being, not a paradox of man that we are dealing with here.[37]

The man-world structure comes about through the ontogenesis of the body and the coming into being of the things by "tours de force." But this process of structuralization also involves acts initiated by man. Here the question as to the identity of man such that his acts contribute to this process is left open:

> To be sure, one can reply that, between the two "sides" of our body, the body as sensible and the body as sentient (what in the past we called objective body and phenomenal body), rather than a spread, there is the abyss that separates the In Itself from the For Itself. It is a problem—and we will not avoid it—to determine how the sensible sentient can also be thought. But here, seeking to form our first concepts in such a way as to avoid the classical impasses, we do not have to honor the difficulties that they may present when confronted with a *cogito,* which itself has to be re-examined.[38]

But we have already learned from *Phenomenology of Perception* that there is no pure consciousness divorced from our bodily opening onto the world. Thus Merleau-Ponty describes in terms of the body those acts initiated by man which contribute to the genesis of the man-world structure. Such acts contribute to the structuralization of the world in which the body is situated as the body "communicates to the things upon which it closes over that identity without superposition, that difference without contradiction, that divergence between the within and the without that constitutes its natal secret." Such acts also contribute to the structuralization of the body itself as the body welds "to one another the two outlines of which it is made, its two laps." And finally, such acts do not contribute to the structuralization of things and of the body in such a manner that things and the body could possibly evolve in universes apart from one another with no communication between them, but rather such acts contribute to the genesis of a man-world structure, in which man and the things are mutually transcendent and yet mutually related.

> For if the body is a thing among things, it is so in a stronger and deeper sense than they: in the sense that, we said, it *is of them,* and this means that it detaches itself upon them, and, accordingly, detaches itself from them.[39]

The dynamic milieu, cohabited by elements mutually transcendent and yet mutually interrelated, which in *Phenomenology of Perception* Merleau-Ponty called "existence," reappears in *The Visible and the Invisible* as Being. The "paradox of Being," which the flesh requires we affirm as an ontological paradox and not solely a logical paradox,[40] is not limited to the access that man has to things that are nevertheless transcendent to man. It involves as well the mutual relationships between the various "senses," which nevertheless must be fully affirmed in their specificity.[41] The "paradox of Being" also involves the mutual relationships of parts of the body, which nevertheless must be fully affirmed in their specificity.[42] The "paradox of Being" also involves our access to other persons, who nevertheless are transcendent to us.[43] The "paradox of Being" also involves what we may call man's "linguistic situation." *Phenomenology of Perception* disclosed that man speaks and hears words that already have their meanings. The realm of the flesh suggests how this is to be understood. The same reversibility is at work in speaking and hearing language as is at work in vision and touching.

As there is a reflexivity of the touch, of sight, and of the
touch-vision system, there is a reflexivity of the movements of phonation and of hearing; they have their sono-
rous inscription, the vociferations have in me their motor
echo. This new reversibility and the emergence of the
flesh as expression are the point of insertion of speaking
and thinking in the world of silence.[44]

Just as Merleau-Ponty has described Visibility as simultaneously involving seeing and being seen, so may we describe the special domain of what Merleau-Ponty has called
"living language" as simultaneously involving speaking and
being spoken to and simultaneously involving hearing and
being heard, and just as in the case of Visibility it is not a
question of first seeing something and subsequently seeing
ourselves, here it is not a question of successive inter-
changes in the course of a conversation with another person. Furthermore, just as in the case of Visibility Merleau-
Ponty does not propose what amounts to an anthropomorphism, so here no anthropomorphism is involved, but
rather the affirmation that while language is transcendent to
man and never falls under man's complete control, man
nevertheless does speak and does hear language that already has its meaning, and speaks it and hears it precisely
as such, just as man has access to the things themselves
that he perceives. Language is no more created by man
than are the things man touches and sees, yet it is somehow
destined to be spoken and heard by man just as the things
man touches and sees are destined to be touched and seen
by the body, this "set of colors and surfaces inhabited by a
touch, a vision. . . ."

But these are mysteries that call for much more work,
beginning with a thorough exploration of "the flesh."
Merleau-Ponty does go as far as to call language a "less
heavy, more transparent body" but nevertheless flesh,[45]
and to suggest an analogy, in terms of the reversibility inherent in the flesh, between the relationship of one's body and
that which it senses and the relationship between language
and the other dimensions of Being:

[J]ust as my body sees only because it is a part of the visible in which it opens forth, the sense upon which the arrangement of the sounds opens reflects back upon that arrangement. For the linguist language is an ideal system, a fragment of the intelligible world. But, just as for me to see it is not enough that my look be visible for X, it is necessary that it be visible for itself, through a sort of torsion, reversal, or specular phenomenon, which is given from the sole fact that I am born; so also, if my words have a meaning, it is not *because* they present the systematic organization the linguist will disclose, it is because that organization, like the look, refers back to itself: the operative Word is the obscure region whence comes the instituted light, as the muted reflection of the body upon itself is what we call natural light. As there is a reversibility of the seeing and the visible, and as at the point where the two metamorphoses cross what we call perception is born, so also there is a reversibility of the speech and what it signifies.[46]

This affirms what was learned in *Phenomenology of Perception*, to the effect that language is involved in processes of mutual determination with other phenomena involved in other dimensions of man's life, that language *has* its meaning—language acts, and the advent of language, not only in the historical sense but also in reference to all instances of speaking, marks foundational change in man and his world.

Man and the things themselves to which man has access in perception, the various senses, the various parts of the body, myself and other people, man and language that *has* its meaning, language and the phenomena involved in other dimensions of man's life—all the mutually transcendent elements that in *Phenomenology of Perception* were disclosed as cohabiting the dynamic milieu that in that work Merleau-Ponty called existence—now reappear as dimensions of Being. But the point of view of a subject who perceives a world already constituted in perception has been totally abandoned in order to begin at that point where perceiver and perceived come into being. Consequently, the full "paradox of Being" may be expressed thus: Being is radically dynamic and man initiates acts that bring about the existence of the world such as it is, and yet there is *the* world prior to any acts initiated by man, and the world that is, is constituted by elements that are transcendent to one another and yet dynamically mutually interrelated. This paradox echoes in each dimension of Being, including language. As it is found in language, this paradox may be expressed thus: Language is radically dynamic and man initiates acts that bring about the existence of Language such as it is, and yet there is Language prior to any acts initiated by man, and Language is constituted by originary instances of speech that are transcendent to one another and yet dynamically mutually interrelated. Thus Merleau-Ponty writes:

> [T]he signification is what comes to seal, to close, to gather up the multiplicity of the physical, physiological, linguistic means of elocution, to contract them into one sole act, as the vision comes to complete the aesthesiological body. And, as the visible takes hold of the look which has unveiled it and which forms a part of it, the signification rebounds upon its own means, it annexes to itself the speech that becomes an object of science, it antedates itself by a retrograde movement which is never completely belied—because already, in opening the horizon of the nameable and of the sayable, the speech acknowledged that it has its place in that horizon; because no locutor speaks without making himself in advance allocutary, *be it only for himself;* because with one sole gesture he closes the circuit of his relation to himself and that of his relation to the others and, with the same stroke, also sets himself up as *delocutary,* speech of which one speaks: he offers himself and offers every word to a universal Word.[47]

Once again, the question that appeared in *Phenomenology of Perception* is posed: how is it philosophically cotenable that Being is radically dynamic and yet, there is *the* world?

Now the task at hand is not that of transforming perception in order that the original content of perception be affirmed before it is overlaid with unwarranted objectivistic perceptual habits, but rather is that of laying bare those elements, transcendent to one another yet dynamically mutually interrelated, which constitute that which is. What is called for is an act of speaking in the fullest sense, which would be the utterance of language that, as originary, would mark a transformation throughout language and throughout the mute dimensions of Being, and yet would not break the silence either of language as it is or of the mute dimensions of Being. The question as to how this act is to be performed has not been answered by Merleau-Ponty.

> We shall have to follow more closely this transition from the mute world to the speaking world. For the moment we want only to suggest that one can speak neither of a destruction nor of a conservation of silence (and still less of a destruction that conserves or of a realization that destroys—which is not to solve but to pose the problem). When the silent vision falls into speech, and when the speech in turn, opening up a field of the nameable and the sayable, inscribes itself in that field, in its place, according to its truth—in short, when it metamorphoses the structures of the visible world and makes itself a gaze of the mind, *intuitus mentis*—this is always in virtue of the same fundamental phenomenon of reversibility which sustains both the mute perception and the speech and which manifests itself by an almost carnal existence of the idea, as well as by a sublimation of the flesh.[48]

C. The Visible and the Invisible

Merleau-Ponty's discussion in "The Intertwining—The Chiasm" does suggest how it may be possible to understand how certain originary structuralizations of Being involving acts initiated by man, including originary instances of language, can at the same time be the taking up in full of man's situation in the world as it is. Merleau-Ponty explicitly underscores the point that the flesh is not matter. Indeed, the flesh is thoroughly lined with that which is called idea:

> [W]e spoke summarily of a reversibility of the seeing and the visible, of the touching and the touched. It is time to emphasize that it is a reversibility always imminent and never realized in fact. My left hand is always on the verge of touching my right hand touching the things, but I never reach coincidence; the coincidence eclipses at the moment of realization, and one of two things always occurs: either my right hand really passes over to the rank of touched, but then its hold on the world is interrupted; or it retains its hold on the world, but then I do not really touch *it*—my right hand touching, I palpate with my left hand only its outer covering. . . . But this incessant escaping, this impotency to superpose exactly upon one another the touching of the things by my right hand and the touching of this same right hand by my left hand, or to superpose, in the exploratory movements of the hand, the tactile experience of a point and that of the "same" point a moment later . . .—this is not a failure. For if these experiences never exactly overlap, if they slip away at the very moment they are about to rejoin, if there is always a "shift," a "spread," between them, this is precisely because my two hands are part of the same body, because it moves itself in the world, because I hear myself both from within and from without. I experience—and as often as I wish—the transition and the metamorphosis of the one experience into the other, and it is only as though the hinge between them, solid, unshakeable, remained irremediably hidden from me. But this hiatus between my right hand touched and my right hand touching, between my voice heard and my voice uttered, between one moment of my tactile life and the following one, is not an ontological void, a non-being: it is spanned by the total being of my body, and by that of the world; it is the zero of pressure between two solids that makes them adhere to one another. My flesh and that of the world therefore involve clear zones, clearings, about which pivot their opaque zones, and the primary visibil-

ity, that of the *quale* and of the things, does not come without a second visibility, that of the lines of force and dimensions, the massive flesh without a rarefied flesh, the momentary body without a glorified body. . . .

We touch here the most difficult point, that is, the bond between the flesh and the idea, between the visible and the interior armature which it manifests and which it conceals.[49]

Rather than a bond between two disparate elements, what is at work here is a profound intermingling of idea and flesh, which Merleau-Ponty expresses, in a deceptively simple proposition, by stating that the idea is the invisible *of* this world:

With the first vision, the first contact, the first pleasure, there is initiation, that is, not the positing of a content, but the opening of a dimension that can never again be closed, the establishment of a level in terms of which every other experience will henceforth be situated. The idea is this level, this dimension. It is therefore not a *de facto* invisible, like an object hidden behind another, and not an absolute invisible, which would have nothing to do with the visible. Rather it is the invisible *of* this world, that which inhabits this world, sustains it, and renders it visible, its own and interior possibility, the Being of this being.[50]

The fact that the reversibility immanent in the flesh is always imminent and never realized, that is, that at any given moment my experience is weighted in favor of either my hold on the world or the world's hold on me, is the source, in articulations of man's commerce with the world, of either a "subjective" accent, according to which that which is called knowledge is primarily a creation by man and man's access to that which is is limited in principle, or an "objective" accent, according to which that which is called knowledge can be reduced to the processes at work in a world, including man, as portrayed by realism. But, if the idea, the hinge at work in the "transition and metamorphosis" of one experience into another, is to be found within the flesh, that realm which is neither interior to a subject nor external to a subject but the place at which perceiver and perceived come into being, a possibility is opened for articulating man's commerce with the world in such a way as to avoid the impasses of the epistemological subject-object dualism, which is discredited in *Phenomenology of Perception*.[51] Furthermore, to trace how the idea inhabits the flesh may enable us to understand how certain originary structuralizations of Being involving acts initiated by man, can at the same time be the taking up in full of man's situation in the world as it is:

> When Husserl spoke of the horizon of the things—of their exterior horizon, which everybody knows, and of their "interior horizon," that darkness stuffed with visibility of which their surface is but the limit—it is necessary to take the term seriously. No more than are the sky or the earth is the horizon a collection of things held together, or a class name, or a logical possibility of conception, or a system of "potentiality of consciousness": it is a new type of being, a being by porosity, pregnancy, or generality, and he before whom the horizon opens is caught up, included within it. His body and the distances participate in one same corporeity or visibility in general, which reigns between them and it, and even beyond the horizon, beneath his skin, unto the depths of being.[52]

The horizonal character of the context of perception appeared in *Phenomenology of Perception* as that characteristic of things perceived whereby simultaneously the perceiver has direct access to them, and thus does not know the thing by a process of interpretation of perspectives, but rather knows perspectives as perspectives of the same thing, and the thing resists the perceiver inasmuch as it is not thoroughly determinate in explicit perception and could only be so if the body and the world in which it is situated were fully determinate in explicit perception, which is not the case. If the body and the world were fully determinate in explicit perception, all would be transparent, or in other words, there would be nothing. Merleau-Ponty speaks of the world as the "horizon of horizons."[53] This is because it is not experienced as a horizon at the limit of the content of perception, but rather is experienced in the experience of each thing perceived precisely as that to which the perceiver has access through the perceiver's overall bodily intentionality, and yet resists the perceiver because it is not fully determinate in explicit perception. Having discovered a realm that lies neither inside a subject nor outside a subject but is that place at which the perceiver-perceived structure comes into being, Merleau-Ponty has discovered that place at which "exterior" and "interior" horizons come into being. Originary structuralizations of Being involving acts initiated by man take up and transform these horizons now understood as themselves a "type of being, a being by porosity, pregnancy, or generality," and in this way such originary structuralizations of being involving acts initiated by man reach beyond the explicit content of perception, beyond the horizon, beneath the skin, and are the taking up in full of man's original situation in the world as it is.[54]

The suggestion that to trace how the idea inhabits the flesh may enable us to understand how certain originary structuralizations of Being involving acts initiated by man, can at the same time be the taking up in full of man's situation in the world as it is, is developed in "Eye and Mind" as Merleau-Ponty explores the nature of an originary work of art. He begins by focusing on one art, namely, painting. First, he recalls that the painter seeks depth. The painter's vision permits him to liberate, in painting, dynamic relationships among factors by which the world he sees is composed, factors that are incompossible yet together. Next Merleau-Ponty considers ingredients of paintings, space and color, in terms of which the painter seeks depth. He notes that Cézanne at one time made space his overriding concern. Nevertheless, color was present in these paintings and one may say that, precisely because color was not mastered, it threatened to sabotage these attempts to find depth.

> Cézanne knows already what cubism will repeat: that the external form, the envelope, is secondary and derived, that it is not that which causes a thing to take form, that this shell of space must be shattered, this fruit bowl broken—and what is there to paint, then? Cubes, spheres, and cones (as he said once)? Pure forms which have the solidity of what could be defined by an internal law of construction, forms which all together, as traces or slices of the thing, let it appear between them like a face in the reeds? This would be to put Being's solidity on one side and its variety on the other. Cézanne made an experiment of this kind in his middle period. He opted for the solid, for space—and came to find that inside this space, a box or container too large for them, the things began to move, color against color; they began to modulate in instability.[55] Thus we must seek space and its content *as* together. The problem is generalized; it is no longer that of distance, of line, of form; it is also, and equally, the problem of color.[56]

But if color becomes the primary concern, space is still present and may reassert itself and demand to be balanced with color.

> Yet (and this must be emphasized) there is no one master key of the visible, and color alone is no closer to being such a key than space is. The return to color has the merit of getting somewhat nearer to "the heart of things,"[57] but this heart is beyond the color envelope just as it is beyond the space envelope. The "Portrait of Vallier" sets between the colors white spaces which take on the function of giving shape to, and setting off, a being more general than the yellow-being or green-being or blue-being.[58]

Merleau-Ponty suggests that Cézanne's last works do achieve a harmony of space and color:

[I]n the water colors of Cézanne's last years . . . space (which had been taken to be evidence itself and of which it was believed that the question of *where* was not to be asked) radiates around planes that cannot be assigned to any place at all: "a superimposing of transparent surfaces," "a flowing movement of planes of color which overlap, which advance and retreat."[59]

Next Merleau-Ponty asks why it is, given that neither the means of expression nor the creative gestures involved in painting, drawing, and sculpture are equivalent, that often a good painter can also make good drawings or good sculpture. In order to focus attention on an ingredient common to these media, namely, the line, Merleau-Ponty considers the works of Paul Klee, in which the line is a primary concern. In these works the line is not a copy of a line as a would-be property of objects in the world in itself, that is, as an outline of an object or a border between areas, but rather is a means of rendering visible the system of equivalences of factors that compose the world that emerges in vision. The development of a line in a painting involves all of these factors and, in particular, those lines which enter into this system of equivalences, those lines which are "always between or behind whatever we fix our eyes upon; [those lines which] are indicated, implicated, and even very imperiously demanded by the things, but [which] themselves are not things."[60]

For henceforth, as Klee said, the line no longer imitates the visible; it "renders visible"; it is the blueprint of a genesis of things. Perhaps no one before Klee had "let a line muse."[61] The beginning of the line's path establishes or installs a certain level or mode of the linear, a certain manner for the line to be and to make itself a line, "to go line."[62] Relative to it, every subsequent inflection will have a diacritical value, will be another aspect of the line's relationship to itself, will form an adventure, a history, a meaning of the line—all this according as it slants more or less, more or less rapidly, more or less subtly. Making its way in space, it nevertheless corrodes prosaic space and the *partes extra partes;* it develops a way of extending itself actively into that space which sub-tends the spatiality of a thing quite as much as that of a man or an apple tree. This is so simply because, as Klee said, to give the generating axis of a man the painter "would have to have a network of lines so entangled that it could no longer be a question of a truly elementary repre-sentation."[63]

Although Merleau-Ponty does not explicitly make the ob-servation, it may be said that the dynamic relationships among certain factors, which enter into the system of equivalences of factors that compose the world that emerges in vision, may be best rendered visible in lines that can best be rendered in particular media—in painting or drawing or sculpture.

Klee "let a line muse." The line "extends itself actively" into space. In a painting considered as an object, that is, as blotches of pigment on a canvas, a line is stationary. In a painting considered as a painting, a line is in motion. Mo-tion itself may become a primary concern of an artist. Merleau-Ponty cites Rodin's account of how motion may be presented by a work of art:

Movement is given, says Rodin,[64] by an image in which the arms, the legs, the trunk, and the head are each taken at a different instant, an image which therefore portrays the body in an attitude which it never at any instant really held and which imposes fictive linkages be-tween the parts, as if this mutual confrontation of incom-possibles could, and could alone, cause transition and duration to arise in bronze and on canvas.[65]

These "incompossibles" are stationary on a canvas or in a sculpture, but in their "mutual confrontation" on the canvas or in the sculpture, they are in motion.

This presence, in a line in a work of art, of those lines which enter into the system of equivalences of factors that compose the world that emerges in vision; this presence, in stationary ingredients of a work of art, of motion; this presence, in the color dimension of a painting, of the spatial dimension; and this presence, in the spatial dimension of a painting of the color dimension—all indicate that a specific originary work of art that transforms the field of painting does so while taking up that field fully, as it is.

Every visual something, as individual as it is, functions also as a dimension, because it gives itself as the result of a dehiscence of Being. What this ultimately means is that the proper essence of the visible is to have a layer of invisibility in the strict sense, which it makes present as a certain absence. "In their times, our bygone antipodes, the impressionists, were perfectly right in making their abode with the castaways and the undergrowth of daily life. As for us, our heart throbs to bring us closer to the depths. . . . These oddities will become . . . realities . . . because instead of being held to the diversely intense restoration of the visible, they will annex to it the proper share of the invisible, occultly apperceived."[66]
Because depth, color, form, line, movement, contour, physiognomy are all branches of Being and because each one can sway all the rest, there are no separated, distinct "problems" in painting, no really opposed paths, no partial "solutions," no cumulative progress, no irretrievable options.[67]

This nature of an originary work of art by the painter who "thinks in painting"[68] illustrates how it is that the process of tracing how the idea, the hinge at work in the "transition and metamorphosis" of one experience into another, inhabits the flesh, may enable us to understand how certain originary structuralizations of Being involving acts initiated by man, including originary instances of language, can at the same time be the taking up in full of man's situation in the world as it is.

Conclusion

In *The Visible and the Invisible* Merleau-Ponty explicitly affirms that his effort is directed toward performing an act of speaking in the fullest sense that would make manifest what language is—an act that would not be a response to a world as constituted in perceptual consciousness but would be an originary act, one that would mark a change in the speaker, his listeners, and their world that would not be vulnerable from other "perspectives," would not be open to the possibility of being "crossed out," as Merleau-Ponty, following Husserl, says every vision or "partial visible" that would definitively come to naught is "crossed out" by the "principle of visibility," which "invokes the true vision and the true visible." Such would be the nature of this act of speaking because, at the same time as it would be an act initiated by man, it would also be the things themselves speaking, and—to go one step farther—it would be Language itself speaking. Such an act is one that would return the philosopher to Wild Being in order that he may lay it bare. "The Intertwining—The Chiasm" concludes with these words:

> In a sense the whole of philosophy, as Husserl says, consists in restoring a power to signify, a birth of meaning, or a wild meaning, an expression of experience by experience, which in particular clarifies the special domain of language. And in a sense, as Valéry said, language is everything, since it is the voice of no one, since it is the very voice of the things, the waves, and the forests. And what we have to understand is that there is no dialectical reversal from one of these views to the other; we do not have to reassemble them into a synthesis: they are two aspects of the reversibility which is the ultimate truth.[69]

Merleau-Ponty's study of art yields two results that bear directly on the search for the precise means of philosophically speaking in the fullest sense, which would make manifest what language is. First, in the simultaneity in vision of seeing and being seen, Merleau-Ponty has discovered a realm that lies neither inside a subject nor outside a subject, but is that place at which perceiver and perceived come into being, that place at which the philosophic act of speaking in the fullest sense is to begin. Merleau-Ponty calls this realm "the Visible." When explored in "The Intertwining—The Chiasm," it opens onto all dimensions of Being and becomes what Merleau-Ponty calls "the flesh." Second, Merleau-Ponty's exploration of the nature of an originary work of art discloses how a specific originary work of art, that transforms the field of painting, does so, while taking up that field fully, as it is. This exploration of an originary work of art illustrates how the process of tracing how the idea—disclosed in "The Intertwining—The Chiasm" as lining the flesh, as the "invisible *of* this world," as the hinge at work in the "transition and metamorphosis" of one experience into another—inhabits the flesh, may help to determine precisely how a philosophical act of speaking in the fullest sense would transform the philosopher's situation while taking up that situation fully, as it is.

Notes

1. "Cézanne's Doubt," in *Sense and Non-Sense*, pp. 18–19.
2. "Indirect Language and the Voices of Silence," in *Signs*, p. 79.
3. *Sense and Non-Sense*, p. 21.
4. "Eye and Mind," trans. Carleton Dallery, in *The Primacy of Perception and Other Essays*, p. 161.
5. *Signs*, p. 52.
6. "The constitution of a level always presupposes another given level . . . space always precedes itself. But this remark is not a mere admission of defeat. It enlightens us concerning the essence of space and the only method which enables us to understand it. It is of the essence of space to be always 'already constituted,' and we shall never come to understand it by withdrawing into a worldless perception. We must not wonder why being is orientated, why existence is spatial, why . . . our body is not geared to the world in all its positions, and why its coexistence with the world magnetizes experience and induces a direction in it. The question could be asked only if the facts were fortuitous happenings to a subject and an object indifferent to space, whereas perceptual experience shows that they are

presupposed in our primordial encounter with being, and that being is synonymous with being situated. . . . Generally speaking, our perception would not
comprise either outlines, figures, backgrounds or objects, and would consequently not be perception of anything, or indeed exist at all, if the subject of
perception were not this gaze which takes a grip upon things only in so far as they
have a general direction; and this general direction in space is not a contingent
characteristic of the object, it is the means whereby I recognize it and am conscious of it as of an object. . . . Thus, since every conceivable being is related
either directly or indirectly to the perceived world, and since the perceived world
is grasped only in terms of direction, we cannot dissociate being from orientated
being, and there is no occasion to 'find a basis for' space or to ask what is the level
of all levels. The primordial level is on the horizon of all our perceptions, but it is a
horizon which cannot in principle ever be reached and thematized in our express
perception" (*Phenomenology of Perception*, pp. 252–53).

7. *Signs*, p. 50.
8. Ibid.
9. Ibid., p. 54.
10. Ibid., p. 66.
11. Ibid., p. 67.
12. Ibid., p. 80.
13. Ibid., p. 81.
14. *The Primacy of Perception and Other Essays*, p. 166.
15. Ibid., p. 167.
16. Ibid.
17. Ibid.
18. Ibid.
19. Ibid., p. 173.
20. Ibid., p. 177–78.
21. B. Dorival, *Paul Cézanne* (Paris, 1948), pp. 103 ff.; Merleau-Ponty's note.
The Primacy of Perception and Other Essays, p. 178.
22. *The Primacy of Perception and Other Essays*, p. 162.
23. Ibid.
24. Ibid.
25. Ibid., p. 164.
26. Ibid.
27. Ibid., pp. 163–64.
28. It would certainly be an error to regard this segment as a substitute for the
effort that was to have followed or to mistake indications contained therein for
what the studies that were to have followed may have established. Nevertheless,
this portion of the text does present the scope of the project and in addition is of
particular interest in regard to the problematic of language inasmuch as the full
import of the problematic is affirmed here in terms of the scope of the project. The
nature of this portion of the text is unique. As an introductory discussion, it does
in a sense contain the ideas that were to have been laid out in the studies to follow.
But these ideas are there in a rough, jagged manner, as though their development
had been torn from the text and annihilated. This adds to the unfinished nature of
the manuscript itself of this portion of the text. In order not to stuff into the
terminology of this text any development that one may guess would have followed, by rashly hypostatizing such elements as "the visible" and "the invisible"
as though they were to be the final yield of the ontological effort that Merleau-

Ponty commences here, in this discussion and the one that follows, "The Visible and the Invisible," the development in the text will be followed as closely as possible, even where a risk of duplication is run by the inclusion of citations at length when necessary, as the location of the text in the context of Merleau-Ponty's steps toward saying precisely what language is, is determined. Merleau-Ponty himself writes during the discussion of particular methodologies that precedes "The Intertwining—The Chiasm":

"Philosophy does not decompose our relationship with the world into real elements, or even into ideal references which would make of it an ideal object, but it discerns articulations in the world, it awakens in it regular relations of prepossession, of recapitulation, of overlapping, which are as dormant in our ontological landscape, subsist there only in the form of traces, and nevertheless continue to function there, continue to institute the new there" (*The Visible and the Invisible*, pp. 100–101).

29. Ibid., p. 130.

30. Ibid., p. 134.

31. Ibid., pp. 133–34.

32. "There is vision, touch, when a certain visible, a certain tangible, turns back upon the whole of the visible, the whole of the tangible, of which it is a part, or when it finds itself *surrounded* by them, or when between it and them, and through their commerce, is formed a Visibility, a Tangible in itself which belongs properly neither to the body qua fact nor to the world qua fact—as upon two mirrors facing one another two indefinite series of images set in one another arise which belong really to neither of the two surfaces, since each is only the rejoinder of the other, and which therefore form a couple, a couple more real than either of them. Thus since the seer is caught up in what he sees, it is still himself he sees: there is a fundamental narcissism of all vision. And thus, for the same reason, the vision he exercises, he also undergoes from the things, such that, as many painters have said, I feel myself looked at by the things, my activity is equally passivity—which is the second and more profound sense of the narcissism: not to see in the outside, as the others see it, the contour of a body one inhabits, but especially to be seen by the outside, to exist within it, to emigrate into it, to be seduced, captivated, alienated by the phantom, so that the seer and the visible reciprocate one another and we no longer know which sees and which is seen. It is this Visibility, this generality of the Sensible in itself, this anonymity innate to Myself that we have previously called flesh, and one knows there is no name in traditional philosophy to designate it" (*The Visible and the Invisible*, p. 139).

33. Ibid., p. 135.

34. Ibid., pp. 139–40.

35. This sign is inserted by Claude Lefort in order to mark terms that are illegible in the original manuscript.

36. Here, in the course of the text itself, between brackets, these lines are inserted: "One can say that we perceive the things themselves, that we are the world that thinks itself—or that the world is at the heart of our flesh. In any case, once a body-world relationship is recognized, there is a ramification of my body and a ramification of the world and a correspondence between its inside and my outside, between my inside and its outside" (editor's note).

37. *The Visible and the Invisible*, pp. 135–36.

38. Ibid., pp. 136–37.

39. Ibid., p. 137.

40. This affirmation is presaged throughout Merleau-Ponty's work. In Merleau-Ponty's first book, *The Structure of Behavior,* this theme is at work in the treatment of the physiological and psychological accounts of human beings, neither of which is reducible to the other but both of which, properly understood, are tenable. This same type of relation is involved among the three "orders" in man, the physical, the vital, and the human. One can neither explain the "higher" by the "lower" nor the "lower" by the "higher," and yet all three are constitutive of human existence. Similarly, the various senses are related in this manner. In our experience, the senses are integrated in a manner that prevents accounting for the total experience in terms of contributions of the individual senses and yet each is specific, as is attested by situations in which alterations of one produces specific results in the total experience. These analyses are furthered in *Phenomenology of Perception.* ("Man taken as a concrete being is not a psyche joined to an organism, but the movement to and fro of existence which at one time allows itself to take corporeal form and at others moves towards personal acts. Psychological motives and bodily occasions may overlap because there is not a single impulse in a living body which is entirely fortuitous in relation to psychic intentions, not a single mental act which has not found at least its germ or its general outline in physiological tendencies. It is never a question of the incomprehensible meeting of two causalities, nor of a collision between the order of causes and that of ends. But by an imperceptible twist an organic process issues into human behavior, an instinctive act changes direction and becomes a sentiment, or conversely a human act becomes torpid and is continued absentmindedly in the form of a reflex" [*Phenomenology of Perception,* p. 88].) ("Thus the connecting link between the parts of our body and that between our visual and tactile experience are not forged gradually and cumulatively. I do not translate the 'data of touch into the language of seeing' or vice versa—I do not bring together one by one the parts of my body; this translation and this unification are performed once and for all within me: they are my body itself" [*Phenomenology of Perception,* pp. 149–50].)

The theme of the tenableness in existence of apparent contradictions appears at each stage of *Phenomenology of Perception.* Sexuality is coextensive with our bodily existence and yet neither is reducible to the other. (See *Phenomenology of Perception,* pp. 168–71. In a footnote to this discussion, Merleau-Ponty treats the relationship between economics and history in the same manner.) The relationship between the individual sense properties of a thing and the thing as an intersensory entity is understood in the same manner. (See *Phenomenology of Perception,* pp. 317–20.) Indeed, the mystery of the world, which in its unity remains the same through my life and yet which is constantly changing, reflects this same quality of existence. (See *Phenomenology of Perception,* pp. 327–34.)

The existence of the other person is transcendent for me and my existence is transcendent for the other person, and yet we know one another, we coexist. ("We have discovered, with the natural and social worlds, the truly transcendental, which is not the totality of constituting operations whereby a transparent world, free from obscurity and impenetrable solidity, is spread out before an impartial spectator, but that ambiguous life in which the forms of transcendence have their *Ursprung,* and which, through a fundamental contradiction, puts me in communication with them, and on this basis makes knowledge possible" [*Phenomenology of Perception,* pp. 364–65].)

In the concluding part of *Phenomenology of Perception,* "Being-for-Itself and

Being-in-the-World," Merleau-Ponty demonstrates that man must be understood as both situated, as in the world in a particular manner, prior to any act by man, and as acting in such a way as to structure this situation and bring about its existence such as it is. Neither aspect of man is reducible to the other and yet together they define man. It is understandable that Merleau-Ponty's has been called a "philosophy of ambiguity." (See Ferdinand Alquié, "Une Philosophie de l'ambiguïté: L'existentialisme de Maurice Merleau-Ponty," *Fontaine* 2, no. 59 [April 1947]: 47–50; A. de Waelhens, *Une Philosophie de l'ambiguïté: L'existentialisme de Maurice Merleau-Ponty,* 4th ed. [Louvain: Éditions Nauwelaerts, 1970].) But this explicit affirmation of the "paradox of Being," which once again takes up themes found throughout Merleau-Ponty's work, makes it clear that for Merleau-Ponty, existence, or later Being, is not ambiguous if by ambiguous we mean that we cannot decide between the contradictories it sustains because then we could not say of it that it is ambiguous but rather that our knowledge of it is muddled. Rather, it may be said that existence is ambiguous because we must simultaneously maintain the contradictories involved in it.

41. Merleau-Ponty makes this point in terms of vision and touch: "There is double and crossed situating of the visible in the tangible and of the tangible in the visible; the two maps are complete, and yet they do not merge into one. The two parts are total parts and yet are not superposable" (*The Visible and the Invisible,* p. 134).

42. "My two hands touch the same things because they are the hands of one same body. And yet each of them has its own tactile experience. If nonetheless they have to do with one sole tangible, it is because there exists a very peculiar relation from one to the other, across the corporeal space—like that holding between my two eyes—making of my hands one sole organ of experience, as it makes of my two eyes the channels of one sole Cyclopean vision. A difficult relation to conceive—since one eye, one hand, are capable of vision, of touch, and since what has to be comprehended is that these visions, these touches, these little subjectivities, these 'consciousnesses of. . . ,' could be assembled like flowers into a bouquet, when each being 'consciousness of,' being For Itself, reduces the others into objects. We will get out of the difficulty only by renouncing the bifurcation of the 'consciousness of' and the object, by admitting that my synergic body is not an object, that it assembles into a cluster the 'consciousnesses' adherent to its hands, to its eyes, by an operation that is in relation to them lateral, transversal; that 'my consciousness' is not the synthetic, uncreated, centrifugal unity of a multitude of 'consciousnesses of . . .' which would be centrifugal like it is, that it is sustained, subtended, by the prereflective and preobjective unity of my body. This means that while each monocular vision, each touching with one sole hand has its own visible, its tactile, each is bound to every other vision, to every other touch; it is bound in such a way as to make up with them the experience of one sole body before one sole world, through a possibility for reversion, reconversion of its language into theirs, transfer, and reversal, according to which the little private world of each is not juxtaposed to the world of all the others, but surrounded by it, levied off from it, and all together are a Sentient in general before a Sensible in general" (*The Visible and the Invisible,* pp. 141–42).

43. In the chapter of *Phenomenology of Perception* entitled "Other People and the Human World," Merleau-Ponty points out that solipsism is based on the presence of myself to myself, my being-for-itself, which persists "on the hither side" of the particular acts in which man engages (*Phenomenology of Perception,*

p. 357), and which I apparently cannot find duplicated elsewhere, outside myself. But solipsism is self-contradictory, because in claiming that I cannot know the other, I speak of the other whom I allegedly cannot know. Merleau-Ponty's studies in *Phenomenology of Perception* demonstrated that being-for-itself and being-in-the-world are inseparable. If I attempt to conceive of my being-for-itself alone, that is if I attempt to conceive of my presence of self to self as not in the world, as inaccessible to another, it is on the basis of my original situation in the world with the other that I arrive at this theoretical position that is solipsism. If I attempt to conceive of the other as solely being-for-itself, inaccessible to me, it is only on the basis of my knowledge of the other as in the world with me that I can arrive at this theoretical conception of the other, which is also solipsistic. If I attempt to conceive of the other as only being-in-the-world, I can do so only on the basis of an assumption I make that the other will not act so as to "shatter the image that I have formed of him" (*Phenomenology of Perception*, p. 361). In short, I arrive at this theoretical conception of the other only by turning away from his being-for-itself. And if I attempt to conceive of myself as only being-in-the-world, I can do so only on the basis of an assumption that I make that I can no longer act so as to bring about the structuralization of my world including a structuralization of the other as he is found in that world. In short, I turn away from my being-for-itself. Solipsism is refuted once it is recognized that its basis in experience, namely, being-for-itself, necessarily implies being-in-the-world with the other. However, this does not resolve the issue of why there is an other for me. In *Phenomenology of Perception* Merleau-Ponty began with being-for-itself and being-in-the-world and disclosed that the two are inseparable. The task became that of conceiving of man as the two simultaneously. The problematic of interpersonal relations raises this fundamental issue posed by *Phenomenology of Perception*. How is it that man, who is in the world prior to any act on his part, comes to act so as to bring about the structuralization of his world such as it is? When I act so as to bring about the structuralization of my world such as it is, I am known to myself and at the same time other persons appear in my explicitly perceived world, giving rise in the first place to the question as to whether these others are illusions or are truly others knowable by me. To seek a means of resolving this issue, it will be necessary to begin not from the point of view of the perceiver who already perceives others and asks whether they are illusions or not, but from the point, so to speak, at which the structure myself-other comes into being. The realm of the flesh, as neither inside a subject nor external to a subject but rather the place where perceiver and perceived come into being, holds open the possibility of resolving the issue of interpersonal relations left open in *Phenomenology of Perception* and raised once again in the affirmation of the "paradox of being":

> "If we can show that the flesh is an ultimate notion, that it is not the union or compound of two substances, but thinkable by itself, if there is a relation of the visible with itself that traverses me and constitutes me as a seer, this circle which I do not form, which forms me, this coiling over of the visible upon the visible, can traverse, animate other bodies as well as my own. And if I was able to understand how this wave arises within me, how the visible which is yonder is simultaneously my landscape, I can understand a fortiori that elsewhere it also closes over upon itself and that there are other landscapes besides my own. If it lets itself be captivated by one of its fragments, the principle of captation is established, the field open for other Narcissus, for an 'intercorporeity.' If my

left hand can touch my right hand while it palpates the tangibles, can touch it touching, can turn its palpation back upon it, why, when touching the hand of another, would I not touch in it the same power to espouse the things that I have touched in my own? . . . The handshake too is reversible; I can feel myself touched as well and at the same time as touching, and surely there does not exist some huge animal whose organs our bodies would be, as, for each of our bodies, our hands, our eyes are the organs. Why would not the synergy exist among different organisms, if it is possible within each? Their landscapes interweave, their actions and their passions fit together exactly: this is possible as soon as we no longer make belongingness to one same 'consciousness' the primordial definition of sensibility, and as soon as we rather understand it as the return of the visible upon itself, a carnal adherence of the sentient to the sensed and of the sensed to the sentient. For, as overlapping and fission, identity and difference, it brings to birth a ray of natural light that illuminates all flesh and not only my own" (*The Visible and the Invisible,* pp. 140–42).

44. Ibid., pp. 144–45.
45. Ibid., p. 153.
46. Ibid., pp. 153–54.
47. Ibid., p. 154.
48. Ibid., pp. 154–55.
49. Ibid., pp. 147–49.
50. Ibid., p. 151.
51. If the idea is acknowledged as the hinge at work in the transition and metamorphosis of one experience into another, specifically the transition and metamorphosis of one originary structuralization of Being into another, then we may be in a position to approach the inexhaustible wealth of ideas that has been referred to as "pure ideality" but that is not, as Merleau-Ponty has said history is not, an "external idol" (*Signs,* p. 75), but exists, in a manner that has yet to be learned, as *the* world that is, even as it emerges in a radically dynamic manner, and is transformed in originary acts.

"But once we have entered into this strange domain [i.e., the flesh inhabited by ideas], one does not see how there could be any question of *leaving* it. . . . [There] is to be sure a question as to how the 'ideas of the intelligence' are initiated over and beyond, how from the ideality of the horizon one passes to the 'pure' ideality, and in particular by what miracle a created generality, a culture, a knowledge come to add and recapture and rectify the natural generality of my body and of the world. But, however we finally have to understand it, the 'pure' ideality already streams forth along the articulations of the aesthesiological body, along the contours of the sensible things, and, however new it is, it slips through ways it has not traced, transfigures horizons it did not open, it derives from the fundamental mystery of those notions 'without equivalent,' as Proust calls them, that lead their shadowy life in the night of the mind only because they have been divined at the junctures of the visible world. It is too soon now to clarify this type of surpassing that does not leave its field of origin. Let us only say that the pure ideality is itself not without flesh nor freed from horizon structures: it lives of them, though they be another flesh and other horizons" (*The Visible and the Invisible,* pp. 152–53).

52. Ibid., pp. 148–49.
53. *Phenomenology of Perception,* p. 330.
54. The accession of acts in the fullest sense by man to man's original situation

in the world was demonstrated in part three of *Phenomenology of Perception,* "Being-for-Itself and Being-in-the-World," and confirmed in "On the Phenomenology of Language." See above, in particular, chapter 2A, 1, chapter 2A, 3, and the Conclusion to Chapter 3.

55. F. Novotny, *Cézanne und das Ende der wissenschaftlichen Perspective* (Vienna, 1938); Merleau-Ponty's note.

56. *The Primacy of Perception and Other Essays,* p. 180.

57. Klee, *Journal. . . ,* French trans. by P. Klossowski (Paris, 1959); Merleau-Ponty's note.

58. *The Primacy of Perception and Other Essays,* p. 181.

59. George Schmidt, *Les Aquarelles de Cézanne,* p. 21; Merleau-Ponty's note. *The Primacy of Perception and Other Essays,* p. 181.

60. *The Primacy of Perception and Other Essays,* p. 183.

61. Henri Michaux, *Aventures de lignes;* Merleau-Ponty's note.

62. Ibid.; Merleau-Ponty's note.

63. W. Grohmann, *Paul Klee* (Paris, 1954), p. 192; Merleau-Ponty's note. *The Primacy of Perception and Other Essays,* pp. 183–84.

64. Rodin, *L'art.* Interviews collected by Paul Gsell (Paris, 1911); Merleau-Ponty's note.

65. *The Primacy of Perception and Other Essays,* p. 185.

66. Klee, "Conférence d'Iena" (1924), according to Grohmann, *Paul Klee* (Paris, 1954), p. 365; Merleau-Ponty's note. *The Primacy of Perception and Other Essays,* p. 187.

67. The Primacy of Perception and Other Essays, p. 188.

68. See above, this chapter, section A, 2.

69. *The Visible and the Invisible,* p. 155.

Conclusion

WHAT we have learned from following Merleau-Ponty's treatment of language permits a preliminary statement of what language itself is. Language is constituted by originary instances of speech, each of which effects a thorough transformation throughout language and yet allows other originary instances of speech to be what they are. Language itself is not an ideal system that subsists independently of speech and that is instantiated in individual occurrences of speech. Rather, the language that is spoken whenever a person speaks is those originary instances of speech, as each takes up all the other originary instances of speech as what they are, with the transformation that each originary instance of speech effects throughout language, and what each originary instance of speech establishes that other originary instances of speech will have to take into account.

A philosophical act of speaking in the fullest sense is required in order to reveal fully what language is. Merleau-Ponty's manner of proceeding toward determining the precise nature of such an act displays what may be called a circularity, which first becomes apparent in his study of art. Merleau-Ponty's effort is ultimately directed toward determining as thoroughly as possible what one domain of man's world, namely art, is, in order that the philosopher may be that much closer to a position in which man's situation may be taken up fully, as it is, in order to perform a philosophical act of speaking in the fullest sense. Only when the means to perform such an act are determined precisely, enabling the philosopher to lay bare what is, will the philosopher be able to say fully what art is. Working notes for *The Visible and the Invisible* indicate that Merleau-Ponty intended to engage in studies, similar to the study of art in "Eye and Mind," of other areas of man's life, including language itself, and that he was aware that only after the precise nature of a philosophic act of speaking in the fullest sense had been determined would he be in a position to return to these areas of life and say fully what they are. Merleau-Ponty concluded that this is the only manner of proceeding that could succeed. One working note says:

> Ontology would be the elaboration of the notions that have to replace that of transcendental subjectivity, those of subject, object, meaning—the definition of philosophy would involve an elucidation of philosophical expression itself (therefore a becoming conscious of the procedure used in what precedes "naïvely," as though philosophy confined itself to reflecting what is) as the science of pre-science, as the expression of what is before expression *and sustains it from behind*—take as theme here the difficulty: if philosophy wishes to be absolute, it contains itself. But in reality all the particular analyses concerning Nature, life, the human body, language will make us progressively enter into the *Lebenswelt* and the "wild" being, and as I go along I should not hold myself back from entering into their positive description, nor even into the analysis of the diverse temporalities—say this already in the introduction.[1]

Another working note says:

> Circularity: everything that is said at each "level" anticipates and will be taken up again: for example, I make a description of the aesthesiological *Einfühlung* which is neither false, nor "true" in the absolute sense: for it is obviously a "layer" separated abstractly—It is not false either, since all the rest is anticipated in it: that is, the *Einfühlung* of the I think. What is constantly and principally implied throughout this whole first part is the λόγος: I speak of the things as if that did not call language into question! The thematization of language overcomes

another stage of naïveté, discloses yet a little more the horizon of *Selbstverständlichkeiten*—the passage from philosophy to the absolute, to the transcendental field, to the wild and "vertical" being is *by definition* progressive, incomplete. This is to be understood not as an imperfection (a *Weltanschauung* philosophy, unhappy consciousness of the Encompassing) but as a philosophical *theme:* the incompleteness of the reduction ("biological reduction," "psychological reduction," "reduction to transcendental immanence," and finally "fundamental thought") is not an obstacle to the reduction, it is the reduction itself, the rediscovery of vertical being.—

There will therefore be a whole series of layers of wild being It will be necessary to recommence the *Einfühlung*, the Cogito several times.—

For example, at the level of the human body I will describe a pre-knowing; a pre-meaning, a silent knowing. . . .

But I will then have to disclose a non-explicitated horizon: that of the language I am using to describe all that— And which co-determines its final meaning. . . .

I will finally be able to take a position in ontology, as the introduction demands, and specify its theses exactly, only after the series of reductions the book develops and which are all in the first one, but also are really accomplished only in the last one. This reversal itself—*circulus vitiosus deus*—is not hesitation, bad faith and bad dialectic, but return to Σιγή the abyss. *One cannot make a direct ontology.* My "indirect" method (being in the beings) is alone conformed with being—"negative philosophy" like "negative theology."[2]

The ultimate purpose of the study of perception in "The Intertwining—The Chiasm" was to bring the philosopher closer to being in a position of performing a philosophical act of speaking in the fullest sense. The study of perception in *Phenomenology of Perception* is called for by *The Structure of Behavior*. In Merleau-Ponty's first book he demonstrates that the concept of what he calls "form," borrowing from gestalt psychology, is extremely helpful in describing what scientific study discovers in the physical order, the organic order and the human order, and he proposes this concept of "form" as an alternative to physicalistic ontology that contradicts results of scientific work. Merleau-Ponty finds traditional gestalt theory deficient in regard to ontology, inasmuch as it falls back on a physicalistic account where the ontological issue is concerned. The "forms" employed in theoretical accounts of man and his world, such as the scientific analysis of behavior philosophically scrutinized by Merleau-Ponty in *The Structure of Behavior,* are forms derived from perception. Therefore, in order to determine what is, it becomes necessary to disclose the original content of perception, and this is the task of *Phenomenology of Perception.* That work demonstrates the inadequacy of the account of perception that portrays it as an automatic process at work between the world and a subject portrayed as somehow set apart from the world. Man is in-the-world even to the extent that those acts by man which bring about the existence of the world such as it is originate not in a subject set apart from the world but rather in the world, understood as subsuming man. However, the studies that constitute *Phenomenology of Perception* are based upon the perceiver-perceived structure and to that extent maintain holdovers of both the subject-object dualism and objectivistic ontology. Consequently, in order to determine what is, Merleau-Ponty finds it necessary to begin where the perceiver-perceived structure comes into being. Thus he speaks of the necessity of doing a phenomenology of phenomenology. Inasmuch as subjectism must be abandoned, the task at hand cannot be accomplished from the point of view of a perceiver viewing the world as constituted in perceptual consciousness. The task at hand is that of doing ontology. In *The Visible and the Invisible,* Merleau-Ponty commences to do ontology and begins in the realm of "the flesh," which is neither internal to a subject nor external to a subject but is where the perceiver-perceived structure comes into being. Once again Merleau-Ponty turns to perception. But here the task is not that of disclosing the original content of perception but of taking up perception as one domain of man's life in an effort to take up fully man's situation in the world as it is and speak in the fullest sense. Merleau-Ponty does go to the extent of calling the realm that is neither internal to a subject nor external to a subject, and that requires us to affirm the "paradox of Being" in all its facets, "the flesh," which underscores the primacy of perception. Furthermore, Merleau-Ponty goes to the extent of describing language as "another less heavy, more transparent body," as another sort of "flesh." But we must recall that "the flesh" is lined with ideas—hinges at work in the transition and metamorphosis of one experience into another, which Merleau-Ponty describes as "the invisible *of* this world" in order to indicate that the idea is not an absolute invisible. If this is the case, the visible is not an absolute visible, the sensible is not an absolute sensible, and we are immediately beyond perception in a narrow sense and open to other domains of Being. Nevertheless, there is this decentering that underscores the primacy of perception. Once again, it is perception that allows Merleau-Ponty to present a fundamental tenet, there is *the* world. Working notes for *The Visible and the Invisible* indicate that this tenet was to have been fully affirmed in that work in terms of a quality of Wild Being that Merleau-Ponty called its verticality. This quality of Wild Being surfaces briefly in "The Intertwining—The Chiasm":

> One should not even say, as we did a moment ago, that the body is made up of two leaves, of which the one, that of the "sensible," is bound up with the rest of the world. There are not in it two leaves or two layers. . . . To speak of leaves or of layers is still to flatten and to juxtapose, under the reflective gaze, what co-exists in the living and upright body.[3]

Similarly, to describe in terms of leaves or layers the depths of the beings in the world with which man has commerce— that thickness which at the same time as it separates man from the things themselves is the reason why man has access to the things themselves in virtue of the flesh of the body—is to distort the upright or vertical quality of these beings. In a working note titled "The Invisible, the negative, vertical Being," Merleau-Ponty describes how the vertical quality of Wild Being confirms the tenet there is *the* world:

A certain relation between the visible and the invisible, where the invisible is not only non-visible[4] (what has been or will be seen and is not seen, or what is seen by an other than me, not by me), but where its absence counts in the world (it is "behind" the visible, imminent or eminent visibility, it is *Urpräsentiert* precisely as *Nichtpräsentierbar,* as another dimension) where the lacuna that marks its place is one of the points of passage of the "world." It is this negative that makes possible the *vertical* world, the union of the incompossibles, the being in transcendence, and the topological space and the time in joints and members, in dis-junction and dis-membering[5]—and the possible as a claimant of existence (of which "past" and "future" are but partial expressions)—and the male-female relation (the two pieces of wood that children see fitting together of themselves, irresistibly, because each is the *possible of the other*)—and the "divergence," and the totality above the divergencies—and the thought-unthought relation (Heidegger)— and the relation of *Kopulation* where two intentions have *one sole Erfüllung*[6]

The vertical world is there, upright, never leveled, always calling for acts in the fullest sense by man, by means of which man may assume his place in the vertical world.

Why is it that perception is preeminently suited to present Merleau-Ponty's fundamental tenet, there is *the* world? A passage in "Eye and Mind" responds to this question:

Here is the Cartesian secret of equilibrium: a metaphysics which gives us decisive reasons to be no longer involved with metaphysics, which validates our evidences while limiting them, which opens up our thinking without rending it.

The secret has been lost for good, it seems. If we ever again find a balance between science and philosophy, between our models and the obscurity of the "there is," it must be of a new kind. Our science has rejected the justifications as well as the restrictions which Descartes assigned to its domain. It no longer pretends to deduce its invented models from the attributes of God. The depth of the existing world and that of the unfathomable God come no longer to stand over against the platitudes [and flatness] of "technicized" thinking. Science gets along without the excursion into metaphysics which Descartes had to make at least once in his life; it takes off from the point he ultimately reached. Operational thought claims for itself, in the name of psychology, that domain of contact with oneself and with the world which Descartes reserved for a blind but irreducible experience. It is fundamentally hostile to philosophy as thought-in-contact, and if operational thought rediscovers the sense of philosophy it will be through the very excess of its ingenuousness. It will happen when, having introduced all sorts of notions which for Descartes would have arisen from confused thought—quality, scalar structures, solidarity of observer and observed—it will suddenly become aware that one cannot summarily speak of all these beings as *constructs*. As we await this moment, philosophy maintains itself against such thinking, entrenching itself in that dimension of the compound of soul and body, that dimension of the existent world, of the abyssal Being that Descartes opened up and so quickly closed again. Our science and our philosophy are two faithful and unfaithful consequences of Cartesianism, two monsters born from its dismemberment.

Nothing is left for our philosophy but to set out toward the prospection of the actual world.[7]

The apparent impasse is this: if philosophy fully affirms its situational nature, it becomes aware of its own limits, it becomes aware that it must be a perpetual questioning of what it itself establishes. But if philosophy accepts the absolutized limits built into contemporary scientific constructs, it fails to recognize that its situational nature is precisely what gives access to that which is, that the freedom to say something in the fullest sense, to say what is, does not await the determination of those universal categories which in their would-be applicability to every situation would be applicable to none. Merleau-Ponty's recourse is to turn to perception, which itself underlies scientific experimental study of the actual world and is the source of objectivistic constructs, and demonstrate that perception does not set man apart from the world such that man's dealings with the world are limited of necessity to that operationalism which confines itself to its own constructs without defining their limits or interrogating their origins. Rather, perception is a means by which the philosopher may enter Wild Being in order to lay it bare.

The study of how the question concerning an originary act of speech comes to be posed by Merleau-Ponty's work and of Merleau-Ponty's effort toward answering it makes evident the cohesion of Merleau-Ponty's philosophical life. *The Structure of Behavior* called for the effort to disclose the original content of perception that became the task of *Phenomenology of Perception*. Inasmuch as it involved displacing objectivistic characteristics from an unwarranted dominating role in the content of perception and inasmuch as one source of such unwarranted domination is the cultural influence of science, which affects the very way in which man orients himself toward his world, the task at hand in *Phenomenology of Perception* calls for the type of rigorous study of the work of science, which determines the limits of the scientific enterprise, that was accomplished in *The Structure of Behavior*. On the other hand, in drawing on scientific results in the course of *Phenomenology of Perception* in order to point up more emphatically the original content of perception, Merleau-Ponty reiterates the need for attentiveness to the work of science inasmuch as scientific findings, properly understood, even to the extent of any ontological implications of these findings, are not to be overlooked by the philosopher. *Phenomenology of Perception* called for a phenomenology of phenomenology to begin where the perceiver-perceived structure comes into being, called for doing ontology, which Merleau-Ponty undertakes to do in *The Visible and the Invisible*. Inasmuch as the view of perception according to which it is an automatic, objectivistically conceived bodily process that intervenes between perceiver and perceived and limits man's access to that which is—or even precludes speaking of that which is—distorts perception and is thus an obstacle that prevents the philosopher from taking up his perceptual situation as it is, in an effort to perform an act of speaking that returns the philosopher to Wild Being, the ontology of *The Visible and the Invisible* calls for Merleau-Ponty's effort in *Phenomenology of Perception* to stand alongside it. In addition, inasmuch as scientific constructs do contribute to the philosopher's situation, the task of taking up that situation such as it is, in an effort to say something in the fullest sense, calls for such consideration of science as is comprised by *The Structure of Behavior,* which affirms the truth of science within its proper limits. This is confirmed in a working note for *The Visible and the Invisible:*

The search for the "wild" view of the world nowise limits itself to a return to precomprehension or prescience. "Primitivism" is only the counterpart of scientism, and is still scientism. The phenomenologists (Scheler, Heidegger) are right in pointing out this precomprehension which precedes inductivity, for it is this that calls in question the ontological value of the *Gegen-stand*. But a return to pre-science is not the goal. The reconquest of the *Lebenswelt* is the reconquest of a *dimension,* in which the objectifications of science themselves retain a meaning and are to be understood as *true* (Heidegger himself says this: every *Seinsgeschick* is true, is part of the *Seinsgeschichte*)—the pre-scientific is only an invitation to comprehend the meta-scientific and this last is not non-scientific. It is even disclosed *through* the constitutive

movements of science, on condition that we reactivate
them, that we see that left to themselves they *verdecken*.[8]

Merleau-Ponty's successive works cannot be understood
as strictly logical extensions of previous works or as attempts to overcome previous failures to deal adequately
with particular issues. This is not to say that in writing *The
Visible and the Invisible* Merleau-Ponty did not recognize a
need to rework certain issues already treated in his earlier
work. But what must be appreciated is the philosopher's
faithfulness to shifting concerns within the same philosophical quest, which is made evident by his taking up his earlier
works as they are—as speech that fundamentally, rather
than rendering thoughts that the philosopher already acquired, brings thought into existence—and precisely
thereby proceeding to express himself anew. In the ways
just described, each of Merleau-Ponty's works calls for the
others to stand alongside it.

This approach through the cohesion of his works to the
Merleau-Ponty who may continue to speak to those who
may hear what he has to say, may take a place—in a manner suggested by Merleau-Ponty at the outset of his approach to Husserl in "The Philosopher and His Shadow"—
beside accounts of those who see Merleau-Ponty's work as
facts in the context of the full philosophical life that he lived
and that they perhaps witnessed:

> Just as the perceived world endures only through the
> reflections, shadows, levels, and horizons between things
> (which are not things and not nothing, but on the contrary
> mark out by themselves the fields of possible variation in
> the same thing and the same world), so the works and
> thought of a philosopher are also made of certain articula-
> tions between things said. . . .
>   We should like to try to evoke this unthought-of ele-
> ment in Husserl's thought in the margin of some old
> pages. This will seem foolhardy on the part of someone
> who has known neither Husserl's daily conversation nor
> his teaching. Yet this essay may have its place alongside

other approaches. Because for those who have known the visible Husserl the difficulties of communicating with an author are added on to those of communicating with his works. For these men, certain memories helpfully supply an incident or a short-circuit in conversation. But other memories would tend to hide the "transcendental" Husserl, the one who is at present being solemnly installed in the history of philosophy—not because he is a fiction, but because he is Husserl disencumbered of his life, delivered up to conversation with his peers and to his omnitemporal audacity.[9]

Questions specifically concerning language that open up in the course of Merleau-Ponty's work are not fully resolved with the unfinished last work. Precisely how is an act of speaking in the fullest sense to be performed? What is the precise relationship between sedimented language—language that has already been spoken and is available as a stock of words and expressions the meanings of which are assumed to be common knowledge—and living language, which is constituted by originary instances of speech, each of which thoroughly transforms language and yet allows other originary instances of speech to be what they are? How does sedimented language subsist in view of the fact that it is not constantly employed by man? What is language?

Questions of a more general nature that have a bearing upon the problematic of language and that open up in the course of Merleau-Ponty's originary philosophic endeavor are not fully resolved with the unfinished last work. How is man to be philosophically conceived as simultaneously situated in the world prior to any acts on man's part and yet as the one who acts so as to bring about the existence of the world such as it is? Who is man who acts in this manner? Is it possible to speak of a Self as acting in this manner? How does sedimentation—the store of structures such as gestures, attitudes toward the world and cultural institutions that result from man's acts and subsist as available structures for man to employ again—contribute to man's situation in the world? How is it philosophically cotenable that Being is radically dynamic and yet there is *the* world? Two issues that Merleau-Ponty named in the prospectus of work to follow *Phenomenology of Perception* as primary topics of future work still remain open—first, the question concerning what truth is; second, the general problematic of human interrelations.[10]

Whether or not these questions can be resolved on the grounds that Merleau-Ponty has cleared in his works is left to his successors to decide. One temptation that must be avoided is that of hypostatizing the Visible, the Invisible, the flesh, Wild Being, or Vertical Being and turning this terminology into a theoretical explanatory scaffolding. Even a metaphysics of realism that avoids the explanatory devices of traditional metaphysics by confining itself to terminology that derives its meaning from our perceptual contact with the world does not meet the "paradox of Being" that echoes in all dimensions of Being but merely names it. Merleau-Ponty warned against this in *The Visible and the Invisible:*

> [T]he words most charged with philosophy are not necessarily those that contain what they say, but rather those that most energetically open upon Being, because they more closely convey the life of the whole and make our habitual evidences vibrate until they disjoin. Hence it is a question whether philosophy as reconquest of brute or wild being can be accomplished by the resources of the eloquent language, or whether it would not be necessary for philosophy to use language in a way that takes from it its power of immediate or direct signification in order to equal it with what it wishes all the same to say.[11]

Another temptation that must be avoided is that of describing originary structuralizations of Being while forgetting that such structuralizations involve acts in the fullest sense initiated by man, and forgetting as well that the originary philosophical speech that takes up such structuralizations of Being as what they are, involves an act of speaking in the fullest sense initiated by man. This would amount to severing Merleau-Ponty's twofold effort of, on the one hand, determining the precise nature of a philosophical act of speaking in the fullest sense and, on the other, speaking in such a manner.

Merleau-Ponty's efforts were directed toward a philosophical act that says something in the fullest sense. As for the task that lay ahead, all that is available are rough outlines in the working notes for *The Visible and the Invisible* that indicate that Merleau-Ponty intended to engage in studies of nature, life, the human body, the logos of Wild Being, the arts, language, philosophy, subjectivity, intersubjectivity, and history, in an effort to return to Wild Being and lay it bare.[12] This goal that motivates the project permits us to ask the question as to what is to become of philosophy, which has as its own proper responsibility the gaining of access to Wild Being, if man comes to speak the Language that gains him access to Wild Being and sustains him there. Merleau-Ponty was aware of the issue. A working note for *The Visible and the Invisible* reads:

the idea of *chiasm*, that is: every relation with being is *simultaneously* a taking and a being taken, the hold is held, it is *inscribed* and inscribed in the same being that it takes hold of.

Starting from there, elaborate an idea of philosophy: it cannot be total and active grasp, intellectual possession, since what there is to be grasped is a dispossession—It is not *above* life, overhanging. It is beneath. It is the simultaneous experience of the holding and the held in all orders. *What* it says, its *significations,* are not absolutely invisible: it shows by words. Like all literature. It does not install itself in the reverse of the visible: it is on both sides

No *absolute* difference, therefore, between philosophy or the transcendental and the empirical (it is better to say: the ontological and the ontic)—No absolutely pure philosophical word. No purely philosophical politics, for example, no philosophical rigorism, when it is a question of a Manifesto.

Yet philosophy is not immediately non-philosophy—It rejects from non-philosophy what is positivism in it, militant non-philosophy—which would reduce history to the visible, would deprive it precisely of its depth under the pretext of adhering to it better: irrationalism, *Lebensphilosophie,* fascism and communism, which do indeed have philosophical meaning, but hidden from themselves[13]

Philosophy is not realized in absolute nonphilosophy when acts of speaking in the fullest sense appropriate to dimensions of man's life other than philosophy no longer require a preceding philosophical effort to gain access to Wild Being. There is no guarantee that, once having gained access to Wild Being, man will not encounter situations with elements of "militant non-philosophy" that require that he entrench himself in the philosophical effort in order to maintain himself in Wild Being.

Merleau-Ponty speaks of the philosophies that constitute the history of Western ontology as "cultural apparatuses" that cannot be comprehended through an effort to constitute them in intellectual immanence; rather, they can be comprehended only by apprehending them by coexistence, laterally, by their "styles."[14] Whether Merleau-Ponty's work may become such a cultural apparatus or whether it may lead to the Language that gains man access to Wild Being and sustains him there, the Language that would "supersede all others,"[15] is left for his sucessors to determine. The philosopher is aware of the irony of that radical contingency of Being which may come to "cross out" his efforts to say something in the fullest sense, but he is aware of this only insofar as he does make the effort to speak the Language that is the speaking of the things themselves, and the speaking of Language itself.

The philosopher speaks, but this is a weakness in him, an

inexplicable weakness: he should keep silent, coincide in silence, and rejoin in Being a philosophy that is there ready-made. But yet everything comes to pass as though he wished to put into words a certain silence he hearkens to within himself. His entire "work" is this absurd effort. He wrote in order to state his contact with Being; he did not state it, since it is silence. Then he recommences. . . . One has to believe, then, that language is not simply the contrary of the truth, of coincidence, that there is or could be a language of coincidence, a manner of making the things themselves speak—and this is what he seeks. It would be a language of which he would not be the organizer, words he would not assemble, that would combine through him by virtue of a natural intertwining of their meaning, through the occult trading of the meta-phor—where what counts is no longer the manifest mean-ing of each word and of each image, but the lateral rela-tions, the kinships that are implicated in their transfers and their exchanges.[16]

What steps has Merleau-Ponty taken toward this Lan-guage? *Phenomenology of Perception* brings us face-to-face with the silence that the philosopher meets when he engages in the effort to take up his situation fully and say something in the fullest sense. In "Eye and Mind" and *The Visible and the Invisible* Merleau-Ponty presents the dis-covery of "the flesh," a realm that is neither internal nor external to a subject but is where the perceiver-perceived structure comes into being, the place where a philosophical act of speaking in the fullest sense is to begin. In *The Visible and the Invisible* he begins to explore "the flesh." In *The Visible and the Invisible* Merleau-Ponty suggests how an act of speaking may take up fully the philosopher's situa-tion as it is. This suggestion is developed in "Eye and Mind" in terms of the act of painting. If it seems that, for all this, we are left a long way from Language, the distance between Merleau-Ponty's efforts and Language is not a void but rather is spanned by his writings.

Notes

1. *The Visible and the Invisible*, p. 167.
2. Ibid., pp. 177–79.
3. Ibid., pp. 137–38.
4. Or *possibly* visible (in different degrees of possibility: the past has been, the future will be able to be seen); Merleau-Ponty's note.
5. It is the same thing: the [?] is *Kopulation* (Husserl); Merleau-Ponty's note. The sign (?) is inserted by Claude Lefort to mark terms that are illegible in the original manuscript.
6. *The Visible and the Invisible*, pp. 227–28.
7. *The Primacy of Perception and Other Essays*, p. 177.
8. *The Visible and the Invisible*, p. 182.
9. *Signs*, p. 160.
10. "Now if we consider, above the perceived world, the field of knowledge properly so called—i.e., the field in which the mind seeks to possess the truth, to define its objects itself, and thus to attain to a universal wisdom not tied to the particularities of our situation—we must ask: Does not the realm of the perceived world take on the form of a simple appearance? Is not pure understanding a new source of knowledge, in comparison with which our perceptual familiarity with the world is only a rough, unformed sketch? We are obliged to answer these questions first with a theory of truth and then with a theory of intersubjectivity. . . . I am now working on two books dealing with a theory of truth." (*The Primacy of Perception and Other Essays*, pp. 6–7.) (One of the projected works, *Introduction à la prose du monde*, was abandoned by Merleau-Ponty. What work he did on it has been published: *The Prose of the World*, trans. John O'Neill, Northwestern University Studies in Phenomenology and Existential Philosophy [Evanston, Ill.: Northwestern University Press, 1970]. The other is *The Visible and the Invisible*, which originally bore the title *L'Origine de la vérité*.)
    Merleau-Ponty writes of preliminary studies for *L'Origine de la vérité*: "For these studies on expression and truth approach, from the epistemological side, the general problem of human interrelations—which will be the major topic of my later studies. The linguistic relations among men should help us understand the more general order of symbolic relations and of institutions, which assure the exchange not only of thoughts but of all types of values, the co-existence of men within a culture and, beyond it, within a single history. . . . [There] is a history of humanity or, more simply, *a* humanity. In other words, granting all the periods of stagnation and retreat, human relations are able to grow, to change their avatars into lessons, to pick out the truth of their past in the present, to eliminate certain mysteries which render them opaque and thereby make themselves more translucent" (*The Primacy of Perception and Other Essays*, p. 9).
11. *The Visible and the Invisible*, pp. 102–3.
12. See, e.g., *The Visible and the Invisible*, pp. 165–69, 176–79, 183, 185–88.
13. *The Visible and the Invisible*, p. 266.
14. Ibid., p. 188.
15. *Phenomenology of Perception*, p. 190.
16. *The Visible and the Invisible*, p. 125.

Selected Bibliography

Works by Maurice Merleau-Ponty

Adventures of the Dialectic. Translated by Joseph Bien. Northwestern University Studies in Phenomenology and Existential Philosophy. Evanston, Ill.: Northwestern University Press, 1973.

Consciousness and the Acquisition of Language. Translated by Hugh J. Silverman. Northwestern University Studies in Phenomenology and Existential Philosophy. Evanston, Ill.: Northwestern University Press, 1973.

Humanism and Terror: An Essay on the Communist Problem. Translated with notes by John O'Neill. Boston: Beacon Press, 1969.

In Praise of Philosophy. Translated by John Wild and James M. Edie. Northwestern University Studies in Phenomenology and Existential Philosophy. Evanston, Ill.: Northwestern University Press, 1963.

Phenomenology of Perception. Translated by Colin Smith. International Library of Philosophy and Scientific Method. London: Routledge and Kegan Paul, 1962.

The Primacy of Perception and Other Essays. Edited by James M. Edie. Northwestern University Studies in Phenomenology and Existential Philosophy. Evanston, Ill.: Northwestern University Press, 1964.

The Prose of the World. Translated by John O'Neill. Northwestern University Studies in Phenomenology and Existential Philosophy. Evanston, Ill.: Northwestern University Press, 1970.

Sense and Non-Sense. Translated by Hubert L. Dreyfus and Pa-

tricia A. Dreyfus. Northwestern University Studies in Phenomenology and Existential Philosophy. Evanston, Ill.: Northwestern University Press, 1964.

Signs. Translated by Richard C. McCleary. Northwestern University Studies in Phenomenology and Existential Philosophy.
Evanston, Ill.: Northwestern University Press, 1964.

The Structure of Behavior. Translated by Alden Fisher. Boston:
Beacon Press, 1963.

Themes from the Lectures at the Collège de France, 1952–1960.
Translated by John O'Neill. Northwestern University Studies
in Phenomenology and Existential Philosophy. Evanston, Ill.:
Northwestern University Press, 1970.

The Visible and the Invisible; Followed by Working Notes. Edited
by Claude Lefort. Translated by Alphonso Lingis. Northwestern University Studies in Phenomenology and Existential Philosophy. Evanston, Ill.: Northwestern University Press, 1968.

Secondary Sources

Bannan, John F. *The Philosophy of Merleau-Ponty.* New York:
Harcourt, Brace and World, 1967.

De Waelhens, Alphonse. *Une Philosophie de l'ambiguité: L'existentialisme de Maurice Merleau-Ponty.* 4th ed. Bibliothèque
de philosophie de Louvain, vol. 9. Louvain: Nauwelaerts,
1970.

Geraets, Theodore F. *Vers une nouvelle philosophie tran-
scendantale: La genèse de la philosophie de Maurice Merleau-
Ponty jusqu'à la Phénoménologie de la perception.* Préface par
Emmanuel Levinas. Phaenomenologica, vol. 39. The Hague:
Martinus Nijhoff, 1971.

Halda, Bernard, *Merleau-Ponty ou la philosophie de l'ambiguité.*
Archives des Lettres Modernes, vol. 72. Paris: Les Lettres
Modernes, 1966.

Heidsieck, François. *L'Ontologie de Merleau-Ponty.*
Bibliothèque de Philosophie Contemporaine. Paris: Presses
Universitaires de France, 1971.

Kwant, Remy C. *From Phenomenology to Metaphysics: An In-
quiry into the Last Period of Merleau-Ponty's Philosophical
Life.* Duquesne Studies: Philosophical Series, vol. 20.
Pittsburgh, Pa.: Duquesne University Press, 1966.

Madison, Gary Brent. *La Phénoménologie de Merleau-Ponty: une recherche des limites de la conscience.* Préface de Paul Ricoeur. Publications de l'Université de Paris X Nanterre: Lettres et Sciences Humaines, Série A: Thèses et Travaux, no. 20. Paris: Éditions Klincksieck, 1973.

Moreau, Joseph. *L'Horizon des esprits: Essai critique sur la Phénoménologie de la perception.* Paris: Presses Universitaires de France, 1963.

O'Neill, John. *Perception, Expression, and History.* Evanston, Ill.: Northwestern University Press, 1970.

Philippe, M.-D. *Une Philosophie de l'être est-elle encore possible?* fascicle IV, *Néant et être: Heidegger et Merleau-Ponty.* Paris: Éditions P. Téqui, 1975.

Robinet, André. *Merleau-Ponty: Sa vie, son oeuvre, avec un exposé de sa philosophie.* Paris: Presses Universitaires de France, 1963.

Thévenaz, Pierre. *What Is Phenomenology? and other Essays.* Edited with an Introduction by James M. Edie. Translated by James M. Edie, Charles Courtney, and Paul Brockelman. Preface by John Wild. Chicago: Quadrangle Books, 1962.

Index

the artistic gesture, 32; compared with language, 188–89; kinship with language, 181–89; and man as simultaneously one who acts so as to bring about the existence of the world such as it is and situated in the world prior to any acts on man's part, 181–83; originary work of, 211–15

Behavior, 38

Behaviorism, 38

Being, 24, 26, 32 n. 10, 33 n. 11, 33 n. 14, 33 n. 16, 79, 80, 97 n, 139, 148 n. 42, 201–2, 205–7, 217, 237, 238, 239; and existence, 139, 195–96, 203, 205; and the Flesh, 195–96; of language, 159–60, 162; paradox of, 201–7, 236; paradox of, and Language, 205–7; paradox of, and "linguistic situation," 203–5; paradox of, and tenableness in existence of contradictories, 220–21 n; radical dynamism of, and affirmation "there is *the* world," 206–7, 236; radically dynamic, 25, 27. *See also* Existence; Ontogenesis; Ontology; Vertical Being; Wild Being

Being and Nothingness, 85, 147 n

Being and Time, 97 n

Being-for-itself, and being-in-the-world, 101–2, 104, 112, 129–30, 133–35

Being-in-the-world, 25, 31, 47–48, 55, 82; and act by man that brings about the existence of the world such as it is, 129–32; and act in the fullest sense, 148 n. 35; and being-for-itself, 101–2, 104, 112, 129–30, 133–35; and bodily motility, 48, 50, 96 n. 31, 163; body and world as perceived as poles of intentional structure of, 96 n. 31; the body as vehicle of, 94 n. 17; and the *cogito,* 133, 137; concept of, full ontological import, 102,

130, 134–35, 162; and consciousness of mathematical entities, 106–9; contingent, 161; currents of, 57, 139–42, 164–65; and Descartes's step beyond realism, 104–12; dynamism of, portrayed as causal, mechanistic process or indeterminate flux, 95 n. 24; and feeling, 106; and freedom, 127–32, 137; and geometry, 108–9; and habitual acts, 127–32; and the human world, 97 n; and institutions, 128; and intentionality, 59; and knowledge, 106; language as current of, 59, 86, 102; and "living language," 151–56; and love, 106–8; and meaning, 47–48, 50; and the natural world, 96–97 n; and ontogenesis, 50; and the other person, 97 n, 162; and phenomenal body, 96 n. 31, 127; radical dynamism of, 114, 132–37; and the senses, 98 n. 39; and sedimentation, 127–28; and sexuality, 96 n. 31; and space, 96 n. 31; strains or tensions in, 48–50; strains or tensions in, and originary acts, 163; strains or tensions in, and speech, 80, 88, 152–53, 163; structuralizations of, 148 n. 35; and "synthesis of one's own body," 96 n. 31; and temporality, 117–21, 137; and the thing, 96–97 n; and will, 106–8. *See also* Situation in the world

Bergson, Henri, 93 n. 10, 168–70, 197

Biological order, 39

Body, the: and being-in-the-world, 94 n. 17, 96 n. 31; bodily intentionality, 83, 109; bodily intentionality directed toward words, 54–55, 65–73, 86, 102, 132, 133; bodily motility, 46–51, 57–58, 96 n. 31, 143 n. 2; bodily motility, and strains or tensions in being-